S0-BYN-171

JOURNEYING EARTHWARD

by

Edith and John Rylander

Big Swan Press: MN
P.O. Box 999
Grey Eagle, MN
56336
ejryland@meltel.net

Copyright © Edith and John Rylander, 2002
All Rights Reserved

Published by Big Swan Press: MN
Printed by Sentinel Printing Co., Inc.

ISBN 1-59196-084-3

Other books by these authors

John and Edith Rylander

Whats's in a Poem, Dickinson
A Personal Chronicle, Big Swan Press: MN

Edith Rylander

Rural Routes: Essays on Living in Rural Minnesota, North Star
Press of St. Cloud
Dancing Back the Cranes (poetry), North Star Press of St. Cloud

for Dan, Shireen, and Eric

who deserve an explanation

and for others who have asked

Note: This book is a collaboration. The initials under the titles, "E" or "J", indicate authorship. When two initials follow a title, the first initial designates the primary author.

Though we have written in a popular style, without footnoted attribution, readers may wish to know the sources of information when those are not indicated in the text. For general background, we have used the Encyclopedia Britannica, Fifteenth Edition; The Oxford History of The American People, by Samuel Eliot Morison; the Audubon Nature Encyclopedia, First Edition; and The Birdwatcher's Companion, by Christopher Leahy. For environmental issues, we have relied on publications from the Worldwatch Institute and the Minnesota Department of Natural Resources. For phenology, we are indebted to Bruce Watson's WCCO Radio Weather Almanac 1975, and Jim Gilbert's Nature Notebook.

As background on the Dakota Conflict we have used Dee Brown's Bury My Heart at Wounded Knee. For Ahnishinaabe history and culture, our sources are Gerald Vizenor's Summer in the Spring: Ojibwe Lyric Poems and Tribal Stories, and The People Named the Chippewa; Ignatia Broker's Night Flying Woman; John L. Peyton's The Stone Canoe; and assorted articles by Robert Treuer in the Minneapolis Star-Tribune.

An absolutely invaluable source has been Todd County Histories, assembled and printed by the Todd County Bicentennial Committee. Especially important were the writings of Otis B. DeLaurier, whose township by township, family by family interviews of surviving old settlers in the 1930's and 1940's were supplemented by copious research into original records. This son of a Civil War veteran had taught in one-room schools, practiced law, been a Justice of the Peace, farmed, organized town fire companies, and been a school principal and county superintendent of public schools before becoming, in his retirement, a gifted local historian. Without his work, our account of Native American-settler relations, the fur trade, and local lumbering would have been briefer, more vague, and duller.

We are grateful to the Todd County Historical Society, the Todd County Bicentennial Committee, and to Dr. James Hammersten, who rescued the back files of the Grey Eagle Gazette from a trip to the recycler, and donated them to the Grey Eagle-Burtrum Community Library, thus enabling us to discover the saga of the Little family. Thanks are also due to Edith's cousin C.R. (Rick) Birkeneder, for taking care of her father's log books and Operation Budworm memorabilia, and giving them to her just in time to incorporate their data into this book, and to Dr. Max Partch, for permission to use his plant inventory.

TABLE OF CONTENTS

TO EARTHWARD

Love at the lips was touch
As sweet as I could bear:
And once that seemed too much;
I lived on air

That crossed me from sweet things
The flow of—was it musk
From hidden grapevine springs
Down hill at dusk?

I had the swirl and ache
From sprays of honeysuckle
That when they're gathered shake
Dew on the knuckle.

I craved strong sweets, but those
Seemed strong when I was young;
The petal of the rose
It was that stung.

Now no joy but lacks salt
That is not dashed with pain
And weariness and fault;
I crave the stain

Of tears, the aftermark
Of almost too much love,
The sweet of bitter bark
And burning clove.

When stiff and sore and scarred
I take away my hand
From leaning on it hard
In grass and sand,

The hurt is not enough;
I long for weight and strength
To feel the earth as rough
To all my length.

Robert Frost, New Hampshire, 1923

WALDEN ONCE TOO OFTEN
J.

> I went to the woods because I wished to live deliberately, to front only the essential facts of life, and see if I could not learn what it had to teach, and not, when I came to die, discover that I had not lived. I did not wish to live what was not life, living is so dear; nor did I wish to practice resignation, unless it was quite necessary. I wanted to live deep and suck out all the marrow of life, to live so sturdily and Spartan-like as to put to rout all that was not life, to cut a broad swath and shave close, to drive life into a corner, and reduce it to its lowest terms, and, if it proved to be mean, why then to get the whole and genuine meanness of it, and publish its meanness to the world; or if it were sublime, to know it by experience, and be able to give a true account of it in my next excursion.

Walden, Henry David Thoreau

In 1964 I was thirty-five years old, married, the father of a son and a daughter. I was teaching at the public high school in Carmel, California. Carmel is a mid-coastal community with a world-wide reputation as an arts center and vacation destination. Carmel High students were, almost without exception, talented and hard working. It was a lovely place to be teaching; the pay was good and the psychic income incredible.

However, there were some troubling aspects to life on scenic Monterey Bay in those early sixties. During our four-year residence on the Monterey peninsula, we often drove out into the Carmel Valley, back into coast range canyons full of redwood trees, down along the spectacular vistas of the Big Sur coast where white surf line fell away into the deep blue of offshore water, looking, as young families do, for a place to make our home. There was nothing in any of those beautiful locales that we could afford to buy on a teacher's single income, and every reason to think that whatever the real estate cost this year, by next year it would cost more. The notion of parking Danny and Shireen with a baby sitter and both climbing on the work treadmill, so we could in some nebulous someday live the way we wanted to live, frankly never occurred to either of us. We wanted the good life now.

Economic growth and expansion were the unquestioned secular religion of California, and they showed no signs of sparing Carmel and environs. Cannery Row in Monterey, where in an earlier avatar I had drunk buck a gallon wine with people who knew John Steinbeck, was starting its transition from proletarian/Bohemian to upscale chic. Bulldozers growled up and down pine-covered hills. Everywhere roads were being built to accomodate five-acre "ranches" and quarter-acre "estates". Chain-saws whined as the pines around Tor House, pines planted by poet Robinson Jeffers, fell to the needs of the developers.

By the middle of the 1963-1964 school year, I was suffering from serious burnout. Too many papers, too many students, too much to do, too little time for myself or my family. To live in a beautiful place you have almost no time to enjoy while it is gobbled up around you brings its own special frustrations.

I had taught Henry David Thoreau's Walden to my three classes of juniors for the second year in a row. We spent nearly ten weeks on this seminal American work. As the class was in its third or fourth day of discussing the question, "What would you do if you could live your own <u>Walden</u>? How would you live and where?" I found myself internalizing the question. Repeatedly the image of a cabin on the shores of Big Swan Lake in central Minnesota floated into my mind.

Eventually a student asked me the classic question. "What would you do if you could live your own <u>Walden</u>, Mr. Rylander?" I found myself constructing a life with my family in that cabin, in that area, with a self-bought sabbatical.

I told Edie about that discussion. Before long we were both talking about that cottage, at first as a kind of escape fantasy, but, before long, as a serious possibility.

By February or March we had reached an agreement.

LEAVING IT ALL BEHIND
E.

We left at four-thirty in the morning, in the darkness of a pre-dawn June in California. Everything we owned, except for the house, was packed into either the home-made trailer or the International Scout, along with our two children. Daniel was five; Shireen was fourteen months.

At the last minute we found there was no room for a bag of laundry and a bag of ironing. John woke my cousin who lived up the street, and asked Rick to mail this excess baggage to J. and E. Rylander, General Delivery, Grey Eagle, MN.

We were leaving it all behind, as much as a person can leave it all behind. We were leaving the three bedroom, bath and a half house with patio and fenced yard in the hands of a realtor. (Only the year before, we had turned the carport into a Japanese-style dining room.) We were leaving John's job teaching English at Carmel High, where the student body, in 1964, was well-groomed, ambitious, and ready to tackle an enormous reading list. We were leaving the world of suburban lawns and driveways and neighborly barbeques, which I had lived in from age seven to age twenty-nine. We were leaving the almost-new kitchen range and double-door refrigerator, in matching tones of Aztec Bronze.

We were heading for a cabin back in Flyoverland, a two-bedroomed lakeside cottage providing about five hundred fifty feet of living space. The cabin had wood heat, no insulation, an old-fashioned two-holer outhouse, and a well a hundred and twenty-five feet away. We were leaving the sun coast and the comparative sophistication of Steinbeck country for borrowed accomodations, seventeen miles from Sinclair Lewis's Gopher Prairie. Just when half the country was moving south and west, we were moving north and east.

It was (we both felt this, as we bedded sleepy children down in the back seat of the Scout) a grand gesture, a life-changing gesture.

Why would two otherwise sensible young college educated Americans, in the presidentiad of Lyndon Johnson, do something like this?

It was clear what we were doing affected other people, positively and negatively. Not many asked us why we were leaving the coast in a tone of voice that encouraged rational discourse. Many of the people who heard about our plans said, "Really? That's terrific!" The phrases "getting back to nature", "ticky-tacky boxes" and "all this jazz" surfaced in these conversations.

And people gave us things. A beautiful pedigreed English Springer Spaniel named Bet Bouncer, who could not be kept fenced in Carmel. A spiffy going-away party, complete with champagne. (We hardly *knew* those folks.) The Carmel High class of '64 gave John a copy of In Wildness, a book of Thoreau quotations and Eliot Porter photographs.

Not everyone was so enthusiastic. Some people seemed to feel we were leaving our post of duty in battle, though what post and what battle were obscure. "Why are you doing this?" one narrow-eyed woman said, and when, happy to talk about our plans, we began to explain why, her eyes narrowed yet further and she said, "Why are you so defensive?"

Explanations shift with time. Why you do a thing, and why you think you do a thing, are not always the same. The man and woman writing this narrative, looking back across thirty-eight years, are not the same people who tried to stuff in the laundry bag and found it wouldn't fit. In part, they are different people because they loaded that car and turned it east and north.

Part of the reason for the journey was woods and the dream of woods, John's memories of childhood stays on his grandparents' farm, of hunting and fishing, of playing Capture the Flag in the woods around the house where Charles Lindbergh lived as a boy.

The year I was sixteen, a miserable year in a miserable high school experience, I dreamed, night after night, about a cottage in deep woods, near water. I still remember falling into that dream, walking down that woodland path, opening that door, night after night thinking, "I'm home". It was an image of order and centered living which the deepest part of me craved, to live in a house like that with a man I loved, and to write.

It may also have been the house where the Dwarfs meet Snow White, where Robin Hood has friends, where the Weird Sisters spin, where The Good Witch or The Wise Hermit may answer questions, if the questions are asked right. The house where Old Tom Bombadil pours the ale and leads the singing. The House-in-the-Woods is an enduring place in the human mind.

We had stayed briefly in Mother Rylander's cottage, when we visited John's family in Minnesota in the summer of '61. I had seen for the first time the intense luminous green of a northern deciduous forest. (I had imagined the whole midwest would be gray and flat, like the Kansas of The Wizard of Oz.) The wide blue waters of Big Swan Lake were just out the picture window of that cottage. On that lake I had caught my first fish just as we were ready to bring the boat in, had for the first time felt that sudden rush and flurry on the end of the line. I had landed a two pound Northern Pike while my excited two year old son crawled all over me.

We were at the cottage the night Ernest Hemingway shot himself. I remember sitting in the dark, on the Philosopher's Bench which John had built, smoking one of the cigarettes I would soon abandon and thinking long thoughts about life and art, fame and mortality, "Up in Michigan" and "Big Two-Hearted River", then as the darkness and the mysterious small woods noises sank into me, not thinking at all.

All these memories and dreams must have been working inside us.

Sometime in the winter of '64, in my California bedroom, I woke up sobbing at three a.m. and told my husband, "I just can't do this anymore."

What "this" was it I couldn't do? Surely not just the stuff I had been reading about in Betty Friedan's The Feminine Mystique, the mix of childcare and writing, neither of which I wished to abandon, neither of which I would abandon.

But the house, the neighborhood, the very state and nation spoke of aspirations and unasked questions. In houses not built to outlast their mortgages, women who dressed as much as they could afford to like models in Seventeen cooked dinner on their Aztec Bronze ranges while Dad washed the station wagon, and the television said over and over, Isn't this a great life!

The good life of midcentury America proliferated steadily over the farms and orchards and brown California hills, as if it would fill all time and space, constantly praising itself.

The very three a.m. dark whispered, "Progress, Development, Trade Up". And John said, "Maybe we could go back to Mother's cabin for awhile."

A college friend wrote indignantly, asking how we could run away to the woods, when children were being blown up in Birmingham? An extraordinary thing to say, as if Minnesota was the moon, as if the same voices had not spoken the Cuban Missile Crisis and the death of John Kennedy into all our living rooms, from sea to shining sea.

Oddly enough, she made me feel that I needed to defend myself. I wrote her, "I live in a predatory country. I can't do anything about that, but at least I don't have to participate in it."

Bad biology. (I would learn a few things about predators in the life I was moving toward.) Bad biology and worse politics. In surrendering a social status based on our three bedroom bath and a half home, our forced air heat, and our flush toilet, we were not surrendering our franchise. Instead of voting in a building where a small but elegant bust of Robinson Jeffers kept a tight eye on the voters, we would be voting henceforth at the Burtrum Firehouse in Burnhamville Township, with the grease stains on the cement floor. That was all.

So we packed it all in, except for the dirty laundry and the wrinkled ironing, and eased out into our suburban street.

We took the freeway, lurching towards Minnesota at a top speed of about forty five mph, the kids' hobby horse lashed to the roof of the trailer, a galloping domestic totem.

A long hard trip toward what we planned as a brief time out, a year of reflection, a Walden interlude.

We were traveling toward thunderstorms, tornadoes, droughts, blizzards, chainsaws, barbed wire, manure, lambing, weeding, egg-picking, canning, freezing, butchering, building in every way there was to build, harder work than I had ever imagined I was capable of doing.

We weren't leaving it all behind, but we were leaving a whole lot.

We never went back, except briefly to visit. I've never been sorry.

STAYING PUT
E.

What after all is so remarkable about taking off, cutting out, packing your trunk and making your getaway, lighting out for the territory when they threaten to civilize you? It's what Americans have always done.

From Sweden, England, Ireland, Canada, John's ancestors and mine had fled overpopulation and war, military conscription and unjust government, unemployment and heartbreak and rigid social codes.

And those were the admitted motives for flight.

They had come west, west, ever west, in search of work, in flight from misery and hard times. Family tales told of black lung and cheating business partners, lost mansions and dirt floored cabins, women fetching water from the creek barefoot in snow, leaving bloody footprints. There was an aunt whose jailed bootlegger husband had provided all the family's living. After the Feds left, she and the orphaned twelve year old nephew who lived with the family found the scattered parts of the broken still, and the boy who would be my grandfather put it back together, reconstituting the family business. No wonder he went west when he was grown and had a family of his own to care for.

When the wife nagged, when the church thundered, when the children cried, when the well went dry, when the game gave out, when the farm blew away, centuries of Americans have hit the trail west.

When we left Pacific Grove, the social fabric of triumphant trendsetting California closed without a rent behind us. The real estate brokers and consumer indexes of California certainly never missed us.

Taking off, however good it felt in that June dawn, was old traditional stuff, nothing remarkable.

Staying put, that's remarkable.

Today we live about a five minute walk from that first borrowed cottage. We are thirty miles from John's boyhood home, Little Falls. For thirty-eight years we have lived mostly on food we grow ourselves. Our children grew up knowing precisely where their fried chicken and mashed potatoes, sliced tomatoes and apple pie came from.

For the last twenty-nine years, we have lived under roofs we built ourselves, with lumber we cut ourselves, heated by wood we cut and stacked, split and burned. The house we live in now is earth sheltered, half cave, half greenhouse. Grass grows unmowed on our roof.

For the last twenty-five years we have used self-built composting outhouses for at least the warmer parts of the year. We know with absolute intimacy what we consume, and where it goes after we consume it.

"Divorce is
The sign of knowledge in our time,
Divorce! Divorce!"

So William Carlos Williams said, in "Paterson", and every night the television reconfirms his insights, bringing us news of our fellow human beings who cannot live together without killing each other, and cannot live on the

7

earth without destroying it.

But we have chosen marriage, marriage to spouse and place, deliberate sustained connection with each other and with the earth that feeds us.

We made our one move. Since then, we have stayed put.

FREE FOOD
E.

The two-lane county road we took north from the village of Grey Eagle was still graveled in that summer of 1964, so that the traveler approached Mother Rylander's cabin on Big Swan Lake in a cloud of dust.

To get to the cabin, you turned off the county road onto a dirt access road.

The turnoff to the Rylander cottage was near the top of the hill, an abrupt left turn, the car plunging from sunlight into deep shade under the arching boughs of basswoods, maples, oaks, and elms. Transplanted suburbanite that I was, in that summer those trees seemed to me a dense druidical forest, though they were second or even third growth.

Back a little way from that narrow, rutted road, on our right as we drove in, were fruit trees Mother Rylander had planted—Whitney and chestnut crabs, a Fireside apple tree, a pear. There were lilac bushes too, purple and white, and in the spring lilies of the valley pushed tubular green spathes and cool-scented sprigs of little white bells up through brown leafmold over a sizeable patch of forest floor. The flowers had been planted by the wife of a man named Shortridge. They had been the last family to try to make a living farming this land, which many local people still called the old Shortridge place.

Opposite the apple trees and lilacs was a scuffed, sunken place where the Shortridge's house had stood. Once there had been two rooms, one upstairs, one down. But no one who had not been told could look at that patch of earth and say, "Somebody's house was here, somebody lived here." The woods were rapidly taking back every sign of human habitation.

A little further along on that side of the road were some handsome young plum trees of Mother Rylander's planting. Across from the plums, on the right side where the road curved, was another Shortridge artifact, a ruinous old chicken coop.

Then the road went out of shade into sun, making a long swooping curve downhill. On the right side of the road was a tangle of trees and brush. The rather steep field on the left side was rented out to a neighboring farmer. In that summer it was planted to corn, though it was really too steep and erodible for a row crop.

At the foot of the hill, where the road made a sharp left turn, several rows of plowed land had been planted to vegetables. We had sent the instructions and money for seed back to Mother Rylander, and she had planted here with the help of a nephew before she left on a pilgrimage to Sweden, the homeland of both her parents.

This was our first Minnesota garden, the first garden I ever took responsibility for, the first garden I ever thought of as "mine".

Past the garden, the road curved around between corn-planted hill and woods and vine-tangled ravine, upslope and around, past the combined toolshed-privy, dead-ending next door to the square gray cottage with its fireplace chimney.

We were out in the garden within two or three days of our coming, long before we had everything unpacked. And high time too, for in the weeks since they were sown, our little plants had disappeared in weeds. Without Mother's row-markers, I don't know if we could have found them.

John and I progressed like those pilgrims who move along the Stations of the Cross on their knees, in a worshipful grubbing whose intended end was not so much food as it was independence.

Danny knelt beside us—sometimes—and actually weeded a little, or, at least, pulled stuff up. (In that tangle of growth it was not easy to tell weed from planted crop even for adults.) Occasionally helpful, he was always curious, always full of questions. Shireen ran (the precipitate, joyous, unsteady run of someone for whom bipedal locomotion is a fairly recent and novel adventure) and tumbled over things, and absorbed a good part of our attention.

I was in that part of my life where two invisible strings ran from my vitals outward, constantly loosening or tightening as the children were close to me or moved away. If for any length of time they were not at the center of my awareness, the tug at those invisible threads snapped me back.

Hand-weeding plants is, fortunately, an activity which allows for divided attention. As I scuffled along, finding the skinny, pallid, sun-hungry stems of peas and beans among the pigweed and lambs' quarters, giving these preferred plants space to grow, I thought about women who had done this before me. Both my grandmothers. Numerous peasant ancestors. Women clear back to the Neolithic, alternately bending over in concentration on their weeding, and rocking back on their heels to see what the kids were up to.

Four years earlier I had written a pretentiously bad play, about Democracy. Not about any particular person or persons trying to live democratically, but about Democracy. Also Tyranny. And The Survival of the Human Race. With two Choruses, a Chorus of Townsfolk and a Chorus of Women. Creeping along through the dense tangled green, the foot-high jungle of an unweeded garden, I recalled one of those Choruses, the Women singing,

"We shall come back to the dibbling stick
And the seed husked in the hand—"

I couldn't remember much of the action in the play, but that Chorus was supposed to predict what would happen after a nuclear calamity. (I had been writing in 1960, when it was possible to imagine a full nuclear exchange which left pockets of surviving human life.)

I had imagined that after the big blast, the men having blown everything up, women would go out and plant things with their bare hands, thus starting civilization over again. The ancient but ordinary skills of gardening—planting, weeding, hoeing, harvesting—had figured in my mind as heroic gestures.

And here we were, husband and wife and tumbling children, doing as a matter of choice what I had pictured nuclear survivors doing after a terminal catastrophe.

How strange that play seemed now, as the robins sang, the dampness in the soil crept up through the knees of my jeans, and my fingers took on the green-black stain of plant sap. As if I had thought the skills necessary to raise food were on the other side of some great divide which modern persons could not or would not cross, unless nuclear holocaust blasted them there.

The words which had as much as any to do with why I was knee-walking across Minnesota with sweat in my eyes, were the words on my mother's budget and shopping lists when I was a girl.

They were written on those little pages from the notebooks banks and insurance agencies hand out, or on the coarse, blue-lined paper of a Big Chief tablet. They would look like this.

House...$XXX.XX
Car..XXX.XX
Gas...XXX.XX
Loan..XXX.XX
Furniture..XXX.XX
PG and E..XXX.XX
Ins..XXX.XX
Food...XXX.XX

I have not listed the figures because I don't remember them, and of course they changed from month to month, year to year. "Food" was always the last item on the list. It was the number which shrank when the other numbers grew. Prosperity (my father back from a crop dusting job in another state or even another country, with Seagram's Crown Royal in his luggage) meant steak on the table, shrimp in the salad. When prosperity proved illusory, as in the long run it always did, we ate meatloaf cut in thin slices. If I sneaked an extra slice of cake I would be scolded, not for theft or greed, but because by taking more than my assigned share of the treat I had upset a lot of careful planning. Because I had more, somebody else would have less. There was only so much to go around and it was always just enough. "The poorhouse" (a real and terrible place) was where people wound up when they took too much.

To this day, even if there are adequate funds on hand to pay for them, I find myself automatically cutting back on expensive ingredients when I cook.

Long before I understood anything about economics, I knew that those numbers could make my loving parents yell at each other behind closed doors. The word "Poorhouse!" would rise up out of my father's angry mutterings, my mother's placating murmurs, like a firework whose illumination lit up a dismal and terrifying future.

One time I found one of those lists of numbers crumpled in the wastebasket. After all the listing and the revisings downward, especially of "Food", my churchgoing mother had written, "Oh hell!"

I suppose most children have overheard money arguments between their parents. Most American children seem to learn from these arguments that more is better. They go on to structure lives aimed at making more.

I have never outgrown my childhood fear of the windowed envelope. I still think economic dependence puts hooks in the soul.

It's understandable why Henry Thoreau's budgets in <u>Walden</u> appealed so strongly to me. And we on our Minnesota land, working together, we could do better than molasses and Indian meal. I thought of this particularly the July morning John and Danny went out picking raspberries, and came back with enough to top our breakfast cereal, all picked in the time it took me to get fully awake and put the food on the table. Raspberries were a fruit which we never bought, when I was a girl, a luxury too grand even for Christmas. Spooning generous portions onto our cornflakes, I thought gloatingly, "Free food!"

There was plenty of it around. The first garden quickly provided us with peas, snap beans, beets, spinach, and carrots, and later with sweet corn, potatoes, onions, squash, tomatoes and peppers. The second garden, which John planted on the slope of the hill to the north of the cabin, consisted of eleven rows of Navy beans (originally nine, but this seemed too much like Yeats' "Nine bean rows I will have there") and four or five rows of turnips—plants which we hoped would grow fast enough to allow us a crop later. The beans did not amount to much, but the turnips were wonderfully prolific. We ate turnips in the fall till John begged for mercy.

Nor did the non-supermarket provender end at the garden's edge. In a poem written the following summer I enumerated "blackberries...raspberries, strawberries, thorny gooseberries for pie,/ Astringent chokecherries, inedible goose plums/for jelly to make an epicure lick his chops." Since that poem was about wild fruit, I did not include the domestic crabapples and Fireside apples up on the hill, the domestic Mantet apples (two beautiful arching trees) on the slope below the cabin, the domestic plums which bore a magnificent crop that summer, the domestic pie-cherry tree. And I left out the wild grapes.

There were also all kinds of readily available foodstuffs we did not yet think of as foodstuffs. The woods were full of edible mushrooms, but it would take a number of years before we felt confident picking them. There were sugar maples on the place, and it has been at least twenty years now since we bought syrup.

The very weeds we pulled and composted, that first summer, were many of them edible. For years now, the lambs' quarters I weed out of the garden have been a desirable and important part of our diet. Sometimes I have considered deliberately sowing lambs' quarters, so I will have enough next year. But then I would lose that great pleasure of getting something for nothing.

We have eaten all kinds of weeds—purslane, pigweed, dandelions—but lambs' quarters (scalded and served with olive oil and lemon juice) are the best.

Big Swan Lake was full of fish—sunfish, crappies, bass, northern pike, walleyed pike—some of which we caught and ate. The woods were full of edible game. In the fall the skies were full of ducks. John would take our Springer Spaniel Bet Bouncer in his boat and go out into the rushes and come home with a game bag full of feathers and blood and warm dark meat. We ate duck that fall roasted and fricaseed, in pilaf and in soup.

The soil which can grow vegetables can grow alfalfa for hay, corn and oats for feed. Within a few days of our arrival we bought fifty day-old chicks, little bundles of cheeping yellow fluff which we carried from the hatchery in a sturdy compartmented box. For the first couple of weeks they pecked and scratched in the shelter of a no-longer-used privy, while John built them a solid, sturdy chicken coop.

Then there were the rabbits, twenty-nine rabbits (three of them bred does) plus their hutches, plus a hundred pounds of feed, for thirty-two dollars. As I noted in the diary I kept at the time, "A teenaged boy's mother was getting sick of feeding and watering Sonny's hobby." We not only ate those rabbits, we sold them, dressed, to some of our neighbors.

And in the years since we have raised laying hens, sheep, pigs, feeder calves—

But surely we worked at this? What about that kneewalking? What about "earning our bread by the sweat of our brow"? What about blackberry thorns, sweat, the mosquitoes and deerflies which descend on people whose two hands are both busy picking wild fruit? What about poison ivy?

And if we are talking about animals, what about pens and fences? What about hauling feed and water? What about shoveling manure? Not to speak of the dark side of any meat eating, the gun, the chopping block, the heat of a body cavity when hands plunge into it to pull out the viscera. The stickiness of blood, the stink of body secretions on the skin, under the nails.

How could we call it "free food" if, often, we fell into bed sticky and tired? Didn't we, haven't we, spent a good part of our lives ingloriously laboring, getting sweaty and dirty and sore, merely so we could feed ourselves?

We have not even been free from the money economy. We drive a car, we use electricity, we pay taxes, we pay for medical care. Money (as they used to say) doesn't grow on trees, and even when apples grow on trees, you have to pick them. Simpler to buy, simpler always to buy—

"When we talked in California about living largely off the place," I wrote in my diary that summer, "It sounded slightly absurd. But it's quite possible."

Possible is not the point. "This spending of the best part of one's life earning money in order to enjoy a questionable liberty during the least valuable part of it," said Henry Thoreau, in the intervals of hoeing his beans, "Reminds me of the Englishman who went to India to make a fortune first, in order that he might return to England and live the life of a poet. He should have gone up garret at once."

After hoeing my beans that summer, I wrote, "It is neither possible nor practical to drive myself in the old housewifely way...The first few strokes are clumsy and fatiguing, then things fall gradually into more and more of a rhythm until everything is easy and free flowing. Fatigue when you stop is almost a surprise."

That word again, free. Do I mean, "available without cash payment?" Do I mean "politically self-determining"? Do I mean, "achieved without effort", as in those beer commercials where jollity, friendship, and sexual possibility come in the modestly-priced, name brand can?

I mean, no matter how hard we have worked for it, no matter how much of our time has gone into growing and tending and preparing it, the stuff that came off the place has always seemed like free food to us. Breaking home-made bread with sore and callused hands, we have felt like a free man and woman, people with a minimal complement of hooks in the soul.

Also that summer I wrote, "It is probably only possible to explain why we are here to people who immediately understand why—and they don't need any explanation."

But that is snobbery. The experiences of one human being can be conveyed to another human being, given some mutually-shared language to express them in.

It was in search of such a language that we came to the cottage. It is in search of such a language that I write these words.

COUNTRY DARK
E.

Early childhood memory: I am lying on my back on a lawn.

(But when I was a small child, we lived in Gold Hill, Nevada, among old mine diggings, in a small house surrounded by dry desert scrub. Who did we know with a lawn?)

I am with my mother and father and some relatives, Cousin Albert and his wife Isabel, and we are watching for shooting stars. It is dark. It is very late. It is the first time in my life I can remember Staying Up After My Bedtime. In fact, it is three in the morning.

(Staying Up After Bedtime is possible, but would have been extremely and impressively rare. Three in the morning is preposterous.)

The dark of night is over us, and the glory of stars, including, on this night, shooting stars. One micro-meteorite and then another streaks down the face of the heavens. Adults say, "Ah!"

My father points. "There, Edie," he says, "That's the Big Dipper."

Probably eighty per cent of this memory is garbled out of all semblance of reality. But I am sure about the dark and the stars.

Later childhood memory: we are living by now in Sunnyvale, California, a canning and manufacturing town with a population of four thousand. I must have been nine or ten when my parents bought the set of World Book Encyclopedias, with the constellation maps.

We lived at the edge of town in Homewood Subdivision, in a two-bedroom stucco bungalow on Orchard Avenue. Beyond Orchard Avenue the streetlights gave out and the country began.

My father was willing, now and then, to come out into the soft California night and hold the heavy open book for me, while I moved back and forth from flashlit diagram to sky. Those nights in 1944 and '45, standing in a suburban yard in the Santa Clara valley, a child could easily learn the major constellations. The Milky Way blazed across the darkness as it had through all the centuries since stargazers named those constellations.

I did not wholly desert star-watching as I grew up, and the edges of town expanded. Only there were fewer and fewer nights when the Milky Way was visible. Often as not, you were lucky to locate the Big Dipper.

I began to think of those sky fire nights as part of childhood, in the way that the almost unbearable anticipation of Christmas morning is part of childhood. Reindeer did not literally touch down on our roof annually. The vision of starlight brilliance was a tribute to a happy childhood.

There was even a kind of spurious maturity to this conclusion. Life, from this point of view, naturally becomes duller and less charged with glory and magic as one ages. Glory and magic do not exist except in the eye of the child, i.e. the ignorant, beholder.

When we pulled up in front of the cottage at Big Swan Lake at nine-thirty on a heavily-overcast June evening, I had never been in so dark a place before.

Fear of darkness is writ large across our language and our mythology.

The sermons of my childhood described the heathen as living in darkness. It is said of heaven that there will be no night there. When Joseph Conrad wanted to write about moral corruption, he called his narrative The Heart of Darkness.

How much of modern illumination is for need or comfort? How much is an ideological banishing of heathenness, an attempt to make literal the metaphors of faith, a mechanical keeping-at-bay of the dark impulses? And how much is simply because if you can turn night into day, you do?

When we moved to the lake cottage, it had been many years since I lived beyond the reach of a street-light. A continuous low-grade wash of light from passing automobiles and other peoples' houses had bathed all my nights, without my being particularly conscious of it.

At Big Swan we were three and a half miles from the nearest streetlight, and no lights came from the empty cottage.

When the headlights of the car switched off, along with the engine, it was as if black dense fabric pressed against my eyes. I felt a moment's pure physical shock, before the solid forms of trees and buildings began to emerge from the darkness, along with the faint sounds and dense smells of woods at night.

A night or two later, I went, flashlight in hand, to the outhouse. On my way back I stepped out into the open, switched off my flashlight, and said, "Ah!"

The sky above my head blazed with stars. Every constellation I'd learned in my childhood, and all the other foreign suns, burned as they had for Homer and Keats.

It was not the realism of age which had taken the stars away. It was human-produced hydrocarbons and light pollution.

And of course I *knew* that. Yet I had, without knowing I was doing it, come to accept a smogged-up and washed out night sky as the normal appearance of the heavens.

Just so, I suppose, millions of humans have come to accept overgrazed pasture as grassland, lumber company plantations as forest.

It is hard to miss what we have not known. But I had known the sky in full glory. I had become willing to write off my own memory as childhood illusion and exaggeration, so that I could feel at ease under the skies I knew.

Now the stars were returned to me, as if they had never been gone.

They never had been gone. I had let the place and time in which I lived hide them from me.

Now I was back under a true night sky, I planned to stay.

But what about all those other human beings, who had been robbed, and increasingly did not know they had been robbed, of darkness and the stars?

PRESERVING
E.

I worked very hard, that first lakeside self-sufficiency summer.

It's one thing to walk out into the garden and pick fresh peas for dinner. It's something else to view that garden as the source of all, or most, of your winter food supply. Especially when the accumulated meteorological wisdom of the area says no tomato plant is safe in the garden till after Memorial Day, and that from the first of September on you should sharpen your ear to the phrase "frost warnings" on the radio. We have known years in Minnesota when it freezes in late August.

To feed yourself and spouse and children for ninety days, in an area with a ninety day growing season, you will only have to plant, cultivate, weed, water, pick, clean, and cook. To feed yourself and spouse and children for three hundred and sixty five days off the produce of a ninety day growing season, you will also need to preserve.

My previous experience in the preserving line consisted of a few quarts of pears and a batch of apricot jam, made from fruit I picked from trees that grew in the yard of a rented house in Arroyo Grande, California. My next door neighbor there, a spry white-haired woman in her seventies named Mrs. Crites, was willing to give the bride next door instruction in the female mysteries of the waterbath canner and sterilization by boiling. She was simply a little baffled as to why any woman in the year of our Lord nineteen hundred and fifty nine should want to learn these things. "Not too many people want to do this any more," she said. "Most of these young girls, they'd rather buy it in a store."

I could never tell whether Mrs. Crites was grateful for the opportunity to pass on some of her accumulated housewifely skills to a new generation, or thought I was crazy. But having looked at my mother's shopping lists, I knew all about buying food in a store.

So among the household goods we shoehorned into the trailer and the car when we made the move from California were the granitewear waterbath canner we had picked up in a California second hand store, and two cook books with sections on home canning. In the summer of '64 I added to these supplies a vegetable blancher, for freezing, and stocks of plastic freezer bags, plus canning jars, lids, and rings.

Freezing in particular presented a challenge. Having heard the usual horror stories of people who had died of botulism after eating home canned green beans, and having eaten my fill of mushy, tasteless, commercially canned vegetables on school lunch menus, I wanted the fresher quality of frozen vegetables if I could manage it. In the Big Swan Lake cottage, this took some doing.

First of all, we had no freezer. The cabin's old, small refrigerator had a cubbyhole on top, enough spaceto hold ice cubes and a carton of ice cream. But it was possible to freeze food in it, a few packages at a time.

And there was a locker plant in town. We could rent a locker and transfer our frozen food into it as the cubbyhole on top of the refrigerator filled up. It filled up often.

Then there was the problem of blanching. Most vegetables must be blanched—exposed to boiling water or hot steam for a measured length of time, then plunged into cold water for twice as long—to stop the enzyme action, which continues after they are picked. You can't toss a fresh carrot into the freezer and expect it to taste like a fresh carrot when thawed.

The blanching water, said Mrs. Rombauer's dependable Joy of Cooking, should have a temperature around forty-five degrees.

In the years since, when I have had a freezer of my own, I have always kept quart size ice blocks on hand, to chill the blanching water. But of course in the Big Swan cottage, we needed the space in the tiny freezer compartment for the vegetables we were freezing.

No problem. Water as it came from the pump registered just over forty-five degrees.

Of course, the pump was downhill about a hundred and twenty-five feet. A long-handled red pitcher pump, it perched on a hollow steel shaft that went down seventeen feet and ended in a sand point, which looked like a giant sharpened metal pencil end covered with colander holes.

All the water we drank, washed dishes with, washed ourselves with, blanched vegetables with had to be pumped up to the surface, then carried uphill in buckets.

Periodically today I look at the ads on television for fitness centers, and remember all the times I skimmed down and then up that hill in the summer of sixty-four. Two five gallon buckets of water carried a hundred and twenty-five feet up a fairly steep hill will do fine things to the muscles and give the carrier a brisk cardiovascular workout.

To have water on hand was sufficient for drinking or washing, but water for blanching had to be fresh from the pump, if it was to be cold enough. This meant that vegetable freezing was a two-person operation. The coordination of blancher and cold water supply was essential. When we were freezing, it was usually John who raced off down the hill with those empty buckets, and charged back up with full, cold ones.

The peas and beans and corn and greens piled up in the little refrigerator-top freezer, then in the frozen food locker in town. We did not make it quite through till next year's harvest, but we came close.

What could be frozen, I froze. What had to be canned, I canned. I canned tomatoes, stewed and as sauce. I canned dill pickles, sweet pickles, bread and butter pickles, crabapple pickles. I made plum jam, wild plum jelly, wild grape jelly, crabapple jelly, chokecherry jelly, apple butter.

The kitchen was often full of steam. Frequently, I found the job took longer than I had expected, and I would wind up alone with steam and the bumping sound of a boiling waterbath canner and the mixed smells of hot water, hot metal, vinegar or tomato juice or jelly, the only person awake in the house. Outside, loons and owls calling in the summer dark. Inside, the hard grown-up work of preserving the summer.

Lying in bed, feeling the assorted aches go out of my arms and back and feet, I would listen for the small "ping!" sound a jar lid makes as it seals properly. I would fall asleep feeling that I had done a good day's work.

Often, in those long summer days of '64, I was nearly as exhausted as as I was in my first exposure to the mysteries of food preservation.

That had come when I was seventeen, and took my first "real" job at a cannery in my home town of Sunnyvale, California. It was the first nine to five (actually eight to four-thirty) job I ever had, the first job for which I was paid with a printed check.

It was the summer between my junior and senior years of high school. I was going to need money for senior pictures, for a graduation outfit, for a class yearbook, and beyond that, for college. My parents could afford—just barely—to let me stay at home rent free, but tuition and books and fees and bus fares to San Jose State College would have to be financed by me.

A lot of high school and college girls worked in the cannery, also very large numbers of adult men and women. Beginning workers were paid the minimum wage, a dollar twenty-five an hour. Compared to thirty-five cents an hour for babysitting (fifty cents after midnight), it was big money to me.

Workers under eighteen, who wore a badge with the word "minor" in red letters across their pictured faces, were limited to an eight-hour day and a forty-eight hour week—Monday through Saturday at straight time, no overtime payments. Depending on how busy the cannery was, minors worked from five to seven weeks, starting usually in late June or early July.

Older workers could and did sometimes work ten or even twelve hour days, and got time and a half for work over the forty-eight hour week, with double time for the occasional Sunday or holiday.

Shuckle and Company sat by the Southern Pacific rail line, with company housing, little wood-frame cabins lined up along narrow streets of bare dirt, across the tracks. The cannery itself was a massive, grimy, two and a half story block-long pile, exuding the clatter and scream of machinery, the overripe, heavy smell of whatever was being processed—apricots, peaches, pears, tomatoes, soup.

The main office was across the street from the cannery. White, big-windowed, blandly modern, it could have been a school or a dental office. It did not look as if it had any connection to the cannery or the trucks full of produce or the shacks across the tracks. The main office might have flown to that location off the cover of a magazine called *Architecture for Today*, or *Modern Business Management.*

You did not go to the main office if you were applying for a job in the cannery. You went to the cannery employment office, a wooden box of a building of about the same vintage and charm as the cannery and the employee housing. You walked across the bare dirt, opened the plain wood door, pushed in the screen door, and you were in a rectangular box, badly lit, ill ventilated, with grimy painted walls and ceiling and once-painted wood floor, now worn to the grain by the feet of thousands of employment-seekers.

There may have been some benches against the walls, but I'm not certain. In the cannery employment office there was no nonsense about standing in line and filling out a form. Most of the times I was there, the room was crammed with people, people pushed against each other as closely as decency and an occasional sharp elbow would allow, more people trying to push their way in through the door. They pressed as close as they could to the counter that ran along the back of the room. Behind the counter, opposite the entry door, another door gave access to the back room where the hiring decisions were made.

Periodically a slight blond balding man in his thirties in shirt sleeves and slacks and tie came out of the back room into the space behind the counter. Everybody in the place heaved a little closer. And people called out, in the varied accents of Oklahoma and Mexico, "Murl! Murl! You know me, Murl, I worked peaches last summer! Hey Murl, I got seniority!"

I had never thought of myself as a privileged person, but I knew that his name was Merrill, two syllables, and that this was his last name, not his first. He knew, the first time I pushed my way timidly into that madhouse, that I was coming. My mother cared for his children and did his family's ironing.

What's more, when he found out I was such an economic virgin I didn't have a social security card, he held a job open for me while I went and got properly documented and picked up the full-length plastic apron, rubber gloves, and hair net which were part of the necessary equipment for a job in the cannery.

So I walked with four or five other newly hired girls of sixteen or seventeen, in through those wide doors. We walked on cement which was sticky in places with fruit syrup, or slick from recent hosing down, past long lines of women and girls intent on whizzing conveyor belts. We picked our way between work stations, around big plastic barrels full of canned grapes and maraschino cherries. Steam billowed, machinery clattered and roared, men drove by on fork lifts with barrels on the lift section, people shouted incomprehensibly. If you wanted to hear or be heard, you had to lean in close, and even then you were never sure you'd caught every word.

I was put with other minors on the fruit salad line. I was, as they said, "on pineapple", a big bin of yellow sweet smelling chunks in front of me. Canned pineapple was a rare special occasion food in my family, and on that first confusing day its festive aroma lifted my spirits.

I would come to hate that cloying effluvium of Hawaii in a can.

I learned the job in two minutes, but that didn't make it easy. Tall cans sailed down twin conveyors, being filled by other cannery workers with measured quantities of pear halves, peach halves, apricot halves, grapes, pineapple chunks, and maraschino cherries. A "can boy", aproned and rubber-booted, worked inside the belts, keeping our bins full by dumping the contents of yet other cans into them. At the end of the belt the filled fruit-salad cans were lifted away, passed on to another work station, another machine that would fill them with syrup and put lids on them.

There was not much time to think about anything but my tiny corner of this process, which took mixed fruit from God knows where and sent it off to potential buyers. I never knew, for instance, what label went on the fruit salad cans I helped fill, for Shuckle and Company had no brand label. So if I had wanted to, I could not have gone into the grocery and bought a can and tasted the fruits of my labors.

And of course no can was or ever would be the fruits of *my* labors.

"Five chunks in each can," the woman in the white uniform yelled at me, leaning in so I would hear over the din. She was the floorlady on the fruit salad line; each line had its female supervisor. "Five in each hand, no, no, don't stop to look, you stop to look you go too slow, just grab and feel there are five and drop them in, okay? Just keep your mind on your work and make sure there are five." Flashing five fingers in my face; "Five! Okay?"

I was offended by the five finger prompting. Did she think I was a moron? Then two or three weeks after I was hired, a plump cinnamon colored woman came to work on my right, and faintly, through the racket of the cannery in full clattering cry, I heard the floorlady explain the process in Spanish. "Cinco! Cinco!" Flash of fingers. "Cinco, okay?"

"Yais," the new worker said, nodding, nodding.

"Yais," was most of her English, and may have been all of it when she was hired. She quickly caught on to yelling, "Pineopple!" at the can boy when her bin got low. And once, when she was talking with other Spanish speakers, "Paycheck" swam out of the Hispanic music.

My grown bin-mate would smile, nod, shrug shoulders and stretch her neck to signal shared fatigue, roll her eyes and pouch her mouth at the floorlady's back, sometimes lift a gloved hand and shake it in a little gesture of shaking off the yelling, the rules, the boss. Sometimes we giggled together. Shared language of the fruit salad line.

It was the summer Rosemary Clooney's "Come On a My House" was a big hit. The pineapple girl on the other side of me, a blond "minor", worked for seven weeks perfecting a Clooney imitation. By layoff time in the fall, she had it down pat, right to the cheery concluding, "That'sa nice!" She probably sang it thirty times a day. Remembering it even now brings the smell of pineapple syrup to my nostrils.

So, without regard to age or ethnicity, language or grade point average, the women on the lines stood and grabbed and dumped, five and five, five and five, whoops, don't stop, somebody will get a double load but don't stop, five and five. If I screwed up or knocked a can over, the line would have to stop. The floorlady would yell at me and, who knows, might fire me, and then what would I do for the college money which I needed if I wanted to become the next Ernest Hemingway?

The floorlady yelled, all right, and when the line did stop we all stood in our places like good soldiers, hands poised over the fruit bin, but in the relaxation of shoulders, the shifting of tired feet, the heads leaning close to exchange a few words, it was clear that having the line break down was not a catastrophe for the workers who stood behind their bins all day, five and five, five and five.

Life on the line. Stand in one place for two hours, mind on the work, five and five, five and five. Ten minutes off, just time to run to the lavatory with "Please wash your hands before returning to your work place" written over the sinks in Spanish and English, maybe to gulp down a Coke or buy and wolf a candy bar from one of the vending machines. Or maybe to grab a smoke, standing by the big windows overlooking the loading docks, where sometimes a truck or fork lift driver or one of the guys hefting crates would sneak a minute to wave or whistle.

Two more hours of five and five. Lunch (I always brought mine in a brown paper bag) at the long tables of the cafeteria whose windows looked across six feet of packed dirt at the cannery windows. Then back, and two more hours, and break, and two more hours, five and five, five and five, and done, and home.

I walked the mile home that first day trying to find appropriate words, new uncliched metaphors, for the soreness of my hands and arms, the deep ache in the small of my back, the hot needle pricks in my neck and shoulders.

I peeled out of my pineapple-sticky clothes and climbed into a tubful of hot water. My mother, a depression kid for whom the word "job" had a halo around it, made much of me. While I was bathing she brought me the first cup of coffee I'd ever had in my life. I had always disliked the smell, but now it drew me. Soaking and sipping, experiencing the aches and caffeine rush of adulthood, I began to feel heroic.

Of course, I had to go back the next day, be a hero all over again.

Did not know then that I would work there five summers, hating every second of every day. Every spring I looked for a "nice" job. (Like the girls who worked in the white, clean, big-windowed building across the road. The girl who stood in chic office garb behind the pay window at the end of the building, look-ing at pictured badges, thrusting printed paychecks into sticky hands. Lady Bountiful in pressed skirt, nylons, and heels.)

Or—and once for seven glorious weeks I actually *had* this job—work-ing as a camp counsellor. Seven weeks of dawns over redwoods, hikes, warm dusty wild huckleberries, mountain streams. Of reading Byron, Shelley, and *Leaves of Grass* by flashlight, under mountain stars—

But all-summer jobs were hard to come by, and even that counselling summer, I wound up grimly back on the line, indenturing my soul to Shuckle and Co. for tuition money.

Five summers. Hating, consciously, deliberately, all day, every day, hat-ing it.

Do I sound as if I was a soft, indulged, sheltered, sentimental child who had thought shoving the family pushmower around a little square of lawn was work?

Certainly physical labor was more of a shock to me than it would be for my children, who began weeding, picking, filling feeders and hauling water the summer I began preserving. We did not want the world of work to be a mystery to them. It was one of the reasons we had left the suburban house with the hand-kerchief yard and all the gadgets behind.

And it was not the physical effort of the job which fueled my loathing. Within a few days I hardened to the work. I was always tired after a day at the cannery, but no more tired than often in those late nights with the waterbath can-ner.

No, my primary basis for hating life on the line was the brainlessness of the work. Five and five, all day long. When Adam Smith lauded economies of scale and the advantages of the pin-factory, I am sure he never asked himself how much mental stimulus there would be in performing the same motion over and over, day after day. Economists rarely work the line.

There were other shocks and annoyances. At the end of a shift, I was always slightly deaf, and there were people who had worked there twenty plus years. We were regimented in petty ways which seemed to me to have nothing to do with the job. If we sang individually to keep ourselves going, like the blonde Clooney imitator, we got no more than glares from the floorlady, but the few times all of us on the line tried to sing together, we were told sharply, "No singing! You're here to work!"

A few times guys in shirts and ties, with clipboards, came over from the main office, walked along beside our lines, looked over our shoulders, made marks on charts. This made me feel like a monkey in a cage.

Even in 1952, it seemed to me not quite right that women did all the line jobs, all the stuff where you had to stand in one place all day long, while men tended the machines, men got to move around. Male bosses were foremen; female bosses were floorladies.

In my second or third year I worked the night shift. It was an extra nickle an hour and I enjoyed walking home in the starlit (and quite safe) darkness of two a.m.

At night there were parts of the cannery which were cold. To get to some of the jobs, you needed to climb stairs and walk along raised catwalks over the heads of other workers, including men.

The younger nightshift workers wore jeans, sensible garb for a cold and dirty job.

Somebody in the office across the road must have decided we didn't look respectable. A directive came down from on high that all female workers were to wear skirts, regardless of where they worked, no exceptions. One sorority girl I knew came to work with jeans on under her skirt, a display of purely nominal compliance which I admired then and admire today.

Worse than the boredom of the job, worse than the noise and stench and ugliness of the place, worse than the petty tyranny and regimentation which treated us workers as machines and slapped us down when we tried to remember we were human, was a single phrase I heard again and again from my fellow workers.

It was, "This is a good job. The time goes fast."

The "good job" part I could understand. Most of the workers were not high school and college kids, but adults. A substantial number of them were people who lived in the employee housing. People like the "pineopple" lady. Or the women with faces straight out of Margaret Bourke White and Walker Evans, who had "come up from Pohteville"—Porterville—"to wuhk in the fruit."

I worked night shift for a while on peaches, opposite a stooped woman with one of those *Grapes of Wrath* faces, sallow behind the Woolworth glasses. It was a relatively quiet part of the plant, and there were just the two of us, in a place where the floorlady rarely looked, so we could actually talk a little.

On the basis on her appearance, I thought the woman who worked with me was in her forties. She was twenty-nine. She had boys named Hershel and Virgil, and a voice like my Missouri-born grandmother. Pushing back lank hair into the knot on the nape of her neck, she said over the peach halves, "My man's a good man and he works hard, but there ain't much work for a man who can't read nor write."

The cannery was unionized—I still have my Teamsters dues book somewhere—and the seniority list was sacred. Once you had seniority, you could not be fired except for cause. You could get on the seniority list and move up till you were working two-thirds of the year, and eligible for unemployment compensation the rest of the time.

It was a better life all the way around than migratory stoop labor with its piece work wages. It was a first step up the ladder to stable residency, educated kids, home ownership, money in the bank.

I could understand why grown men and women, parents of families, would shout and jostle and yell, "Murl! Murl!" in the employment office. I could understand that curing the brainlessness of the job by replacing the line workers with robots would simply mean a lot of hard-working, conscientious people unemployed.

But—no matter how much you needed the work, no matter how much better it was than picking fruit at so much a lug—to say you liked it! Because the time goes fast—

I stood over my fruit bin, hands grabbing five and five, five and five, brain reciting, "And since, to look at things in bloom/ Fifty springs are little room—"

Or, "Shades of the prison house close about the growing girl—"

Or, "Afoot and light hearted I take to the open road—"

I had to be here because I needed the money, but I'd be eternally double damned if I ever pretended to like it. Shuckle and Company could have my hands and the part of my brain which I needed to keep counting "five and five", to keep an eye out for the floorlady, but they couldn't have my imagination.

I recited (mostly with lips closed) all the poems I knew, good and bad. I composed bad poems. (I could not write good poetry on the line.) I sang rock and roll tunes and the kinds of songs college girls used to sing back then when boys and mothers weren't around. "One Bad Stud." "Roll Me Over in the Clover." "Flamin' Mamie."

I would have liked to believe that my co-workers said, "The time goes fast" as if it was an advantage, because for them it was an advantage. I would have liked to believe, as no doubt Adam Smith believed about the workers in his hypothetical pin manufactury, that they were bred to labor as the ox is, so they did not resent the years their labor stole from them. They did not miss things in bloom. They did not expect to press joy's grape against their palate fine, on the line.

I could not quite believe this. I suspected they had the same sort of nervous system, the same capacity for pleasure, the same delight in unstructured time as I did, or why were there so many songs devoted to the joys of Saturday night?

I knew that in the early months of her pregnancy with me, my mother and father had supported themselves and my grandmother with the bad heart, by picking fruit in a northern California orchard. They had lived, the three of them, in a single bare room, a doorless shed once intended for cattle, which they lived in free. They had offered five dollars a month rent—all they could scrape up—but the owner had said, "It's not fit for human beings. But if it's all you can find—"

It was all they could find. If it wasn't for the New Deal, I might have been born there.

It was not any personal superiority of mine which allowed me to spend my falls and winters and springs studying political science and biology and literature at San Jose State. It was the California taxpayers, the excellent public education of the forties and fifties, which was lifting me steadily further away from the danger of having to work jobs like this my whole life.

So who was I, to look at my fellow badge-wearers and decide they were too dumb for boredom, too unimaginative for rebellion?

Besides, they were kind to me. When one of the floorladies tried to lay me off because, "She looks around too much, she's always taking inventory," another one, Rosie of the earth-mother body and seagull voice, sprang to my defense. "That girl got weak eyes! She *got* to look up once in awhile!"

(In truth, I had been eyeing the can boy.)

When we worked on Rosie's line, she encouraged us to sing. "Just get the work out, girls, that's all I ask—"

Besides, again and again, when they found out I was working to go to college, a brightness came into the eyes of my workmates. They always said the same thing, more even than they praised the job because it went fast. Indeed, I heard the phrase so many times it became a cliche to me, and I began to discount it.

Still, they said it with feeling. "Ah! Going to school! Well, you do that, you get your education. Because what you got in your head, they can never take away from you."

They said it as if what was in their heads was of value to them. They said it as if lots of things had been taken away.

I have Shuckle and Company in my head, and it came back to me those long days and late nights of preserving. Adam Smith would have frowned at so much work to pack away twenty pints of corn, six quarts of tomatoes, a batch of chokecherry jelly.

But sitting and waiting for the load to finish, or lying in bed listening for the "ping!" sound of a jar sealing itself, my body would remember sun and the feel of soil under my feet. I would recall the whole process of growth, from dropped seed to sealed packet or jar. Garden row and orchard bough, undergrowth and chattering birds, pump handle and husband's laughter and watching kids, they were all in my mind and all in the freezer bag, all in the jar.

My workmates at Shuckle and Company had learned and mostly accepted that in order to live they must sell their time. Sell their lives in hourly, daily, weekly, monthly packets. As long as that time was gone from them, sold, alienated, it was as well if it went fast.

There was not much of Shuckle you would want to fill your time with, except the camaraderie of the weary, the stolen laughter of the line.

I had not sold my time, not in the summer of '64 and not often since. My labor was mine, mine and my family's. Seed to suppertime, I savored it in my hands and mind.

It was my life I was preserving.

WATER DISCIPLINE
E., J.

World Watch, September-October 1995

When we lived at the cabin, we had two main sources of water.

The real estate ads of small Minnesota towns in the sixties often used the term "modern" or "modernized", a description which had nothing to do with architectural style. "Modern" meant a residence had interior plumbing.

If you grew up in a "modern" house, as I did, the concept of a water source seems strange. All your life, when you want water, you have turned a handle, or pushed one down if the place you want water is a toilet.

When we moved into Mother Rylander's cottage, we moved back in time from the era of tap, bathtub, shower, and toilet to the era of pump, bucket, galvanized tub, and pit privy. In Sand County Almanac, Aldo Leopold speaks of the "spiritual dangers" of "supposing that breakfast comes from the grocery, and...that heat comes from the furnace." I was a child of the modern world. I thought water came from the tap.

Since the cottage was not modernized, water did not come to us. We had to fetch it.

One potential water source was visible out the living room window. When John's father built the cottage in 1950, he sited it among mature elm and maple trees on a hill, with a splendid view of Big Swan Lake. We looked across its expanse to the reed beds and fields and silos on the opposite shore.

Big Swan Lake is an irregular body of water, a remnant of the last glacier to move through this area, a melted chip become a catchment basin. It is three and a half miles long, three quarters of a mile wide at its widest, and (according to the Minnesota Department of Natural Resources) forty-eight feet deep at its deepest point. There was plenty of water in it.

To get to that water source from the cottage meant a brisk downslope walk, the descent of a small steep flight of stairs, then a further walk down a rutted dirt road to the dock where Mother Rylander's boat was tied. A boat path through the reeds led out into open water, reflecting the colors of dawn and sunset.

Some experiences reach back into the deep past, as the doer repeats something done and done across the ages. Building a wood fire is like that. So is dipping a bucket of water into a lake and carrying the contents home. It would have been profoundly romantic to go out to the end of the dock and dip in a bucket and catch the very color of the sky.

Then of course it would have been necessary to carry that bucket all the way up to the house. Our kitchen buckets held around two gallons. Full, they weighed about fifteen pounds.

Also there would have been some health considerations. Since this was a live wild body of water, water was not all it contained. It harbored all the vegetation that likes wild places. Along its margins were willows, alders, osier, horsetail reed, blue flag. Closer to the water were the truly wet-footed plants, like pickerel weed and duckweed. Most of the lake shore was ringed by beds of reeds and cat-tail, interspersed with wild rice. Among the reeds and in the open water grew glossy yellow pond lilies. Yet further out in the lake were lacy underwater forests, plants with names like coon-tail and water lettuce, plants that squished under the feet and left fine green strands on the skin of a swimmer.

The lake also harbored water-striders, backswimmers, larvae of crane-flies and mosquitoes, and the nymphal forms of the delicate blue damselflies and glittering-winged dragonflies which perched on reed tips and sometimes on the tips of our fishing rods. Red-winged blackbirds nested in those reeds and ducks swam among them. Fish of all sizes from nearly-invisible fry to large Northern pike, bass, walleye and carp lived in our lake. Herons and kingfishers and humans harvested them.

The fall of a foot anywhere at the lake margin set off a ripple of retreat. Frogs launched themselves like leggy missiles. Painted turtles slithered off logs and swam away, with only the little peak of their heads visible. Occasionally we saw the sleek head and trailing tail of one of the muskrats that built round houses near the shore.

The lake surface was often dusted with plant pollen and pocked with fallen leaves. In late summer near the shore, it bloomed with algae, green as spilled paint. Like any lake, it contained traces of everything uphill and upstream from it.

In fact Big Swan Lake was not just a source of water, but the center of a whole complex biotic community, of which the four people living in the Rylander cottage were by no means the only members.

We swam in it, usually not by Mother's dock, but down in front of Johnson's cottage, where the bottom was less squishy. Sometimes when the weather was warm and there were no boats out, we bathed in it. We caught its fish and its breezes, took into ourselves its smells and sounds and colors.

We did everything but use it as a household water supply. We did what humans often do; we tapped the watershed further up.

The pump which provided our household water supply was downhill from the cottage, next to the gully. Most of the year there was no water in the gully, only dampness and a perpetual presence of mosquitoes. During spring runoff, or after heavy rain, the gully becomes a temporary stream, running under the lakeside road through a culvert and draining into the lake, not far from the dock, with a small gurgling sound.

Well-drillers talk about "veins of water", a metaphor which emphasizes the organic connectedness of the earth. Our sand point tapped into this particular vein of water, this shallow aquifer, about seventeen feet down.

The pump's long handle and flaring mouth stood in partial shade. Next to the pump stood the priming can, an empty clean number two can which any pump user was supposed to leave full of water. I was familiar with the phrase "to prime the pump" from political discussions of tax policy. But pitcher pumps like ours have to be primed in the literal sense. Water must be poured into them to wet the leathers inside, or the pump will not function. With a hand-pump you always get more out than you put in, but you have to put something in first.

The water-carrier set down her pail where water from the spout would pour into it, emptied the priming water into the flared metal mouth of the pump, then pushed vigorously down on the handle, once, twice, three times. The first couple of pumps produced a dry miserable screech, as if the whole mechanism was protesting the work it was required to do. Then, if the priming water was sufficient and the timing of pump strokes right, there came a gurgling sound rising upward, followed by a silvery gush of water. The water-carrier filled pail or pails, filled priming can, rewarded herself with a cup full of fresh well water, drunk from the shiny tin cup which always sat next to the priming can.

Even in the hottest weather, it was always cool by the pump, and there was usually a puddle or two where water had spilled. As the heat of summer grew, we were not the only creatures for whom the pump provided refuge and sustenance.

Journal Entry, August 3: "The wet wiggly sensation of Pumpy Greengrower, the tree frog who lives in our pump, plopping out into my hand. He is about the size of a fifty cent piece, light green, with pad feet and a cynical eye. Who wouldn't be cynical, being pumped out of his cool wet haven two or three times a day?"

"There are several of the bigger leopard frogs hanging around the pump. They range in color from a bright medium green to a lustrous bronze. The great trick with seeing them is really to look. A quick scanning, the supermarket and cocktail party eye, misses them every time."

Pumpy Greengrower was most likely a striped chorus frog, *Pseudacris triseriata.* The lustrous brown frog was a wood frog, *Rana sylvatica.* I was right about the leopard frogs, *Rana pipiens.*

They had come, like me, for the water, and the water was delicious. Straight out of the earth, it was cold enough to shock the mouth. It tasted of wildness. To drink it was to think of that unseen vein slipping by under my feet, water which would empty into Big Swan Lake, which emptied into the Swan River, which emptied into the Mississippi, which emptied into the Gulf of Mexico, the Atlantic, the oceans of the world.

Where had the water I drank come from, all the years of my life till then? Out of the tap. From what clouds had it fallen, down what mountain slopes had it run? What bogs and marshes had filtered it? What lakes, streams, rivers and veins had carried it to me? What dams, what aqueducts, what pumps and filters and pipes brought it into my glass and my sink, my toilet and shower and tub? It was all a mystery, that "city water" for which we paid at the end of the month.

In the summer of 1964, I would have defended the purity of the water from our pump against any detractor, though the pails it sat in always accumulated a thin layer of grit on the bottom, silt too fine to screen out. And some years later, when Mother Rylander had the water tested before she pumped it away uphill to serve the house she built, it proved, like much water in agricultural country, to have some nitrate contamination. Nitrates restrict the amount of oxygen reaching the brain. In high quantity they can cause infant death from what is called blue baby syndrome.

Our pump was downhill from land which had been plowed, pastured, fertilized, farmed (and more recently treated with herbicide and pesticide) for eighty or ninety years. We hadn't been able to see or taste the contamination, but it was there.

Everything runs downhill. Nothing stays in one place. All water is recycled water. You drink whatever is in it, wherever it came from.

It was profoundly educational to live for a year in a household where every drop of water, for drinking, for washing, for household cleaning, had to be pumped and carried uphill, and, if we wanted hot water, heated on the stove. We probably carried uphill, on average, around twenty gallons a day.

The average resident of Los Angeles uses two hundred and eleven gallons of water daily. Not the average household; the average resident. In Tucson, Arizona they get by on a hundred and sixty per capita, and in Oakland, California, they manage on a hundred and ten. In Las Vegas, where the original ecosystem included creosote bushes, Joshua trees, Gila monsters and chuckwallas, the Southern Paiute used to manage on the average annual rainfall of four inches. Now Las Vegas residents and visitors go through three hundred and sixty gallons daily. Contemporary patterns of living effectively prevent most of those people from ever considering where that water comes from.

Our world is blue as seen from space, because so much of it is water. Water not only quenches thirst and washes everything that needs washing, it lubricates manufacturing, delights the eye, fills swimming pools, greens golf courses, supports fisheries, swimmers, water-skiers, boaters, divers, and the resorts and industries which serve them. Every living thing, including ourselves, is composed mostly of water. The world weather cycle, with its droughts and floods and storm pulses, is driven by water in its various forms, in ways we don't understand completely.

Water is also power, to warm, to cool, to light, to transmit information.

Humanity has been industriously (if not always intentionally) changing the world's water systems with increasing speed. We have dammed, we have channeled, we have drained, we have polluted. What's good temporarily for one group of people or nation in one place is often disastrous for other people, downstream, and in the long run.

As the abundant and varied life of the Big Swan watershed quickly showed us, water used by humans is also used by other forms of life.

In many major river systems, there is far more present human demand than there is water to supply it. The Rio Grande, the Colorado, and the Ganges no longer reach the ocean. The Aral Sea, which used to be the fourth largest lake in the world, has lost half its area, three quarters of its volume, and its valuable fishery. The once fertile fields around it are now salt desert.

The World Bank predicts demand for water will double in the next two decades, with more than fifty countries expected to have water shortages by 2025.

In February 2001, the U.N. Intergovernmental Panel on Climate Change issued a report at Geneva, Switzerland, predicting massive earthwide effects from global warming, which is largely driven by industrial and auto pollution. The Geneva report summarizes a thousand pages of reseach by around seven hundred scientists. It predicts more extreme weather conditions, massive displacement of populations, expansion of tropical diseases like malaria, and extinction of animal species due to habitat destruction.

Changing rainfall patterns, coupled with population growth, will lead to huge pressure on water supplies. It's estimated that 1.7 billion humans currently live in areas of tight water resources. In the next twenty-five years, this number could rise to about 5.4 billion.

Even with good local water supplies and two healthy adult bucket carriers, keeping ourselves provided with water in the summer of 1964 was hard work. It required continuous forethought. At first I was always reaching for the handle that didn't exist, to turn on the tap that didn't exist. The only thing that made me feel more foolish was finding myself in the middle of dinner preparation, or hand washing, or shampooing, with empty water buckets. Especially after dark.

It's worth remembering that much of the world—in many countries, all but the elite—still lives in a world of bucket and basin, as we did that year. Water for them comes from the village well or communal pump. Or it is dipped from the local watercourse, complete with whatever pollutants come into that watercourse from the local human and animal waste disposal systems. Water must be carried for miles, at the arm's end, or balanced on the head. Most often it is carried by women or children. A substantial part of the working day is devoted to securing the necessary water supply.

The Geneva Report properly points out that climate change, with its water scarcity, disproportionally impacts poor nations. The worst impacts will be felt by those people living in the world of bucket and basin, who will have to walk farther, to dip up less water from dirtier sources.

The first thing we learned trudging uphill with our buckets was the extreme luxury of the daily bath. George Orwell writes eloquently, in The Road to Wigan Pier, about coal miners coming home from the pithead coated with coal dust, attempting to get clean in bucket and basin households. He also says in his childhood, he regularly heard middle class people, people with plumbing or servants, say, "The lower classes small."

I never take a shower, or look at pictures of women in the third world carrying water, without remembering the discipline of my days in the Big Swan cottage. My muscles remember the weight of water.

Public health and any decent living standard begin with clean water, accessible water, water not full of disease organisms or industrial poisons. But is the climax of civilization the flush toilet, the sprinkler greening the desert golf course, the tap turned on without thought?

There is a series of science-fiction novels by the late Frank Herbert, about a desert planet called Arakis, also known as Dune. The people who have learned to live there over the long term survive by practicing "water discipline". Every drop of fluid is precious. Dew, sweat, urine, even tears, it all comes back into a closed recycling system. The resident of Dune who does not learn water discipline quickly dies.

The invasive non-residents who live there briefly as representatives of empire display wealth by deliberately wasting water. Not for them the closed "still suits" of the desert Fremen. The invaders wash their hands and faces with a great, unnecessary sloshing; they dump their soggy towels on the floor. Their message is, "We don't have to worry about this stupid little planet; we don't really belong here."

The lowly desert-dwellers working as servants in the Big House sneak in, blot up the spillage, rush it home and wring every drop into the communal reservoir.

Their planet is a closed system, like a space ship. They have figured this out. Our planet too is a closed system.

Most residents of industrial countries on our well-watered Earth see little need as yet to practice water discipline.

Frank Herbert did not get his ideas about water discipline by traveling to planet Arakis. He got them by studying water usage and aquifer degradation on this, our green and lovely Earth.

How are we to learn water discipline, if the tap is always handy? And without water discipline, how are we to keep all those taps running?

The house we now live in, Earthward, is fully "modernized", though we use a composting outhouse during the warm months of the year, and most of our garden irrigation is done with captured rainwater. For laundry, for household cleaning, for personal cleaning, to quench our thirst, the two of us use about seventy-five gallons of water per day.

We pass the English middle-class sniff test. On the other hand, we haven't yet reached the Arakis standard of water discipline. We are thinking about installing a commercial composting toilet, to replace the flush model in our bathroom. So we're working on it.

GRANDPA BRINGS IN THE HAY
J.

I seem to have been born with an aptitude for a way of life that was doomed, although I did not understand that at the time. Free of any intuition of its doom, I delighted in it, and learned all I could about it.

Wendell Berry, The Long-Legged House, 1969

I am six or seven years old. It's 1935 or '36. I don't know it then, but the Depression still holds much of the world, the US, the state of Minnesota and my own family in its grip.

My maternal grandparents live on a small rented farm ten miles west of Little Falls, the town of five thousand where I live with my parents and sister.

Not only are economic conditions bad, our area is also afflicted by hot, droughty weather. Crops wither in the dry heat. My mother will remember her mother sweeping the dust of the Dirty Thirties out of the small farmhouse, sweeping it out the front door and muttering in Swedish, "Dry as ashes."

But I am enjoying myself, because I am "helping Grandpa with the hay."

At least, I am with my Grandpa in the swampy area a half mile from the house and barn. I hold the reins as he pitches the hay onto the hayrack pulled by two of his beloved work horses, Dolly and Brownie. The sky gets dark and ominous. Huge thunderheads form and fly by. Lightning bolts flash as thunder cracks loudly.

Grandpa throws a last big forkful onto the hayrack and scrambles quickly up onto the load of hay. Dolly and Brownie move us slowly out of the bumpy marsh, with the care of long practice.

We are at the road. Grandpa looms above me, shaking the reins, yelling, "Giddyup!" The big slow draft horses move faster and faster, till they rumble into a full gallop down the paved road surface. We hold on tight to the framework of the iron-wheeled old hay wagon as we sway and lurch toward home and shelter.

We slow at the driveway and get safely to the house. The smell of rain is strong in the air, but we have got the hay home dry. Grandpa sends me into the house with a "Good boy, Johnny" in his thick Swedish accent.

I go in thrilled by the ride, admiring my Grandpa's skill and daring. More than sixty years later, those lovely, lively memories of a time now long departed are vivid in my memory.

PUMPY GREENGROWER
E.

TWO STUDIES LINK PESTICIDES TO DEFORMED FROGS (AP)—Pesticides used in agriculture have been linked with some frog deformities in Minnesota, according to two new studies.

The studies are the culmination of 18 months of lab tests on pond water from Minnesota and elsewhere. The results suggest that a combination of chemicals appears to be causing malformations of the frogs' limbs, eyes, mouths, and other parts..
"At this point we can't say that this is something that applies only to frogs," said Jim Burkhart, co-author of the studies and a biochemist.
— *St. Cloud (Minnesota) Times*, October 7, 1999

Earlier in this narrative, I mentioned the small green frog that lived in our pump, whom we called Pumpy Greengrower.

The name came from one of Dan's favorite books, <u>Charlie Yup and The Snip-Snap Boys</u>. I wish I could consult a copy of this engaging narrative to refresh my memory, but it suffered the fate of many well-loved children's books; it was read to pieces, largely in the summer of '64. In the summer of '64 it developed an unforgettable resonance.

As I recall it, the story concerned a boy named Charlie Yup who used his scissors to cut out little paper friends, which came to life and played with him. Flyboy was half-airplane. Scooter had roller skate feet. The Scribble Indians could follow a trail anywhere. Outside Charlie's house was a garden (bright cartoon rows of cornstalks and flowers) which one day suddenly shriveled. (Picture of swooning, near-dead vegetation.) The villain figure, Bad Bart (leer, cowboy hat, huge mustache) had stolen the Pumpy Greengrower!

Hurried consultation among Charlie and friends. Scouting expeditions by Flyboy and the Scribble Indians. Hot pursuit of villain by Charlie and Scooter. Bad Bart is surprised with the Pumpy Greengrower, which he admits he has stolen out of jealousy. "Nobody plays with me. I'm not a bad guy if you give me a chance." Bad Bart returns Pumpy Greengrower, plants leap upright in miraculous revival, Charlie, Bart, and the Snip-Snap boys play happily ever after.

By the time I wrote my journal entry about Pumpy Greengrower the frog, our garden was looking less and less like the sturdy, productive plants we had rescued from their early weeds, and more and more like the near moribund vegetation portrayed in <u>Charlie Yup and The Snip-Snap Boys</u>.

During our first week in the cottage, we had two or three substantial rainstorms. A midwestern thundershower is a dramatic production, from growth of anvil clouds, to distant rumble, to hiss of rain and flash and crack and blue-white dazzle of lightning, to washed and glistening leaves, chorusing birds, rush of plant scents as the storm rumbles on east.

Between those timely rains and temperatures in the eighties, our corn and beans and squash had grown with a speed which suggested a magician's trick, or time-lapse photography.

Then, slowly, the heat intensified and the clouds disappeared. A week went by without rain. A second week. A third.

In late June, when we walked our damp meadows, very small frogs leaped out of the grass ahead of us. By the middle of July, no amphibian wave marked our passage. Instead, tiny, green, still-wingless grasshoppers shot out of the drying grass stems and pattered against the hot hardening dirt, making a small sizzling sound.

All my life I had heard about droughts on the news. Now I was in one. And the plants to which I had devoted days of work and loving care, the plants I planned to feed my family on next winter, were beginning visibly to suffer.

Plants in a drought situation adapt themselves, devoting all their energy to staying alive. Corn leaves go spiky. Squash leaves sag like the fabric of broken-ribbed umbrellas.

We carried water, buckets and buckets and buckets of it, brought from the lake in the back end of the Scout. We were afraid to draw the well down too far; in such weather, wells can be pumped dry. We kept things alive, but that was all. New leaves did not form. Flowers did not open. Seeds did not set.

Uphill from our garden, the field corn planted by our neighbors the Simonitchs "fired", its leaves spiky as cactus, a band of tan moving up the stalks from the roots, replacing the green coloration of healthy corn. We were watching one of the continuing dramas of rural life; is this field going to make a crop? Will it produce enough harvestable product to pay the farmer for his land costs, his seed costs, his fertilizer, his tractor depreciation and fuel and labor? Will he make enough profit on this shriveling corn to support his family?

The man who had planted that corn, renting the land from Mother Rylander, was dying that summer of cancer. That did not mean he and his wife and his son did not worry about the lack of rain. Farming people all over the world live or die with the rain.

Carrying buckets of water, watching thirsty earth gulp it down, lying awake sweating and listening for the faint rumble of distant thunder, we understood the primacy of rain gods, thunder gods, in the mythologies of the world. The world-wide Pumpy Greengrower had developed a small local glitch in its usually reliable operation, the kind of minor instability which will not even make the network news, and even asleep in bed we could feel our garden crying out for rain.

It was our first drought, but there would be others. If you live with the soil, you live with its griefs. In our part of the world, 1987 and 1988 were terrible summers. Whole cornfields turned to spiky earless sticks, good for nothing but low-grade silage. Tree leaves turned brown and shriveled and fell early, not waiting for the coloration of frost. Wild plants were half their normal size. Copious flower bearers produced scant tiny blossoms which went almost instantly to seed. Reproduction was sacrificed to survival. The beets in my garden came out of the earth flabby, as if they had been boiled. They had cooked in the ground.

Along with local drought conditions, the summers of '87 and '88 were times of catastrophe for the global environment. The seals off Scandinavia were dying of a virus. Medical waste, terrifying because of its association with AIDS, was washing up on eastern beaches. The ozone hole was getting bigger. Maple trees in New England sugarbushes were succumbing to acid rain. The tropical rain forest was burning, adding its increment to the process of global warming.

On a morning walk in one of those bad summers, seven-thirty a.m. and the temperature already in the high eighties, I passed an older neighbor who called out, "I think the Almighty is trying to tell us something!"

Droughts always feel like that, apocalyptic and permanent.

Our '64 drought broke in mid-August with a daylong, soaking rain, a steady calm music of change. A robin bathed in one of the puddles by the house.

The spiky leaves of the corn recaptured their normal fountaining curves. The big squash leaves no longer sagged.

The heat did not return. Our late-planted peas, gone in a few days from drought to drown, developed mildew. We began to need a fire to keep the house warm through the night.

THE THRESHING CREW
J.

I am fifteen in 1944. World War II is the nasty backdrop against which boys like me live our adolescent lives in central Minnesota. We wonder if our time to serve, fight, and perhaps die is not far off.

My Uncle Louie owns and operates a thirty-two inch Minneapolis Moline threshing machine, one of the larger ones in the area, pulled by a Minneapolis Moline tractor on steel wheels. He asks my parents, then me, if I can be his crew when threshing season starts in July. Most of the men are off to war. Of course I can.

I'm his "crew" of one. I drive the thirty-five Chevrolet pickup with the gas barrels, oil drums, grease guns and tools loaded on it, following Uncle Louie's threshing machine from job to job. Farmers whose oats and barley we're threshing arrange for the teams, tractors, hayracks and other help needed on the particular job site.

My uncle has decided I can handle the bagging duties. Bagging, I discover, is hot, hard, dirty, repetitive work. The grain, beaten loose from its stalks and chaff by the action of the threshing machine, comes down a chute, one thirty-two pound bushel at a time. The chute is divided at the end, so that one filled sack can be removed while another fills. The filled sack will hold two or three bushels of grain. I pick it up and swing it behind me, to be hauled by others to a granary. There's an occasional break for meals, but otherwise the machine hammers on as long as the grain bundles are dry, or till the job is finished.

Once in a while the bundles will be too damp, or they may have been pitched on too fast. The threshing machine clogs, and Uncle Louie disappears into the hot dusty innards of the iron beast to remove the choking material. Sometimes I hear words echoing from the machine that I didn't know Uncle Louie knew.

Some days Uncle Louie picks me up at five a.m., in near darkness, and I don't get home till ten p.m., also in near darkness. It is real work for a boy, but not uncommon to that time and place.

The work goes on through hot, grueling July and August days. I am happy about the fifty-five cents an hour I get paid, but when school starts in early September I welcome the change.

The images of those two summers are still strong in my mind; the grain pouring down the chute, the horses pulling in wagonloads of bundles, shying as they near the noise and commotion of the threshing rig. The enormous farmhouse meals of meat, potatoes, bread, pickles, pie, all washed down with coffee or milk. The easy camaraderie of the men who cooperated in the tasks. The farmer whose grain was threshed today would be helping on other days with the harvest on the farms of neighbors, who had helped him.

I am reminded powerfully of the contrast with today's harvests. One person drives a huge machine across a field, stopping only to unload into a truck or wagonbox which another person hauls away. The combine operator sits, more often than not, in an air conditioned cab, where piped-in music from somewhere else drowns out equally the songs of field birds and the roar of his machine.

The work I did those summers is exactly the work which modern agribusiness prides itself on having eliminated. Boys anymore seldom have to push their bodies all day long in the company of men, harvesting food for man and beast. They do not chow down on home-canned beef and mashed potatoes, laughing at small jokes, being gently teased about their girl friends.

"Progress" has meant not only larger, faster harvests, but a loss of community, of sharing time and work, dreams and lives.

NIGHT MUSIC

E.

The varying murmurs of a wood fire, after the unvarying hum of a mechanical furnace. A lively nocturnal small talk of flames and fuel. The little ticks and snaps of metal expanding and contracting, as the wood stove heats and cools.

June. Jerking up out of early sleep in a cold sweat, with what I took to be a woman's scream in my ears. Where had that terrible sound come from, in this quietest of places?

Then it came again, less terrified, less human, now recognizable. I was hearing a loon, that handsome black and white swimmer and incredible diver, that notorious producer of nocturnal cries. The call I was hearing that night was probably what ornithologists call a yodel, a loud repetitive complex call which is a feature both of male territorial disputes and of the elaborate loon mating ritual.

In my near-dream, I had construed the sound as a cry of mortal terror uttered by a woman in fear for her life. But this emotional overtone was something I had brought with me. The sound itself was part of a ritualized non-violent male territorial display, or the verbal component to an elegant dance across lake water: a pair-bonding display, an avian pre-copulatory "Whoopee!"

I have heard loon calls often since, and almost certainly so have you, even if you live in downtown L.A. or Manhattan. The softer, mellower loon cries have become established in the sound repertoire of TV and movie producers as a signaler of natural or exotic places, often enough places where no loon has ever touched down. A little loon noise is not infrequently paired with some Native American style flute, after which somebody in the cast talks about Nature in hushed tones.

I am writing these words in the middle of an extraordinarily long, cold, and snowy winter, with all our local loons long gone to their warm-water wintering grounds on the Atlantic coast or the Gulf of Mexico. Nevertheless I recently heard some loon tremolos. They were part of the sound-track of a holodeck program titled "Luau", being played on a twenty-fourth century space ship named Voyager which was lost in the Delta Quadrant.

If I were lost in the Delta Quadrant, the cry of loons would carry me home.

....

Rain after heat: a heaviness in the air, a premonitory quieting of night insects, the rumble of thunder at a distance. Abrupt illumination from far-off lightning barely perceived through closed eyelids.

Closer approach of the heavenly artillery. A sudden sough of wind rustling the leaves, touching bare skin from which blankets and then sheets have been thrown back. The first fat, isolated, slow drops on the roof. That unmistakable smell of rain on hot dry earth and ozone in the air.

Then the full cannonade of the sky, varying from CH-BOOM, with a several-second interval between sound and flash, to the full steel-on-steel slamming BLAM! and the near strike blazing everything in the room alight, leaving an after-image on the eye.

And on the roof the roar, the rush, the baptism of the opened heavens, the drumming into the rain-barrel turning into a steady pour. Delight and relief balanced on a knife-edge, let it slack off now, let it just turn into a good soaker, let there be no raw ruts in the cornfields, no washed out roads, no erosional flush of earth into lakes and streams to ruin the fishing. Let it just come easy, hissing into the marshes, filling the potholes, sliding down grass blades and washing dusty leaves.

Out in the fields the stiffly-angled corn blades and scrunched bean-leaves open themselves outward, the sagged squash leaves rise again, to greet the morning as green umbrellas. Air in the bedroom cools off to that undefinable but desirable temperature called "good sleeping weather." Steady calm roof-drumming and the rumbles and thumps and flashes moving away, to bless other gardens and fields and woods, to shake other sweating sleepers awake and pleasure them down again into soaking and greening dark.

If the rain holds till tomorrow the farm cars will come into town, splashes of mud on the doors, bug screens full of June bugs and broken dragonflies. The farm wives in starched dresses, released from hot kitchens, will look at piece goods and stock up on Mason jars. The guys in clean crisp "town" overalls will visit the hardware, the feed mill, the implement dealer, the cafe. For once in a summer slowed down and not minding it, they will drink coffee and eat pie and look out at the silver curtain and mutter, "She must be up over two inches now. Ya, she's what you call a million dollar rain."

At least, that's how it was in 1964. Most of those stores are closed now. Many of those farms have been swallowed up. And most farm wives, of necessity, have their own full-time jobs.

Only the drama of the thunderstorm endures as it was.

....

Fall night, heavy overcast, that light-eating country dark. A sudden raining-down of notes from the sky, a brilliant rhythmic swell of sound.

Canada geese, invisibly winging south, above our darkness finding the old travel routes. What tone-deaf lout ever used the same word, "honk", to describe this poignant music and the parking-lot blat of a car?

The very same geese which had winged their way across the sentimental skyscapes of my early poems, having flown there from other peoples' poems.

In the cool dark with the sharp damp smells of the woods around me, I hear them for the first time.

....

The single once-every-twenty-four-hours wail of the Burlington-Northern railway train, blowing for the crossing in Grey Eagle. A long gone sound. Today you have to ask around to locate where the track was. Ask older people.

....

42

The rustle and slide of falling leaves across the roof. The furtive scratch and scamper of a deer mouse, driven in by the cold.

....

Deep quiet in the fall house, the fireplace talking, pages turning. Somewhere out in the woods, a little sharp yap.

John raises his head from his book. "Fox," he says.

We listen hard, but the sound does not come again.

....

The even deeper quiet of winter, snow and the lake frozen. A sudden singing zinging sound, halfway between the crack of well-dried wood splitting, and the ringing of a bell.

I have heard this sound in daylight, at lake level, in the angling house, absorbed in jigging my ice-fishing stick in the water which was comfortable to swim in, last June. The hole in the ice, the little window John has augured into the underplace, casts a faintly green luminosity upward, a disk of light that shimmers on the low roof of the fish house. As if the lake whose ice we could now drive across has its own source of light down there, and it is the realm of light and life, and we are the children of darkness.

Looking down, I could see sunfish approach the tiny bait minnow I was twitching. I would make the red eye of the ice-fishing fly bounce, just a little.

The round-bodied sunfish, the deep-tinted bluegills, the golden-flanked pumpkinseeds, all so tasty in beer batter, would open and shut their mouths thoughtfully, then swim off.

I could see twigs on the bottom, fifteen feet down. (Ice fishermen on Swan can't do that today).

Then this great ringing cracking sound came at us with an ice-tingling shudder and went away as fast as a fish darting out of danger, too fast to frighten except in retrospect. "Crack in the ice," John said calmly. "It does that."

This was the same sound, only heard from the house, several hundred yards up the hill. Heard through covering snow and woods in between and the walls of the cottage. ZING. Big Swan Lake stretching a little in the cold. Talking to itself.

WHAT WILL THE ROBIN DO THEN,
POOR THING?
E.

I am standing on the porch which John built onto Mother Rylander's cottage, so that we have a place to put our muddy shoes and hang our raincoats in wet weather. It is October, 1964. The wind is blowing.

Shireen is playing with blocks on the floor of the kids' bedroom. I can hear her talking to herself and her toys. Behind me in the kitchen, the tea-kettle is hissing over a firebox full of split oak and maple. The little portable radio is set on a station which calls itself The Good Neighbor To The Northwest. At the moment it is playing Ian Tyson's song, "Four Strong Winds".

Four strong winds that blow lonely,

Seven seas that run high;

All these things they don't change, come what may:

But our good times all are gone

And I'm bound for movin' on;

I'll look for you if I'm ever back this way.

The fall so far has been bright and golden. Danny has started kindergarten, his first regular away-from-home experience. A photograph shows him holding up the zipped pencil case his Grandma gave him with a grin of mature pride, and trudging up the long path to the top of the hill, our English Springer Spaniel, Bet Bouncer, trotting at his side. Every morning he stands by the mailboxes till the bus comes to take him off to Grey Eagle Independent School Distict, Grades K through 12.

The leaves have changed in a great rush of glorious color, going from late-summer green to the shimmering yellow of birches and aspens, the golds and reds of maples, the maroon and bronze of red and bur oaks. The driveway to the cottage plunges through a breath-taking tunnel of autumn glory.

John has been cutting wood every day. The chainsaw will snarl away back in the woods, then he will haul in a wagon load, then the splitting maul and ax will set up an echoing chorus from the hill behind us. I have helped stack the lighter wood in what are beginning to look like the walls of a fort, Fort Rylander. I have been learning that it isn't easy to stack wood so it stays stacked and doesn't come crashing down on your feet when you take an armload inside.

Last week when John was stacking wood, he heard a crashing in the undergrowth. Expecting a deer, he looked up to see our neighbor plunging down the hillside through the prickly ash. Old Mr. Stuckel, the patriarch of the farm to our south, had heard a rumor that some young folks were planning to spend the winter in the Rylander cottage, and had come over to see for himself if this was true. He had not bothered with the half-mile walk down the road; he had cut through the woods between his farm and our cottage, up hill and down dale. At ninety-seven, he was no more than moderately winded by the walk.

He was friendly and non-committal, as many country people are. People in Minnesota rarely come right out and say, "You guys are crazy." But you could tell he was dubious about our winter plans.

By last week a good many of the leaves had come down, but the fallen foliage was still brilliant and crunched deliciously underfoot. The water of Big Swan Lake reflected back a deep steely blue into the clear vault of the autumn sky. The reed-beds around the lake edges had cured to a rusty gold, like the setting for a ring.

Splitting oak chunks in the sunshine, John had said, "Swedish flag weather," meaning the blue and gold were like the stripes on the little flags which his mother would put on the Christmas tree.

There had been some hard wind last week, too. The woods behind the house had roared on a single exultant note, like a huge deep-toned tuning fork. Now and again a sharper snapping sound signalled the breaking of a dead branch, the overthrow of a weak or old tree. "God's pruning", Mother Rylander called that.

Today the wind was higher-pitched, the bare trees not roaring but screaming. If I had known it, I was right at the peak of honey mushroom season. I could probably have filled an ice-cream pail with succulent dryable, freezable *armillariella mellea* if I had been willing to plunge out into the woods. But that was one of the many things I did not yet know. And the woods did not sound friendly today.

Our garden had frozen dead a month earlier, the tomatoes and squashes to which we had devoted so much attention reduced to black rags. We had picked everything we needed to pick, and it was actually a relief to be done with gardening, but still, there was something about that transition from brisk upright plant to limp rag of dead vegetable matter that came as a shock to somebody from a more temperate state.

And I was beginning to discover that cold here was not like any cold I had ever felt. It leaned into a body, not just mechanically chilling it, but actively sucking out its warmth, as if it wanted to get to the core of me, right down to the marrow of my bones. I could almost believe the weather knew I was a Californian, and was letting me know I lived in Minnesota now.

Big Swan Lake today was not blue, but slate gray, a mean cold gray. The wind had whipped it into whitecaps, cold peaks of foam like pointed teeth. The wood's roar was high and thin and continuous.

I hugged my elbows and listened to the wind, to my daughter's happy prattle, to the teakettle's song and the song on the radio.

If you wait until the snow
Won't be much that you can do,
And the wind it sure blows hard away out there—

All that business about the weather having it in for me was what, in my English classes at San Jose State, was carefully tagged the Pathetic Fallacy. The wind bloweth where it listeth and has no knowledge of who it blows on or what it blows over. "Nature never did betray the heart that loved her" had not been written by somebody who was hauling his own wood and water.

John came in then, arms stacked high with split wood, filling the woodbox with a rumble of potential heat. Brushing bark off his clothes, he smiled at me.

46

"What will the robin do then, poor thing?" he said.

An older song than the one on the radio.

The north wind doth blow,
And we shall have snow,
And what will the robin do then, poor thing?
He'll sit in the barn,
And keep himself warm,
And hide his head under his wing, poor thing.

He wrapped his arms around me. His jacket smelled wildly of bark and leaves and his clothing breathed cold, but the man inside was warm. I burrowed my face into his chest for a minute.

Then Rini came out of the back bedroom, carefully making a square turn around the hot stove as we had taught her, and tugged on my pants for attention.

And I made tea.

FORT RYLANDER
E.

The first snow of my first Minnesota winter fell two days before Halloween.

I went out and danced in it, as I had done in my first Minnesota thunderstorm. That time John had talked me back in—"I really don't want my wife to be hit by lightning." In falling snow, I quickly discovered, one becomes not only cold, but wet. My celebratory Dance of the First Snow was brief.

Still it was a good thing to do. In a climate where the snow falls early and stays long, the purely esthetic pleasure of white feathery flakes descending with their almost imperceptible sound is lost, too soon, in the mechanics of snow removal, jumper cables, the running noses of children, and all the rest of the machinery of survival till spring.

As our pre-Halloween snow fell, we drove into Grey Eagle and bought mittens and scarves for the children. The stores were full; main street was full; people from miles around had found some need to come into town, stock up on supplies, talk about the weather. I have found this a common response to snowstorms in Minnesota. The supplies that are being laid in at such times seem as much social and convivial as physical.

Then we went home, where there were now three or four inches of fluffy snow, joined the children in building a snowman, and took pictures of the whole operation.

Our October snow melted, as did the brief flurries of early November. The real snow, "staying snow", came just before Thanksgiving. The thermometer dropped into the teens. Though we did not know it yet, temperatures would stay below freezing till the end of February.

John had covered the single-glazed cabin windows with plastic, all but the picture window in the living room. He had put as much poured insulation as he could into the overhead crawl space, and stacked insulating straw bales around the house footings. And there was all that wood stacked up, cords and cords of it, the walls we called Fort Rylander. We felt ready.

Our living room fireplace and kitchen range began to eat wood in staggering quantities. Within a few days of Thanksgiving, John and I moved out of our bedroom and began sleeping on the living room hide-a-bed. With its door that opened into the kitchen shut, our bedroom quickly attained and retained a temperature at which frozen vegetables could be stacked on top of the dresser without thawing.

John and I slept under the picture window, which gave us glorious views of moonlight on snow and the occasional snowmobile headlight of an angler riding out on frozen Big Swan Lake, going to or from his ice-fishing house. The window also breathed cold at us.

The children's room had one long wall up against the back of the fireplace, one short wall just behind the kitchen stove. Danny and Rini stayed snug in there.

Christmas came, and for the first time I experienced the generous hospitality of Christmas eve and Christmas day dinners in a Swedish-American home. My children opened gifts in the middle of a milling horde of tow-headed, blue eyed cousins. We ate fruit soup and meatballs and rice pudding and an incredible variety of cookies and bars. We also had the traditional Swedish Christmas eve dish, ludefisk, or, as the Norwegians call it, lutfisk. Ludefisk is lye-cured cod, soaked and cooked and served, at least by my mother-in-law, in a cream sauce over boiled potatoes. Its aroma is pungent, its texture gelatinous, and though generations of Swedish immigrant children have groaned about its flavor, it has hardly any. "It slides down so easy," Mother Rylander said, as assorted family connections looked sideways, to see how I was passing this cultural test.

I had no way of knowing it as that ancient, honorable, and slithery fish slid down my gullet, but I was at a cultural crossroads. Christmas eve of 1964 was almost the last year ludefisk graced Mother Rylander's Christmas eve board. Tradition died in the face of Americanized taste buds. In the last years of her life, John's mother was forced to resort to Lutheran church suppers in small towns, if she wanted some Christmas ludefisk. This is the more remarkable insofar as she was not Lutheran. A desire for the flavors of the past can be more potent than the actual report of the taste buds.

Then the Christmas tree came down, and the thermometer fell even lower. We had bought our first television set that fall, and the station identification logo of the one available channel included current temperatures, as if they were the news, as often they were. Day after day we read them; 8 degrees. Zero degrees. Minus 10 degrees. Minus 20 degrees—

We stoked the fires constantly. By the time we went to bed at night, John would not only have the woodbox filled to overflowing, but a choice supply of big stuff standing around along the wall by the fireplace, a collection of backlogs in the most literal sense. He would waken as the temperature fell, after three hours, two, an hour and a half, roll out of bed in a single efficient flash of nude male, encourage and order and feed that fire, be back in bed and asleep in five minutes. The color of flames would flicker on the basswood-panelled walls and the fire would roar more deeply as the backlog took hold.

John took substitute teaching assignments in five different school districts, Grey Eagle, Long Prairie, Sauk Centre, Swanville, Melrose. Sometimes the night before, but more often on the morning itself, the phone would ring to let him know his services were wanted, and he would coax the 1958 Ford sedan which had replaced our Scout into life, and chug off to work.

Minnesota then (and to some extent still) is a state of numerous small towns, and back then most of them had their own schools. On stormy mornings we listened to Roger Erickson on The Good Neighbor to the Northwest, reading school closings sometimes for five and ten minutes at a stretch. It was a good way for an outlander to get a grasp of geography. After we had heard "Grey Eagle, Long Prairie public and parochial, Melrose, Sauk Centre public and parochial, Swanville", we could relax.

Out in the chicken coop, eighteen hens and two roosters remained from the flock that had come in as yellow fuzzy balls in their little box. The rest had enriched our diet. Now the survivors clucked and scratched. When the roosters crowed, their outcry was visible as a little plume of steam. I discovered that eggs in Minnesota are not gathered, they are picked. I also discovered that if not picked promptly, eggs will freeze in the shell. The yolks and whites of frozen eggs expand, cracking their shells and ruining them for human use.

The temperatures held bitterly cold. At around five degrees, I discovered, the hairs inside the human nose frost up. Below twenty degrees, taking a deep breath chills the lungs deep into the chest. Tradition said the lungs would freeze unless the air was pre-warmed by being breathed through cloth. I learned all the lore of protecting the face from frost, layering for warmth, drying out the boot liners. I also learned from other kindergarten mothers that boots slip on and off little feet more easily if a bread-bag is used as a boot liner.

The walls of Fort Rylander kept shrinking. On the coldest days, when the wind came off the lake over the ice, we could not get our internal living room temperature above fifty-eight degrees Fahrenheit. At the base of the living room walls there was frost on the floor.

We used a chemical toilet in the closet, which smelled foul. Saturday night baths meant a great heating of water, the square galvanized tub as close to the fully-stoked kitchen woodstove as it could get.

The world began to seem permanently white, permanently cold, the hands permanently chapped, the lips permanently split.

Then at the very end of February came two days of thaw. Temperatures above thirty-two degrees! Icicles dripping from the eaves! We drove somewhere, just to get out of the house. Crows were flying and calling.

On March 1, a four-day snowstorm began across most of the state, though we did not get heavy snow till the third. Around a foot that time. But still, March—

We dug out, took a deep breath, listened for the cries of geese.

On St. Patrick's Day the snow came again, with screaming winds. The radio brought us relentless strings of school closings, then highway closings. Endlessly, endlessly snow pelted the house, wind screamed overhead. For three days the state was shut down, no school, most roads and businesses closed, no mail delivery.

When at last on the fourth day the county road was plowed out and mail was delivered, the access road to the cottage was still drifted shut. The snow was waist high. John did not so much walk as swim the two hundred and fifty yards to the mailbox. It was two days before we could get plowed out, and then the plow left five-foot walls along our road.

There would be more snow. Snow fell on April third, just as we were leaving the house to celebrate the birthday Shireen and I share. A few flakes of snow fell on John's birthday, which as it happens is on May 31st.

And when everything melted, as of course it eventually did, there was major flooding in a lot of places in the state.

It was not the beginning of a new ice age. It was merely my first winter in Minnesota.

Everything since has been easy.

WOOD HEAT
J.

That fierce winter of '64-'65, in the cottage at Big Swan Lake, taught us lessons about heating which we have put into practice in later dwellings. We have not had a single winter so long and severe since. (In May of that year, we still had snowdrift remnants in the woods which nesting robins and wood thrushes had to hop over.) But we've had plenty of very cold days. Where we live you expect that.

On Ground Hog Day, February 2, of 1996, our exterior thermometer at Earthward registered -42 degrees Fahrenheit. At the same time, inside the earth sheltered house where we have lived since 1987, our wall thermometer registered 69 degrees. Much of the hundred and eleven degree difference between outside and inside derived from the warmth rising from our cast iron wood stove, a Franklin Scandia model 809.

I had gotten up during the night and chunked more wood into the fire, knowing that the prediction was for bitter cold. We were in the grip of arctic air, which had been blocked over the upper Midwest for a couple of weeks.

Not that the house would have frozen by morning. If I had slept through an unbroken eight hours, the house might have been three or four degrees cooler at breakfast time. The truth is, I take a primitive pleasure in getting up at night to feed the fire so my family will stay warm. We have heated with wood since we moved here from California in 1964.

A quick scan of our well-thumbed Minnesota weather almanac does not record any temperatures as low -42 for the winter of '64-'65, the one we spent in the Big Swan Lake cottage.

That cottage was never intended for winter use. Its "heat machines" were an open fireplace with Heatilator, extraordinarily handsome—my father had faced it with local brick—but cranky when it came to getting a draft going, and tremendously inefficient as a combustion unit. The wood-burning range in the kitchen, with its firebox and warming oven, bake oven and reservoir, was finished in elegant chrome curlicues and faced in porcelain. But forty or fifty years of use, plus sitting unused over winter in a frozen cabin, had begun to rust and loosen its cast-iron parts. Until you got it really drawing, it leaked smoke.

From late October on, hearth and woodstove were never without fire.

In the late summer and fall, I had cut wood by the wagonload and stacked it between trees next to the cabin, in double ranks six feet high and perhaps thirty feet long. In Mother's cottage, that picturesque but minimally insulated and weatherproofed structure, we needed all of it. When we closed off the back bedroom of our five hundred and fifty square foot cabin we had no more than four hundred fifty square feet to heat. We still burned over ten cords of wood that winter.

Just as living in a house without indoor plumbing teaches you a few things about water and waste, living in a poorly-insulated house teaches you a few things about energy conservation. Here in Earthward, we heat about nine hundred square feet, around twice the footage we heated in the cottage that first winter, with two and a half to three cords of wood.

The wood we burn comes off our forty acres. Late each summer and into the fall, I go into the woods to gather dead and downed trees. I cut trunks and limbs into sixteen to twenty inch blocks and haul them to an area near the back door where they are split, stacked, and covered. In addition to the house supply of two and a half to three cords, we need an extra couple of cords to heat the shop where I do woodwork, and to provide fuel for the spring maple syrup cookdown.

I enjoy this work. It has never been an unwelcome task or a dreaded chore to me. The chain saw's roar and fumes are a necessary aggravation. I should, for the sake of my hearing, have started wearing ear protectors sooner. Sometimes my machinery causes trouble. Sometimes the logistics of getting at a tree and hauling it out get chancy or awkward.

But all in all, I love getting out the wood. The fall weather is often glorious. The mosquitoes and deerflies of summer have succumbed to frost. The fall colors and smells are so beautiful I've heard myself saying, "I should have to pay to be out here today."

I realize that for many, the snarl of the chainsaw is a dreaded intrusion on rural silence. It signals the advance of urban sprawl. For me, it has been part of the small-scale, appropriate technology that lets me keep my family warm without depending on the energy companies.

Friends have asked me if I don't worry about cutting down all my trees just for heat. Not a chance. We have excellent natural regrowth on our land, slim little trees which will easily provide fuelwood in forty or fifty years. I can't come close to burning up just the yearly number of dead and downed trees on our forty acres. My guess is that these woods could easily provide heat for five to ten homes the size of Earthward on a sustainable basis.

What about the pollutants that come out our chimneys, what about carbon dioxide?

The carbon dioxide a tree releases when it is burned is the carbon dioxide it has consumed while it was growing. It would release that carbon dioxide as it decomposed, in any case, though of course it would do it more slowly. Unlike fossil fuels, wood releases little sulfur dioxide in oxidizable form.

There have also been major improvements in wood combustion technology since we burned those ten cords of wood in an open fireplace and a 1920's vintage kitchen range. Wood stoves and fireplace systems are available today which provide secondary combustion of much of the material which once went out chimneys.

Of course in areas of high population density and temperature inversion, the smoke from wood fires can become a nuisance, even a health hazard. What's appropriate for an isolated house in central Minnesota or other genuinely rural locations might not be appropriate for every residence anywhere.

According to the World Watch Institute, more than two-thirds of all Third World people rely on wood for cooking or heating. According to the UN Food and Agriculture Organization, as of 1980 nearly 1.2 billion people in developing countries were meeting their fuelwood needs only by cutting wood faster than it could grow. In rural parts of the Himalayas and the African Sahel, women and children spend between one hundred and three hundred days a year gathering fuelwood.

So it is perfectly appropriate, when thinking about wood heat, to ask where the wood will come from, whether it will be harvested in a way which leaves the forest resource undamaged, how efficiently it will be burned. Our answers to those questions are: locally, yes, and very.

If we weren't burning wood, where would our heat be coming from?

A lot of our neighbors burn oil, or LP gas, a petroleum product. As I was writing this essay, an oil tanker ran aground off a wildlife sanctuary in Wales. Final figures on the resultant environmental degradation, on how many birds and fish and seals were oiled out of existence, on how badly and permanently a beautiful place has been changed, will no doubt take time to assemble and also, no doubt, will be contested. And then there was the Gulf War—or Operation Desert Storm, as the Defense Department prefers to call it—which is generally agreed to have had at least something to do with oil.

Many of our neighbors have electric heat. We have electric backup heat ourselves, though we never turn it on except when we are going to be away from home for an extended length of time.

Electricity generation and distribution is by no means pollution free. When we go to Little Falls, the town in the next county where I grew up, we not infrequently get stopped by the long trains going through town, car after car loaded with strip-mined North Dakota coal. When we drive from Grey Eagle to Minneapolis on Interstate 94, we pass three enormous towers near Monticello. The two tall skinny ones vent a coal-burning power plant. That is where a lot of strip-mined North Dakota winds up. Despite stack-scrubbers, emissions from coal burning add to acid rain, global warming, and the visual haze that dims the stars.

The wider, more squat tower emits steam when its nuclear generator is running. Here in Minnesota we are already arguing, and likely to go on arguing, about permanent disposal of the nuclear waste from an older, now decommissioned nuclear generator.

To use electricity for any purpose—heat, refrigeration, cooking, light, the power that sends letters from brain to screen to computer memory—is to split atoms, to dam rivers, to strip-mine. There are of course less destructive modes of electricity production, like windpower and solar cells, but as of this writing, they still provide only a small amount of the world's heat and light. Perhaps this is because most people would just as soon depend on the energy business, and not think too much about where their comforts are coming from.

We know where our heat is coming from. It is manufactured out of soil and sunshine and air. I cut it, often as not, under bright blue skies, working up a good sweat in the process. (When Thoreau said the wood a man cuts warms him twice, he was underestimating.) Alone or with the assistance of my wife and, when they were home, of my children, it gets loaded into the trailer, hauled uphill, split, stacked. As it dries, it gives off the various sweet or nutty or sour or tangy smells characteristic of its species.

In the winter, we store a week's supply of wood in the little tunnel between our backdoor and our storeroom, which we call the trollway. The wood we feed into our stoves provides our house with more than heat. The fire ticks and whispers to itself as it gives up its stored sunshine.

When the last embers are reduced to ash, the ash goes out the back door in a bucket, then into a fifty-five gallon barrel where it is stored until spring. Then it is scattered in our garden, giving its minerals back to the soil.

What tiny percentage of the world's load of environmental damage we have prevented by cutting and burning our own wood, it's hard to say. But we know where our heat comes from.

ORGIES AND CORPSES
E.

Every place has its own spring, and they are not all the same. Spring in the upper Midwest is three seasons—Ice Out, Green Up, Leaf Out.

To properly enjoy any of these spring phases, it is necessary to throw away preconceptions about spring based on the literature of other places. Those springs belong to different latitudes, different climatological zones, a different set of expectations. Milton and Keats and Wordsworth never went through anything like those storms Minnesotans give titles to: the Armistice Day Blizzard, the Superbowl Blizzard, the Great St. Patrick's Day Blizzard. If in Minnesota you wait for shirt-sleeve weather, green grass and "flocks of golden daffodils" before you start enjoying spring, you will miss half of what there is to enjoy.

Every January, a popular nature commentator on a Twin Cities radio station encourages his listeners to "think spring" by watching the beaks of starlings, which start turning from winter dark to yellow in the long-nighted, deep-snowed nadir of the year. Naturalist James R. Gilbert also annually encourages winter-logged Minnesotans to watch for snowfleas.

Snowfleas are not a joke. They are members of the springtail family, tiny primitive wingless insects which live in soil, valuable consumers and reprocessors of leaf litter. Warm (well, comparatively warm) weather will bring them to the snow surface, where they make little visible specks, like a scattering of pepper. Gilbert says, "I notice many snowfleas on the edge of forests near wetlands when the temperature is above 27 degrees Fahrenheit. There they may be as thick as 500 to the square foot on level surfaces. When they accumulate in hollows and depressions such as deer footprints from which they cannot easily escape, they sometimes become a solid mass that could be dipped out with a spoon."

In my first long Minnesota winter I did not know to watch for yellowing starling bills or massed snowfleas. I do remember hearing about horned larks and watching for them on roadsides. They are grayish white birds, smaller than a robin, bigger than a house sparrow, their "horns"—little tufts of black feathers by their faces—a less distinctive field mark than the white outer feathers of their dark brown tails. They feed in open fields, of which there were none that hard winter, and along the margins of graveled country roads. A few of them overwinter; the rest begin to come north in late January or early February. The abrupt small explosions of their flight and the faint tinkling of their song are a welcome contrast to the familiar snaky creeping of blown snow across icy pavement.

The first signs of awakening life are tiny; a color change on a bird's beak, a pepper-scatter of snowfleas, a flash of tailfeathers, the distant cries of crows, which become restless and loud the end of February. But the first breaks in the ice of winter begin coarsely and pungently, with the smell of manure thawing and the waft of startled skunk over the snow.

These are humble beginnings to the glory of spring. But all winter, animal droppings have turned to stone minutes after they were deposited. When the weather is cold enough, a cattle yard can be as inoffensive to the nose as a bank.

Air has been scentless crystal, stiffening skin and nose hairs and putting the lungs on guard.

The first day on which a country passerby can distinguish by smell whether he is passing a dairy barn or a hog barn is a red letter day. On such a day jackets are partway unzipped. On such a day, the seed catalogs which arrived in the RFD mailbox just after Christmas are often opened, and the order sent off right away.

The reek of skunk is the ground-note of that activity for which spring is most noted. The waft of butylmercaptan, that volatile sulfur-alcohol compound which makes the bold-striped skunk so leisurely and unafraid, means that male skunks have left the comfort of warm winter dens, and are trekking maybe miles across the snow on the mere hope of love.

Skunks are not the only February breeders. Raccoons, squirrels, great horned owls, any animal whose young will need to eat the young of other animals to survive, must breed in the cold time, before the ice goes out, before the snow retreats, before the coming of green leaves. The smell of skunk means, not that winter is over—the whole state may yet be shut down by blizzards—but that it has begun to be over.

Most animals in a state of nature breed so they can bear at the time of the new forage, or at the same time as those young that eat the new forage. The white tailed deer of our woods mate in November so they can give birth to their fawns in time for the new browse of May and June.

Human interposition in the natural breeding cycle is as old as the fence to keep the bull away from the heifers, as new as the American Breeders Service truck trundling down the road, with the liquid gold of registered high-quality bull semen stored away in its refrigerated tanks. Despite frozen semen and cloned sheep, the barn lights you see down country roads when snow banks are still deep and mud deeper usually mean birth. Somebody is in there pulling a calf or a lamb, watching as a sow farrows, watching life and next year's crop come into the world, and hoping to God the vet bills won't be too high. Despite the best assistance of science and agri-business, delivery and birth are always perilous and exciting.

Life waits, waits, waits, waits. The snow comes again. The due date passes. Last year's ewe lamb, bred in the fall and round as a barrel, stands chewing and waiting, frosty breath jetting from her nostrils.

Then everything happens at once.

So one day the snow is merely sagged and rippled, grubby at road edges, sinking into melt saucers around the trunks of trees whose dark bark concentrates heat. The livestock tender making her way to the barn, to distribute food and water and see if any animals are in labor, still slogs through snow and slithers over ice. Sometimes the footing is worse than a week earlier, because the top layer of mud has started to thaw over still frozen ground.

Then abruptly, dark patches begin to show on southfacing hillsides. Skunk-cabbage blooms in the woods. Along roadsides, everything the snow has covered, every advertising circular, beer can, and fast food carton surfaces, four months worth of human trash all at once.

A sweeter phenomenon is stirring the veins of the trees. The parapher-nalia of birth is joined by the equipment for maple tapping. The first cries of newborn animals mingle with the "tunk tunk tunk" of maple sap falling into buckets. Smells of meltwater mingle with woodsmoke and the sweetness of syrup, as clear sap boils down to brown goodness.

I list processes sequentially. This hardly means they happen in neat order. At Ice-Out everything—fields thawing, animals giving birth, sap rising in trees—happens at once. The cold familiar castled landscape of tree and hillside and barn-yard goes to bare branches, bone-colored grass, slick mud sometimes in a day.

And all across this changing landscape, the birds return, beginning with the birds of prey. The big red-tailed hawks take back their soaring stations as the fields lose their snow cover. The bald eagles move up river valleys. The bright little American kestrels space themselves out at regular intervals on the telephone wires along country roads.

Now the water birds sail north in their skeins and V's.. Our Chinese and Toulouse geese used to answer the north-going calls of Canada and snow geese, dormant wild instinct stirring briefly in their chubby breasts. Tundra swans and cormorants fly over, as do ducks of every size from mergansers to teal. White pelicans wheel on updrafts. Rarely and wonderfully we see a line of sandhill cranes. Herons, egrets, loons come north as they have for millennia, following the open water. Birds we last saw six months ago plop down with joyous cries into ponds and potholes and those low places in fields some thrifty farmer has-n't yet ditched and tiled. They fly the width of the continent to ride once again the waters of Big Swan lake as the ice draws away from the shore.

"Ice out" is not only a descriptive term, but a technical one. Ice is said to have "gone out" on a lake on the day when ninety per cent of that lake is ice free. John has kept freeze-up dates (the day on which no open water can be seen) and ice-out dates on Big Swan Lake for over twenty years. We have had ice out as early as the first of April and as late as the first of May.

Ice Out was late in '65. Ice that has been thick enough to bear the weight of ice-fishing houses and sizable trucks takes its time to melt. At Ice Out, cracks appear slowly, great lines drawn by the chance geometry of current and weather. The ice begins to pull away from the shore, changing from solid sur-face to floating continents of residual winter. These temporary gray-white Africas and Europes drift and collide on the expanding water. One day there is more ice than water. Then suddenly, as in field-to-ground pictures, water domi-nates, live and blue.

At the last, the eroded and rotten ice becomes slushy, honeycombed with warmth, known in this senescent stage as "black ice". Here and there a pile of ice pushed ashore past the reeds may hang on, as here and there a packed snowbank crusted with grime may linger on the north side of a house or deep under trees. But the snow has melted, the ice is out, and one fine morning noth-ing but anecdote and memory remain to show that land and water were hard as iron for long months.

In the spring of 1973, when we briefly owned a small resort on a lake called Howard, we spent the last night of Ice Out in a cabin built near the water. It was warm enough by then to leave the windows open. A moderate onshore wind was assisting in the last pulverizing of the winter's black ice. All night long we heard ice ring and chime and tinkle and musically disintegrate. It was like being guests at a night-long, silent, enormous cocktail party, a thousand quiet guests meditatively shaking the cubes in their spectral glasses.

Even as the ice-continents of winter dwindle, the first faint traces of color begin in the woods. Willow branches turn yellow, and red osier dogwood flames, while snow is still deep, but the red on birch twigs and the faint green of aspenglow, visible only at a distance, come as the ice goes and the snow boots are put away.

The northward sweep of song birds begins always with red winged blackbirds calling their "konklaree!" from the tops of last year's reeds. Field birds and wood birds, killdeer and bobolinks, robins and the other thrushes, blue-birds, song sparrows and white throated sparrows, swallows and indigo buntings, grosbeaks and orioles, phoebes and pewees and wrens bring their songs, a con-tinuous chorus of territorial assertion and courtship which will swell to full anthem by mid-April. April to July, there is scarcely a moment in these woods and fields, from the faintest light of morning to pitch-black night, when some bird or birds is not singing. A seamless curtain of silver lies over everything, a comely, courteous, but persistent reminder that the business of life is making more life.

With the first bird songs come—or came, for the chorus in recent years has noticeably diminished—the first frog trillings, tree frogs, cricket frogs, leop-ard frogs, wood frogs, American toads. There is a pond at the foot of the hill where our cottage was, that first year, and by June that pond was the site of a con-tinuous amphibious orgy. Frogs two and three deep croaked, chirruped, clung and scrambled over each other, their throats pulsing, their great eyes staring, too besotted with the act of generation to hop away from the vibration of a footfall. The shallows of the pond were clotted with frogs' eggs. On June nights the roar of frog sex filled our ears, almost drowning out the flutes of the wood thrushes. But of course, the wood thrushes too were singing the hymn of procreation.

In Green Up time, under the still leafless trees, the early woods flowers make their glorious succession; jack in the pulpit, bloodroot, hepatica with its delicate whites and pinks and blues, rue anemone, yellow perfoliate bellwort, starry saxifrage, wild ginger, and the various wood and field violets. In the damp, hidden places grow rare showy orchises, which we do not show to just anybody, and those plants the state very properly forbids us to dig, the wild lady slippers. In the really wet places, marsh marigolds lift their golden tufts.

Come the end of May every road and old farmstead will swim in the scent of lilacs, an exotic plant, a child of Persia, but still so intrinsic a part of the American landscape that a time of spring without lilacs is hard to imagine. June will bring wood roses, the briefest of blooms, the one shade of pink, the unim-proved single cup of petals, the wild rose smell no grower has ever bettered. Wild rose time is also, in the expanding shade of the woods, wild geranium and columbine time, neat small nodding flowers, humble cousins to their vastly

60

grander windowbox and border relatives.

Later yet, as woodshade plunges the forest floor into cool summer dark, the field and roadside plants bloom, exotics and prairie remnants tumbled together, goatsbeard and trefoil and sweet clover and thistle and black-eyed Susan making tapestries of color until the highway maintenance crews mow them in the interests of better sightlines for motorists.

In time these roadside beauties are joined by goldenrods and asters, the last of summer's abundance, the turn of the year toward coolness and leaf-fall, first snow and death.

But in Green Up time the anemones push up through leaf mould. Sharp spears of green grass pierce last year's mummified snowbeaten grass on south-facing hillsides. And then very quickly the first leaves are visible, tiny as the fingers of newborn babies, colored even in the sturdiest species a most delicate gold-green. The new leaves expand from day to day, every tree, every shrub thrusting upward and outward, readying itself for germination. Birch, basswood, maple, oak, ash, species by species they open their calendars.

Henry Thoreau is said to have been able to tell, within two or three days, what day of the year it was in the woods around Walden by looking at the vegetation. This is hard to imagine in snowflea time, but quite plausible in Leaf Out.

Tradition says corn should be planted when oak leaves are the size of a squirrel's ear, but in practice, tractors are in the fields as soon as the last mud of snowmelt has dried, and sometimes earlier than that. In central Minnesota small grains like oats and barley and wheat can be grown, and when we first moved here, oats were still common, often as a nurse crop for alfalfa. And in the northern part of our county, on sandy soil, potatoes are grown on a large scale, mostly to make the ubiquitous American potato chip. But the staple field crops of dairy farms, the stuff you grow so your stock can eat it, were then and are still alfalfa for hay and that golden corn the Mexican Indians developed. In a place with a ninety-day growing season, you need to plant your corn early, then pray it does not catch a late spring frost or an early fall one, or drown, or shrivel in drought.

So humans are in the fields early and late, the rumble of the John Deere and the International and the Belarus competing with red winged blackbirds and robins. Good fertile earth when it is newly opened by the plow has its own strong perfume. It is a kind of intoxicant, promising fertility under human control, seeds in the bin, beasts in the barn, a wall to keep out the raiders who haven't been broken to the plow yet; money in the bank to pay other laborers, so the grandsons of the first need not carry dirt under their nails.

Gardeners burn the grass off the asparagus bed, sow the seed crops in their neat rows, fetch out the frost-tender starts of tomatoes, peppers, and eggplant, and get them into the ground as soon as it is warm enough. Vegetables, berries, fruit trees, herbs, flowers, we plant our thirty or forty garden species, while neighboring farmers are plowing, seeding, cultivating, fertilizing, insecticiding, herbiciding their two or three field crops. All around us on the unbroken land, nature pours out its species beyond our powers of identification, if not, quite, our powers of extinction.

Among the earliest and lustiest of these are the insects and spiders. Even in the long cold, the snowfleas and their invisible compatriots are alive and thriving. Indeed, without them we would not be alive and thriving. The leaves of last year and the year before and the year before that would bury the world in hard lignified corpses, without these humble co-inhabitors of the planet to reduce them to plant-usable mulch. The four species of woodpeckers who haunt our winter woods, along with the bug-eating nuthatches and chickadees, let us know our environs are well endowed with eggs and grubs and many-legged adults. Our first mosquitoes hatch from puddles of melted snow water, while snow is still on the ground.

The food chains, the process by which Creature A seems to come into the world primarily to be eaten by Creature B, are more blatant among insects than among the larger species. The first large hatch of mosquitoes is always followed within a few days by a hatch of ten-spotted dragonflies. One day there are none; the next, patrols of the great gauzy-winged mosquito-eaters cruise the fields in neat spacings of flight, as if on military assignment.

The human sensibility which winces at the gutted deer in the pickup bed, the mouse in the cat's mouth, the nestling blown from the nest, is less tender toward the worm in the robin's beak, en route to the nest, or the mosquito sucked out of the air by the dragonfly, before she could find us to suck our blood, before she could lay her eggs. In the great procreative symphony, the voices of the little hummers and biters, the big blundering Junebugs that thump our screens and the confused moths that clutter our lightbulbs play important parts.

By early July, the ground-note of every other utterance, every bird chirp or amphibian trill, is the low continuous drone of insects. Some of it is the domestic sound of the twenty-eight hives of bees which have harvested nectar from the white sweet blossoms of our basswoods, clovers and wild field blooms for some years. Much of it is the song of creatures humans reflexively slap, stomp, swat, and spray.

The immense and reckless abundance of life is perhaps most obvious in the kingdoms of the small, because the individual creatures take up so little space, but their swarms and clouds are so impressive and sometimes so terrifying. Anyone who has read Laura Ingalls Wilder's <u>On</u> <u>The</u> <u>Banks</u> <u>of</u> <u>Plum</u> <u>Creek</u> knows about the grasshopper hordes, relentlessly stripping the fields bare, walking in a steady rippling flood across the ruined fields, walking through the cabin, walking over the baby in her chair with their hard little feet till her cries of distress bring her parents to beat them off. Anyone who has read the Bible or National Geographic knows about locusts and army ants.

I wrote this essay in early summer. One morning I heard on the radio that one of the small cities in southern Minnesota had to turn off its streetlights the night before. A hatch of mayflies (creatures born without mouthparts, living at most a few days, living for the sole purpose of breeding and dying) had grown so dense around the lights that the bodies of mayfly casualties were making the sidewalks too slippery for human pedestrians.

In midsummer Minnesota, along with mosquitoes, biting gnats, wood ticks, deer ticks, deer flies, ladybugs, Junebugs, other bugs, we have an insect called the crane fly. It looks, to the non-entomologist's eye, exactly like a mosquito, only three times bigger. If you have just swatted the last mosquito in your room and you see a cranefly sitting on your window screen, the effect is one Alfred Hitchcock would enjoy. God knows how many craneflies are swatted each summer, with screams and imprecations. And all in error; for despite its suspect shape, the cranefly does not suck human blood. I do not know what the cranefly does, except buzz around and get itself slapped by horrified tourists, who think they have encountered Mutant Mosquitoes from the Pond of Doom!

One midsummer evening in our first year at Big Swan, John was out on the lake in a small boat, fishing. There were no clouds, no distant thunder, no radio reports of tornado warnings, which we take seriously. Nevertheless, when he looked back at the little gray cottage which held his wife and small children, he could see a black funnel dropping out of the clear sky, straight toward that cottage.

He fired up the outboard hastily, pushed the boat ashore without tying it, ran up the hill as fast as a vigorous young man can move. By the time of his arrival, he was breathing heavily, but looking sheepish.

The black descending funnel, the tornado-shape, was merely a huge circling hatch of crane flies.

After the long sterility of winter, after journeys of generation across weary miles of ice, after the struggles for birth in den and barn and nest, after the quieter struggles for sunlight, which means life, among seeds and shoots, the season of birth and abundance is also the season of ample corpses. Beetles thump on the screens, moths incinerate themselves, mayflies grease sidewalks. Windrows of the small dead are swept off porches and drift in the shallows of lakes.

A friend of ours, a wildlife biologist, was confronted in tears by his daughter, holding the corpse of a songbird nestling in her hand. Like a true biologist's daughter, or maybe a budding theologian, she wanted an answer; why do so many of them die? Their parents, after all, flew all the way up from South America, dodging the perils of migration, found territory, found each other, mated, managed to protect their nest from predators, produced a nestling to stuff with worms and mites and bugs, and now the poor little thing lay dead in her hand. "Dad," she said, resentfully (adults should ensure that the world is kind), "Why?"

"Well, honey," he said, "There is just no way all the little birds can live."

He did not pass on the statistical information with which he and all biologists are familiar. In The Birdwatcher's Companion, An Encyclopedic Handbook of North American Birdlife, Christopher Leahy says, "A stable population implies a birth rate in balance with the death rate. Birds tend to have as many young as prevailing conditions, such as the length of season, will allow and do not significantly control their population by manipulating their own birth rates. Birds sustain an enormous death rate, particularly as juveniles. The yearly death rate of *adult* passerines [perching birds] is between 40 and 60 percent or more, but the percentage of *eggs* which reach full adulthood averages only about 12 percent..."

"So integrated into the maintenance of population stability are such normal mortality factors as weather and predation that, viewed objectively, they can be seen as beneficial influences that keep us from being buried in warblers or Dovekies."

Perhaps one becomes an adult when phrases like "maintenance of population stability" can be understood without flinching.

God, I was told as a child, marks every sparrow's fall.

GOD, I recently read on a bumper sticker, IS PRO-LIFE.

Life certainly breaks out of the ice with irresistible vigor, and sustains itself in a thousand ways, many (most) by consuming other life, often while that life is still alive.

God, on the clear basis of the way the world functions, is equally, actively, and enthusiastically pro-death.

DEADHEADS
J.

...What I am has to a considerable extent been determined by what my forefathers were, by how they chose to treat this place while they lived in it; the lives of most of them diminished it, and limited its possibilities and narrowed its future. And every day I am confronted by the question of what inheritance I will leave. What do I have that I am using up...?

Wendell Berry, The Long-Legged House, 1969

It's April of 1945. My friend Archie has called to tell me his father needs some help this coming Saturday at his sawmill on the banks of the Mississippi, just north of the boat works. Archie, Gene, and I show up at eight a.m. A north wind blows over the cold waters of the river, which was covered with ice just days ago.

A pile of large wet logs is ready for the mill. We recognize them as deadheads, logs pulled out of the river by spring deadhead hunters when high water, ice jams, and strong currents break loose logs that have been jammed into the river bottom. These logs might have been cut far up the Mississippi watershed anywhere from thirty to sixty years earlier, when the Minnesota pinery was being sawed down as fast as crews could be got into the woods to do it. In fact this is a salvage operation to recapture what, two or three generations back, the timber industry was willing to waste.

Back then, these logs broke loose from the log rafts in which lumbermen brought their timber downstream to sawmills. Archie's father tells us that some of the islands north of us were actually formed when logs got jammed together and held in place as debris, then dirt, piled up on them. The vegetation on some of these islands now includes large trees, as well as a jungle of wild grape vines and other water-loving vegetation.

The five foot diameter circle saw bites into the first log, sending a plume of spray and sawdust into the air. The first pine slab falls off, and I grab it. It's saturated with water and incredibly heavy.

We each have a job to do. Archie helps his father roll the logs onto the carriage with a cant hook. He also helps turn the log that's on the carriage as it's squared off for final cutting. Gene and I haul off the slabs and the lumber, which is not the yellowish white of fresh cut pine, but a strange bluish color, stained from the many years of immersion in the Mississippi.

A huge log, perhaps twenty feet long and three to four feet in diameter, is laboriously rolled onto the carriage. It is a size of tree today's lumbermen can only imagine. The saw speeds and slows as it bites into the old, soaked log. Repeatedly the carriage stops, the saw regains speed, and again tears into the log. Finally, the slab falls away. Gene and I try to lift it. We can't. Archie comes around to our side. It takes all three of us husky young guys to drag it to the slab pile.

Later, we pile the wet lumber to dry, not realizing we are handling slices of history, remnants of a vast old growth forest, which once produced far more than simply lumber.

That forest, millenia in the making, once stretched from Michigan to Minnesota. Our immigrant grandfathers helped cut it down. They had little time to look at it with awe, although here and there a thoughtful worker must have scratched his head and wondered if all this despoliation was absolutely essential. They (and the timber company owners, financiers, even the foresters of the time) had no systematized knowledge to help them value what they were destroying as a living system. They could only see it as board feet.

Besides, our grandfathers were working men with families to feed. Destroying America's forest was the work the larger culture gave them to do.

Archie, Gene, and I, grandsons of loggers, hauled away the dripping salvage of history and a destroyed ecosystem, with little consciousness of what we were doing, and nobody to explain it to us.

All "deadheads" aren't wood.

THE ARNOLD BROTHERS
J., E.

The marketplace is a dismal failure at telling us what the earth is worth. You can start with a simple question: What's a tree worth?...The marketplace tell us what a tree is worth as pulp or two-by-fours, it doesn't say anything about the impact of the forest as a bank of carbon dioxide, or its role in freeing oxygen...It doesn't tell us how trees keep soil in place...or how they provide habitats for millions of species. It doesn't tell us anything about their beauty.
So what's a tree worth? What's a bird worth? What's clean air worth? If we asked these questions, we'd get some startling answers...

David Brower, interview, "Utne Visionaries Profiles", *Utne Reader,* May/June 1996

My environmental awareness had a growth spurt in the summer of 1965. As the year at the cabin passed, Edie and I began talking about the possibility of not returning to California. High school teaching jobs in Minnesota were plentiful. The opportunity to build our own home near the lake moved in our minds from the fanciful to the possible.

As the dream became stronger, I decided to cut down a number of trees from the wooded forty acres on the far side of the road, to provide at least some of our own lumber. The acreage had ample mature basswood, ash, oak, and birch, so cutting down enough lumber for a house was not difficult, nor would the number of trees cut down even be noticeable after a couple of years. So I set to the job. A young neighbor and an old John Deere B tractor helped me haul the logs out to a clearing near the road.

Logs are not lumber, so the next step was to find a sawmill to convert the logs into lumber and our ideas and dreams into a house. I soon learned of the Arnold brothers, who lived in a nearby town and had a portable sawmill and a reputation for producing quality lumber. In early spring I contacted them and arranged a time in June for them to saw. Their terms for labor and the use of their sawmill were reasonable, if somewhat old fashioned. They included the provision of coffee (which of course meant coffee and sweet rolls or cookies) morning and afternoon, plus noon dinner. Not lunch. Dinner. Meat, potatoes, gravy, vegetables, bread and butter and jam, pickles, coffee, dessert. Noon dinner.

As the time for sawing got closer, my curiosity about the Arnold brothers increased. When they arrived early on the morning of the appointed day, it was clear that they were not young. They were both gray-haired and weathered, but upright, brisk and competent in their movements, and, despite all those noon dinners, on the lean side.

They went right to work setting up their mill, leveling it, installing the power plant and the sawdust elevator. The taller of the two was the sawyer, riding the carriage, making the cutting adjustments, turning the logs as needed. The other brother did the tail sawing, throwing the slab in one pile, the boards in another, except for those that needed to be run through the edger. At times he would help his brother with logs that were especially large or otherwise difficult to turn. He also kept the power plant fueled and oiled.

The engine rumbled. The cut lumber and sawdust piled up. The air filled with the fresh tang of new-cut lumber.

At noon that first day, we all went down to the cottage where Edie had ready a proper Minnesota working man's noon meal. We ate heartily, exchanging small talk about the weather, crops, and pieces of personal history. At one point I commented on how well their sawmill worked and how new it looked. At that point the taller brother, the sawyer, said, "Yes, it's quite new. We drove down to Alabama twelve years ago to buy it and bring it home."

As the conversation went on, we soon learned that the taller of the two was also the oldest. He was eighty-seven. His tail-sawing "kid" half-brother was a mere sixty-six. This meant not only that these two senior citizens were still working at physically demanding jobs, but that the elder had set himself up with a new sawmill at age seventy-five!

Four and a half days of work with the Arnold brothers reduced logs to neatly stacked lumber. In retrospect, I think we both wish we had asked them more questions. As we would find out years later, the Arnold family had settled in Todd County in the 1880's, when it was still raw frontier.

A casual statement by the older brother has reverberated in my mind ever since. He said he could remember, he could still see in his mind's eye, when much of northern Minnesota was virgin timber, white and red pine, fir and spruce.

We have broken bread with a man whose living memory encompassed a wilderness which is now only photographs, and, of course, street, building, and company names that commemorate fortunes made in the lumbering business.
Lumbering in Minnesota began in 1837, when the state was not even a territory as yet. In 1848, an estimated two million log feet of harvested timber came down the Mississippi. The next year the log footage was up to three and a half million feet and by 1850 it had nearly doubled, to six and a half million.

This was the first trickle of a flood. By 1880, when one historian counted two hundred and seventy-five sawmills on the Mississippi and its tributaries, 255.3 million log feet went down river. Riverborn sawdust and lumbering slab (1.5 million board feet in 1880) drifted as far south as Lake Pepin, obstructing navigation and filling in bays. By 1901, which would turn out to be the peak year of Minnesota lumbering, 838 million log feet, enough lumber to build an estimated two million homes, went down the Mississippi. By 1918, the timber flood had slowed to 170.5 million log feet. Over this seventy year period, approximately twenty billion log feet of Minnesota timber had gone down the Father of Waters to market.

In 1837, at the beginning of the lumbering era, the land which would become Minnesota grew an estimated 27,100,000 acres of forest. The most valuable source of lumber was the white pine, a tree which can grow more than two hundred feet tall, reach six feet in diameter, and live for more than four hundred years. The current Minnesota record tree, on state-owned land in Itasca County, is one hundred thirty one feet tall.

When logging began, there were an estimated 3,500,000 acres of old growth white pine forest, exclusive of other forest types, in what was to be

Minnesota. As of 1990, 16,718,000 acres of total forest—all kinds of trees of all ages—remained, with 67,000 acres (again all ages) of white pine. Most of the remaining white pine is less than one hundred twenty years old, what the state Department of Natural Resources calls "semi-mature" trees.

The elder of the Arnold brothers had seen those ancient forest giants with his own eyes. Most of them had been cut in his lifetime and all but a tiny fraction have been cut since. Minnesota has lost 98 per cent of its white pine forests.

This old-growth pinery has largely been converted to a much younger and much less biologically diverse forest dominated by quick-growing jackpine and aspen, trees largely harvested for pulp. The entire ecosystem, not simply the dominant tree species, has changed.

But to the contemporary passer-by, woods are woods, ranks of Christmas trees flashing by the car window. This sort of wholesale change is what the wood products industry glosses over, when it trumpets the claim that "there are more trees growing in the United States now than there ever have been."

Only someone like this old man could remember it as it was. It is hard to register as a loss something we never knew we had till it was gone.

The Big Woods, the mixed deciduous forest of which our forty is a remnant, has not fared much better. In the seventeenth century, there were approximately two thousand square miles of forest dominated by elm, sugar maple, basswood and oak trees, a kind of forest which French explorers called "bois fort" or "bois grand". By the 1930's most of the Big Woods had been converted to cropland, leaving a patchwork of widely-scattered forty to eighty acre farm wood lots which were used for fuel wood, timber, and summer livestock shelter. (This is how our woods survived.) According to the Minnesota Department of Natural Resources, in 1988 only two per cent of surviving Big Woods is in large enough stands to be called forests.

All those trees were still alive that summer in the folds and synapses of a human brain, their immensities preserved in memory.

To have been connected for a few days in the summer of 1965 to someone whose memory encompassed a time now gone and irretrievable has been lovely but bittersweet. We know there was a time close to us, not some remote legendary time, but a time within a then living man's lifetime, when, if other decisions had been made, we Midwesterners could still build homes with local and native lumber, instead of shipping in lumber and plywood and particle board from the western states, and, increasingly, from other countries

We and our children, and you and yours, might have known the complex, self-sustaining beauty of those woods.

In the fall of 1991, traveling through the remaining "big timber" states of Montana, Idaho, Washington and Oregon, we were rarely out of sight of clear-cut logging operations, sometimes on slopes so steep it was hard to imagine how a human being could retain his balance. Whatever lessons might have been learned from the old timers like the Arnold brothers have been effectively ignored.

We forget how incredibly fast the process has been, how a self-reproducing ecosystem can be reduced to living memory, then to photographs and history, within a single human lifetime.

REMEMBERING THAT TREE
E.

Once in his life a man ought to concentrate his mind upon the remembered earth, I believe. He ought to give himself up to a particular landscape in his experience, to look at it from as many angles as he can, to wonder about it, to dwell upon it. He ought to imagine that he touches it with his hands at every season and listens to the sounds that are made upon it. He ought to imagine the creatures there and all the faintest motions of the wind. He ought to recollect the glaze of noon and all the colors of the dawn and dusk.

N. Scott Momaday, The Way to Rainy Mountain, 1969

As John says, at some point in our year at the lake, we decided to stay in Minnesota.

We never sat down and listed pros and cons. As far as I was concerned, there were no cons. Yes, there were mosquitoes. Yes, as the winter of '64-'65 showed us, the weather could be brutal five months out of the year. Yes, the nearest book store was fifty miles away, the nearest motion picture theater seventeen miles away, the nearest live theater in Minneapolis, as was the nearest center of literary activity. Much of what Sinclair Lewis said about small towns was exaggerated, but some of it still rang true. Our neighbors were helpful and friendly, but their social lives revolved around the sort of church we had no interest in joining, the people they had lived among all of their lives, and their web of connections to large, multigenerational families.

None of this mattered. I had fallen in love with the place, with its sounds and smells, with "the glaze of noon and all the colors of dawn and dusk." I felt as one always does in first love, that my senses had quickened in a new way. I wanted what people in love always want, to live intimately with the beloved, shaping my life in patterns that promoted such intimacy. I wanted to live in ways which would do good to the beloved, or, at least, do no harm.

Oh, there were ordinary bread-and-butter pros, if a pro-and-con list had ever been made. Our living expenses would be substantially less in Minnesota. We liked watching our children learn work skills and learn to amuse themselves without needing manufactured pleasures. The poems I was writing had responded to a new environment and a new vernacular in ways which delighted me.

John, I think, had been unconsciously hungering, through fourteen years of exile, for the sights and sounds of farming at his grandparents' place, for the woods and waters where he had hunted and fished with his father. He reveled in passing the skills of a countryman on to his wife and children; how to read the weather, how to bait a hook and cast a line, how to tell weeds from garden produce, how to cut and stack wood, how to build and maintain fires. Coming back into a primary relationship with food and shelter and the tools by which they were produced and maintained had made him a happier man.

Falling in love with a piece of land must be a common human experience, judging by the enormous importance of place and the ubiquity of nature metaphors in literature, across continents and centuries. Yet it is difficult to talk about. Land is talked about as property, as theater for human endeavor, as storehouse of board feet and barrels and bushels, as divine gift, as science textbook.

The characteristic late twentieth century experience is one of placeless-ness. It is walking down the airline concourse stiff from sitting, dull-eared from engine-drone, seeing the little sign that says, "Welcome to Minneapolis-St. Paul" (or Atlanta, or San Francisco, or Pittsburgh), and being grateful for the sign, because, for a blank moment, you can't remember where you are, and the archi-tecture of the terminal gives you no clues.

But you can always, in these anonymous uniform spaces, find the bath-rooms, the food purveyors, the bars, the taxi-stand, the parking lot, just as, on the American interstate freeway, you always know when to enter or exit far in advance, even when you are going seventy. The uniformity of the structure tells you what you need to know, eliminating irrelevancies like the egret in the medi-an strip or the demolished Indian mound incorporated into the off-ramp fill.

Part of this uniformity is necessary. A 747 or Airbus needs a certain amount of glide path, a certain amount of takeoff and landing room, just as a fully-loaded triple-bottom tractor-trailer needs a certain amount of room to pass or stop or turn.

But business has been transacted over the centuries in souks and agoras and log-walled taverns, by men seated at roll-top desks or cross-legged on tata-mi mats. Commerce proceeded before the glass-sheathed skyscraper and the cubicle, before all the city downtowns began to look alike. Recent architectural uniformity answers less to need than to ideology and a curious sort of hope, grounded in deliberate destruction and conscious ignorance. If we junk all those sculptures and pagodas, those gargoyles and palaces, if all the major buildings look like the World Trade Center and all the shopping spaces look like Wal-Mart, will we not, in the glorious baptism of the market, forget all that bloody old past? And if we can do that, won't we all be better off?

One of the unstated premises of capitalism is the irrelevance of place. Industries go where the resources are. Workers go where the jobs are. To fall in love with a piece of land is an impediment to career advancement. To believe that land as land has some intrinsic value is to perversely thwart the invisible hand of the market.

For good or ill, we believe in the relevance of place. We have wanted to learn all we could about the land we love. We have wanted to know what forces shaped it, what it was like before the bulldozer, before the plow, before the double-bitted ax, before the map and the lines on the map. We have seen the land we love, with its resident lifeforms, as having a right to exist and sustain itself, regardless of human convenience.

Sometimes in large ways, sometimes in small, we are often reminded that other people (most of the modern world) feels differently.

In the summer of 1997, the Todd County Highway Department spent the better part of a month rebuilding a modest stretch of County Road 102, which bisects the land we came to live on in 1964. It was a graveled road then. Now it is one of those really short lines on a large-scale state map, four miles of two-lane county blacktop that goes only from Grey Eagle to the Long Lake Y.

County 102 takes off from State Street in Grey Eagle, passes the school, the tennis courts and volleyball courts financed by the Grey Eagle-Burtrum Lions Club, passes the small industrial plant where local women make personal floatation devices and leisure clothing, and goes on out through corn and hay and soybean fields alongside Trace Lake, named for a Swiss settler named Ferdinand Trace.

The land begins to rise a little, into small glacial hills. Here the road borders Lady Lake, named for the yellow lady slipper flower. To the right of the road is a gravel pit, which gets dug out a little bigger every summer. A little beyond that, further uphill, glimpses of Big Swan Lake come into sight to the west of the road, beyond trees and farm buildings.

Then Rylander's place, and the turn-off for the lake cottages on Swan, and a downhill turn, and a long pull uphill. A straight stretch, then a sharp downslope, and one branch of road going off east along the end of Long Lake toward Burtrum, and the other branch roughly north, around Long Lake and off toward Long Prairie.

At the foot of the last hill, on the east side of the road just before the Y, in the yard of a house which has not been used for years, there grew until 1997 an enormous weeping willow tree. Half its branches were dead, as had been true in 1964. Every wind brought down scatterings of brittle twigs. Every summer a storm or two would break off big chunks of major dead branch. Nevertheless there always seemed to be about the same amount of living tree as dead tree.

The trunk was maybe five feet in diameter and sutured with old scars. The living canopy shaded a very large area of lawn. The dead stubs of branches were favorite perches for birds, especially crows, who used to caw warningly at John and me when we went past the place on our morning walk.

The section of the highway which was rebuilt had two major defects. A sizable section of it between our place and the Y runs through swamp, and the pavement there broke up every spring and was repatched every summer. And at the bottom of the hill, drivers turning into County 102 from the west side of the Y were forced to make a blind, steep uphill turn. School bus drivers complained that they could not negotiate this sharp bend without the bus swinging out into the way of oncoming traffic.

So the graders and the big dump trucks and the road gangs were out there, early and late, for over a month. The highest hill was cut down by twelve feet, so on our morning walk we now go through it, rather than over it. The road bed through the swamp was raised by eight feet. Shoulders and margins were widened through most of the repaired area.

A lot of cubic yards of earth were moved. Several acres of wetland were destroyed. The reedbeds where red winged blackbirds nest are now much further back from the roadside than they were, and the road shoulders are higher and steeper. We don't hear nearly so many red winged blackbirds on our morning walks. I once saw a beaver sitting where the road margin now is, preening his chest fur in the morning sun. He would be unlikely to come so far from water and shelter now.

Slices of what were farm cornfields are now part of the highway margin.

And the willow tree is gone. Not so much as stump or sprout remains. No doubt the road crew slugged the traces of remaining root with plenty of herbicide.

County 102 is still pretty much the same road. Judging by the small double-pointed tracks in the road-edge gravel, the deer still cross in about the same places as they used to. The grade is a bit easier on our legs. The sightlines for a motorist are undoubtedly better. This no doubt means road-users will drive faster, which is no great advantage to us residents.

There is still washing and gullying at road edges where the sharp turn goes down into the swamp. The pothole crew still has to do occasional patching.

The blind uphill turn at the foot of the hill is less dangerous than it was, but still requires caution. To eliminate all danger at that turn, it would be necessary to take out the entire hill. I suspect that from the viewpoint of the highway engineer, nobody should live in country that isn't as flat as Kansas.

To anyone who didn't live here, the changes would be almost invisible. To us they are large and obtrusive. And of course, as local taxpayers we helped finance them.

Choosing to live at this place, on this land, did not necessarily have to mean choosing to live in this place, with this land. There are plenty of placeless people with addresses in central Minnesota.

We have chosen to let the land shape us, while shaping it in ways that are as unobtrusive and sustainable as possible. We have chosen to be mindful of the earth's past, in fealty to a future when nobody named Rylander may live anywhere near this chosen ground of our being.

These were choices, and in an era of deliberate placelessness, they are not popular choices.

I understand why the county changed the road. I wish they could somehow have saved the willow tree.

FIRE AND ICE, STONE AND BONE
E.

Human time, regarded in the perspective of geologic time, is much too thin to be discerned—the mark invisible at the end of a ruler. If geologic time could somehow be seen in the perspective of human time, on the other hand, sea level would be rising and falling hundreds of feet, ice would come pouring over continents and as quickly go away. Yucatans and Floridas would be under the sun one moment and underwater the next, oceans would swing open like doors, mountains would grow like clouds and come down like melting sherbet, continents would crawl like amoebae, rivers would arrive and disappear like rainstreaks down an umbrella, lakes would go away like puddles after rain, and volcanoes would light the earth as if it were a garden full of fireflies.

John McPhee, In Suspect Terrain, 1982

When we moved to the shores of Big Swan Lake in 1964, the cottage we moved into, with its sixty-six acre parcel of woods and farm land, was still known locally as "the old Shortridge place", though it had been sold to my husband's parents, Elmer and Elsie Rylander, in 1947. Country custom holds on to old names.

Of course "old" is a relative term. The natural human impulse is to see time as a stage play which begins when we enter. It is always good, in any consideration of history, to remember that our species are latecomers. I find it both informative and humbling to look at maps of continents with names like Laurentia, Laurussia, Pangaea, Laurasia, as they shuffle and skid, jam together and split apart, grow and shrink into the continent of North America. On these maps of the deep past, if the map were of sufficiently large scale, we would be able to see the place which has consumed and nourished us, that portion of the globe which will become a mapped and named sixty-six acres of Burnhamville Township, Todd County, Minnesota, U.S.A., formed and transformed again and again.

For a time the land we now call ours was equatorial. Our land has known a four-hundred day year, a lunar cycle of thirty and a half days, a globe without ice caps and a globe in which massive areas are buried under ice. Our land has risen and fallen, been invaded by oceans and scoured by glaciers, been populated by life in all its increasing complexity, and been swept by tides of mass extinction, at least five of which killed more than half of the world's species.

Relics of this deep past are readily visible to the informed eye on today's land. The tiny club mosses under our trees are descendents of tree-sized Carboniferous flora. Our dragonflies and mayflies are veterans of the same period, along with the little garter and ribbon snakes which like to bask on haybales near our garden. Amphibians, like our chorusing spring frogs, came along during the Devonian. Conifers emerged in the Jurassic, birds in the late Jurassic, flowering plants and placental and marsupial mammals in the Cretacious.

And at least since the first heat of planetary formation cooled down a little, there has been stone.

Much of Minnesota is striated and underlaid by granite. Ely

Greenstone, named for a town in northern Minnesota, is among the oldest rock on earth. Our northern lakes are characteristically cliffed and islanded with granite, stone thinly scurfed with moss, studded with flowers and pines growing in tiny pockets of soil. St. Cloud, where John taught at a state university for years, calls itself "the Granite City". (In 1916 its street sprinkling truck bore the euphonious motto, "Busy, gritty, Granite City.") Granite outcroppings have been quarried there and in nearby Cold Spring since the 1870s. First this ancient and handsome stone became the standard funerary grave marker, replacing shipped-in marble head and foot stones in the local cemeteries in the 1870s and '80s. More recently, St. Cloud and Cold Spring granite has been used for the F.D.R. Memorial in Washington, D.C., as well as for facing in many an upscale office tower or government building, Proterozoic stone sleekly incorporated into the most modern styles of architecture.

Field margins in much of this state are marked by long irregular piles of stone. The farther northeast you get, the bigger these rockpiles are.

Each spring, when the snow is gone, but before the plows and seeders go to work, farm fields bloom with little clusters of people picking rock. Frost thrusts stones upward through the soil. Erosion lowers field surfaces. Every year brings a new crop, from pebbles to fist-sized cobbles to boulders as big as a compact car.

One can buy rock-picking machines of various efficiencies, but most rock is still picked from fields by hand and thrown into the backs of trucks, or onto hay-racks pulled by tractors, or onto flat sledges called stone boats. From there it is hauled to field edges and tipped onto those ubiquitous piles.

We used to use an old car hood for our rock picking, dragged behind a tractor. On bright spring mornings John and the children and I would don heavy boots and gloves. John (or, as he grew into automotive competency, our motorhead younger son Eric) would drive the tractor. Dan and Shireen and I would follow behind, picking this year's crop of old geologies, heaving them into the drag with a resounding clang. Big stones sometimes needed to be pried out of the ground with a fork. For really big stones, crowbar and shovel and chain and the motive power of the tractor were necessary.

Fieldstone has reinforced our building foundations and walls, adorned our fireplaces and chimneys, become ornament, curiosity, and statement. As I write this, the House Spirit is watching me from the corner wall of Earthward, of which he is part. He is a dark, face-shaped stone with two small eyelike hollows into which lighter pebbles have been inserted. We have never been quite sure what his enigmatic face is saying, but it has something to do with fire and age, catastrophe and burial and long silence. With the House Spirit looking over my shoulder, I have to write with a certain gravity. I have to take the long view.

Building requirements aside, neither of us can resist an interesting rock. You cannot take a walk hereabouts without encountering rocks, and a few of the rocks always come home in our pockets. Gradually our windowsills and other flat surfaces fill up with rocks. We have granite in all its forms, we have agate and chert and quartz and chalcedony, but mostly we just have rocks that appealed to us. We have rocks of strange color and shape, rocks like candies and rocks like pyramids, rocks with stripes and streaks, bubbles and enclosures, rocks with red hematite cores and rocks with fossilized snails in them, and quite a few geodes, those round or egg-shaped stones the Dakota called *wakan* stones, spirit stones, power stones, the gift of the Thunderbird.

It's a good thing we're peaceable people, as the entire house is full of blunt instruments and potential missiles.

Some years back John found a big odd slab of tan stone in one of our field-edge stonepiles. The shape interested him. He hauled it home with the tractor. It was sandstone, rippled and striated, here and there harboring fossil shells. No doubt it was once a piece of old lake or ocean bottom. It was also pierced toward one end by a large natural cavity through which a chain could be inserted. It hangs in our front yard from a rough-hewn Torii gate. We call it the Holey Rock, or, in certain moods, the Holy Rock.

Most of those rocks were where we found them because of the Wisconsinan glaciation.

Glaciers, those mysterious sheets of ice which grow and thicken over time, burying continents and lowering sea levels, begin and end for reasons which are not clear to geologists. The Pleistocene Epoch includes seventeen glaciations and seventeen interglacial periods. The Wisconsinan glaciation closed out the Pleistocene, also popularly called the Ice Age. As far as geologists are concerned, we are simply living in the most recent interglacial period.

Some years ago, on a hot August afternoon, John saw a stranger digging near the road in our forty acre woods. Like many country people, we keep our land posted against trespassers. We do not mind walkers, bird-watchers, even hunters, but we like them to ask for permission before they go onto our land.

By the time John had crossed the road from the house and walked up to him, the young man had laid down his tools and was producing identification. He was a University of Minnesota graduate student working on a Ph.D. in geology. He was sampling our rocks and soil. We were happy to exchange those samples for some information about the land we live on.

Over a cold drink, the student geologist talked with enthusiasm about the complexity of Minnesota geology. He was doing his doctoral field work in an area of central Minnesota encompassing around a thousand square miles. His hands moved across our round oak dining room table, sketching the ways in which glacial ice from the northwest, north, and northeast had moved and retreated at least five times across what he believed was one of the most geologically complex areas in the United States. He had seen clear evidence of these advances and retreats, he said, in the layered strata of a gravel pit only a few miles from us.

The world has never seemed quite so solid and unchanging since that conversation.

Glacial ice presses down and scrapes along, carrying stone, much of which it grinds into gravel, sand, silt, and clay. This transported material is called till. The lightest till is carried farthest, which is why the rockpiles at field edges grow bigger as you travel northeast in Minnesota. Under moving ice, clusters of elliptical streamlined hills called drumlins are formed, with their long axes roughly parallel to the direction of ice movement. Drumlins slope steeply toward the direction from which the glacier came and gently toward the direction in which it moved. They vary in height from twenty to two hundred feet and can be several miles long, and are mostly formed of clayey till. Drumlins often form in echelons or belts, so they disrupt drainage, and small lakes or swamps form between them.

I am writing these words in an earth-sheltered house dug into the upper backslope of a drumlin, a fact I did not realize until I did the research for this book.

Most of the state of Minnesota was covered with ice during the Wisconsinan Glaciation. Glacial Lake Agassiz, formed when the Laurentide Ice Sheet blocked the drainage of the northern Great Plains into what today is Hudson's Bay, was seven hundred miles long and two hundred miles wide. The flat, fertile lands of the Red River and Souris watersheds are old Agassiz lake bottom. Canadian Lakes Winnipeg, Winnipegosis, and Manitoba, and Lake of the Woods on the U.S.-Canadian border, are Agassiz remnants. The Great Lakes are also glacial remnants; lobes of ice moved down pre-existing lowlands and scoured out the weak basin rock.

The rich farm land to our south and west was blessed with the lightest, farthest-carried glacial till, fine rock flour to make rich well-mineralized prairie soil, not flat like lake bottom, but gently rolling.

Here in the center of the state, that "geologically complex" area, we are in moraine country, where the heavy stuff landed, the place where the glaciers dumped their load. In addition to scraping and dropping drumlins, glaciers also leave behind them stranded ice masses, great chunks of glacial ice that became partly or wholly buried. The depressions, roughly round because chunks of ice tend to become rounded as they melt, are called kettles. When they retain their water, the resulting lakes are called kettle lakes. They are often interspersed with kames: moundlike hills of poorly sorted drift, mostly sand and gravel, deposited near the glacier terminus. The frequent combination of kames and kettle lakes is called kame and kettle country.

I do not know of any local chamber of commerce which hands out tee shirts reading, "Welcome to Kame and Kettle Kountry", but a Grey Eagle booster group a few years back sold shirts that read, "25 Lakes in a 5 Mile Radius", which is a less geologically exact way of saying the same thing.

Active glaciers melt seasonally, sending large and variable quantities of meltwater and sediment from their margins. Some rivers run in tunnels within the glacier. When the glacier melts, the sediment deposits in the tunnels are left as long ridges of stratified sand and gravel called eskers, which are a frequent source of sand and gravel quarrying today.

Glacial rivers running at ground level left braided channel patterns. They also left thick deposits of sand and gravel in their valleys. As glaciers waste away, river channel patterns change from braided to meandering. Near glaciated areas, rivers erode into glacial outwash and leave a system of stream terraces along the sides of valleys. Modern interglacial rivers are much smaller than their glacial counterparts. Geologists describe them as "underfit"—they look too small for the valleys they move through. So the Swan River, draining Big Swan Lake, slides in S-curves among its reeds, almost invisible in its wide water meadows as it flows to its meeting with the still modest Mississippi south of Little Falls. So the Long Prairie River, flowing in part along the bed of an earlier Mississippi, meanders past its river terraces to join the meandering Crow Wing, which flows into the Mississippi north of Little Falls.

Most of Todd County is barred with green morainic ridges. Nobody who grew up, as I did, in a valley between two branches of the California Coast Range, would refer to these little rounded hills as mountains. Here and there a group of them attains to the dignity of a local name, like the Melrose Hills or the Dromedary Hills. Mostly these drumlins and kames and eskers, interspersed with water and places where water has been, are simply the shape of the land. It looks—certainly it looked, that summer we came to live in it—a rich, a gentle, a motherly country.

As it first emerged from the Wisconsinan ice, it must have been a raw young place, a land of boulders and rocks, mud and sand and seasonal tundra vegetation, a place with all the charm of a gravel pit.

It was, however, a place full of life.

The front page of the Todd County *Country Courier* for August, 1998, displays a photograph of a *bison antiquus* skeleton, rescued piecemeal from the bottom of Longbridge Lake and the Sauk River by a local man named Ron Weinhold. Weinhold has been hauling fossilized bones from the marl beds of the lake and the river for nearly thirty years, since he and the Boy Scout troop he then headed saw vertebrae in the bottom of the river. The marl, "20 to 30 feet of lime from snails and clam shells" marked a one-time bog on the edge of glacial Lake Agassiz, which, like the more famous La Brea Tar Pits in California, became over time a megafaunal graveyard. Weinhold and friends have identified bones of at least twenty-nine ancient bison.

Mammals at the close of the Pleistocene were gigantic. *Bison antiquus* was two-thirds larger than today's buffalo, *bison bison*. Bear, sloth, mammoth, mastodon, horses, all were almost twice as big as their counterparts today, and a lot of their bones are buried in those Sauk River marl beds, and presumably in other places. They are estimated to be from 28,000 to 9,000 years old.

Some years back, a local woman who was car-pooling to St. Cloud State University with John came out of her farmhouse one morning carrying a large oddly-shaped rock. "We've been wondering what this is," she said. "It came out of the gravel pit by Lady Lake. We've been using it as a door stop."

John left the odd stone, with a note, on the desk of a paleontologist colleague. By the time he got to his office the phone was ringing. "John, do you know what you brought me? That's the ninth vertebra of a young mastodon."

This was not the first occasion when local bones were laid on that desk. A contractor with a back hoe, digging up black dirt in the swampy land just north of us, saw chunks of bone coming up with the soil. He knew us, knew our interests and John's academic connections. So a fifty-pound sack of browny-white bones made its way to St. Cloud. The bones, preserved for several thousand years in acidic peaty ground, had belonged to woodland bison. They included the knife-like hump bone of a bull.

The place where they were found, now low-lying forested land on the edge of a swamp, was, when the bison were alive, almost certainly an extended bay of a much larger Big Swan Lake. Since the skeletons of several bison were found together buried in old lake bottom, most likely the big animals had stepped out some winter morning onto snow-covered ice, which broke under them, making them into historical artifacts.

There are mornings when the hilltops around here are in bright sunshine, but as we come over the brow of the hill on our morning walk, the reeds and trees of the marsh disappear into mist. It is not hard to imagine at such a time that bison, or even mastodons, may loom at any minute out of that whiteness.

The beginning of the Holocene brought with it the last of the great extinctions—at least, the last of the great extinctions up to the present time. In a period of approximately two thousand years, from around eleven thousand years before the present era to nine thousand years B.P.E., thirty-two genera of large north American animals vanished. Mastodons were among them, but they also included mammoths, ground sloths, giant beavers, and the American horse.

All the megafaunal extinctions may have been the result of climate change. Glacial times are wet times. (Utah and Nevada and the Sahara had giant lakes.) As the ice receded and the vegetation changed, maybe the big animals simply could not find enough of the right kind of food.

Or, as some paleontologists believe, human hunting pressure may have wiped them out.

The whole question of when _homo sapiens_ first entered North America is currently in flux. But there were probably human beings in Minnesota following the advancing tundra north as the glaciers retreated. The last ice left the state around 8000 years before the present era—in paleontologists' terminology, 8000 B.P.E. These new efficient human predators, hitherto unknown to their big prey, may have tipped all those genera of Pleistocene magafauna over the edge, into extinction.

We do not really know very much about these first Minnesotans, who may have hunted and foraged and lived on what we think of as our land. We do not know when they left Eurasia, how many groups made the migration, what their migration routes were. We do not know their exact genetic connections to the Old World populations they came from, and the New World populations that came from them.

What we have of those people are the more lasting remains of their material culture; projectile points and other stone artifacts, scrapers, mauls, milling stones. Sometimes the projectile points are found at sites where numbers of large Pleistocene mammals were killed and butchered. (There is one such large mammal kill site in Itasca State Park, where the Mississippi River originates.)

Warren Upham's invaluable <u>Minnesota Geographic Names</u> says of the Little Falls area, where John grew up, "The discovery in 1878 by Miss Frances E. Babbitt, a school teacher at Little Falls, of artificially flaked quartz fragments in the Mississippi valley drift, gave evidence of the presence of primitive men here during the closing part of the Ice Age." The Chippewa knew the area as Kakabikansing, "the place of the little squarely cut-off rock."

Stone survives, while wood and fiber, bark and pottery are often destroyed, taking with them inferences we might have made about the kind of people who used them. How much could some future civilization tell about the kind of people we were, if only the stones of our house remained? That we kept on hand a big supply of potential blunt instruments.

One of my most cherished possessions is a white quartz point, found in the early seventies in our Swan Lake garden. That field had been plowed and cultivated and cropped for years, so there is no way of knowing the point's provenance. (It may also have come in with a load of manure scraped from a barnyard belonging to a local farm.) Two inches in length and one inch at its broadest axis, it is bifacially and very delicately flaked. Its tip has been lost to use or erosion. It is not stemmed or notched, as most Archaic Eastern Woodland and later points were. It is what is sometimes called a Laurel Leaf point.

There is no way of knowing who made it, how long ago, even for what purpose, whether the procurement of food or the practice of war, or to accompany the dead.

Like the House Spirit and the Holy Rock, it has a message for me, this time from members of my own species. It says something about workmanship. Could I chip a rock into any kind of cutting surface, let alone a beautiful one? Lithic technology took great skill.

My Laurel Leaf point is a cross-cultural "Kilroy was here."

We know these first Americans by names Euro-American archaeologists of the nineteenth and twentieth centuries gave them. Past the vagueness of Mr. Upham's "primitive man", we have terms like Paleo-Indian, Clovis man, Folsom man, Old Copper Culture, Archaic Eastern Woodland culture, Mississippian Culture, Laurel Culture, Blackduck Culture. These descriptive terms allow us to talk about different forms of projectile point, different types of ceramics, different modes of burial. But none of the people we give them to would have so described themselves.

We have surviving rock art. The Jeffers Petroglyphs of southwestern Minnesota include nearly two thousand glyphs, carvings in a bed of soft pink Sioux quartzite. Some of them are fairly modern, dating probably from 900 A.D. to the seventeen and eighteen hundreds. But there are also glyphs which go back to the Archaic period. They are at least five thousand years old and quite possibly older.

They depict spears and spear points, including point shapes associated with the Old Copper Culture of the Great Lakes area. Veins of native copper were mined and cold-hammered in places like upper Michigan, Isle Royale, and Madeline Island, and show up all over eastern North America. Such points must have been valued trade goods, like shells from the Florida keys and the Gulf of Mexico and obsidian points from western volcanic deposits, which also have very wide distributions. ("Primitive man" was more cosmopolitan than most of us recognize.)

The Jeffers Petroglyphs also have more than eighty images of atlatls, archaic spear throwers which preceded the bow and arrow as weapons.

Archaeologist Kevin Callahan of the University of Minnesota, who has built present day replicas of atlatls, says they increase the throwing force of a spear two and a half times and that, with practice, some people can regularly hit a four inch target from ninety feet away. "With a copper point attached, it's like a flying knife." Atlatls were certainly used to kill mammoths and bison.

Later petroglyphs and pictographs are scattered around the state, often near water. Some of them can be read by contemporary Chippewa. Others are known to have been left by "the old people, the ones who were here before."

Some, not all, of those "old people" left effigy mounds, earthworks in the shapes of birds and animals. Some of them also left burial mounds of various shapes and sizes. The Laurel or Smith Mounds Site on the Rainy River includes the Grand Mound, which is 25 feet high and measures 136 feet by 98 feet. Charred logs from mounds in Otter Tail County, a little west and north of us, have been carbon dated at 690 B.C. Clearly human beings have been burying their dead, or the bones of their dead, for a very long time in this country, but for most of white settlement history, digging for relics was simply a popular amusement, with no scientific goal in mind and no sense of desecration. Steamboats on the Rainy River used to stop to allow passengers to take a crack at digging in the Grand Mound.

Most mounds, especially the common small interments where the bones of one or five or ten individuals were covered with soil, perhaps with the inclusion of grave goods or a food cache, simply disappeared under the plow or the road grader. (The phrases, "previously disturbed" and "reduced by cultivation" occur again and again in Burial Mounds of Central Minnesota, a 1969 publication of the Minnesota Historical Society.) John's childhood memories include a box of arrowheads, picked up by his father when he was a boy working in fields in Culdrum Township, near Flensburg. These remnants, which were at least several hundred and maybe several thousand years old, were treated as curiosities with which the children might play. Nobody in the family seems to know whether they were sold or lost, only that they aren't around any more.

Whoever they were, the people who chipped the stone, hammered the copper, made the pots, buried the dead, they lived here as the land changed. Raw glacial moraine slowly developed topsoil, as clay and gravel broke down into humus at the rate of two or three inches per hundred years. Megafauna were replaced by modern bison, bears, wolves, elk, caribou, moose, antelope and deer. Tundra gave way to forest. The distribution of the boreal forest zone, with its spruce and fir and pine, was probably established by 4500 B.P.E., with its southern limit about where the senior of the Arnold brothers saw it, just north of Highway 27.

Our land today is a northern outpost of what French explorers called "bois fort" or "bois grand"—the strong woods, the big woods. If we drive five miles north, we come to groves of remnant white pine. Seventeen miles west, and we are in Sinclair Lewis's Gopher Prairie, which was an actual prairie before Lewis appropriated its name for his fictionalized Sauk Centre. But right here, where agriculture and logging has not wholly transformed it, we are in deciduous woodlands.

The boreal forest does come close to being Longfellow's "forest primeval", but the big woods in all its spring and autumn glory, our northern deciduous forest of oaks, elms, basswoods, maples, and ashes, with aspens and birches at its edges, is a historical afterthought, a mere three to four hundred year hiccup. Prior to that time, our land was in brush, prairie, and oak savannah, maintained through periodic burning. Then the temperatures cooled off, wild-fires decreased in number and intensity, and the trees crept out of their isolated groves, shading out brushlands and grasslands, as today they creep back into deserted fields.

The people who lived here learned how to live in these changing environments. In addition to the hunting and fishing techniques which are so much part of our image of the "wild Indian", they developed a detailed knowledge of plant types which kept them fed, sheltered, and medicated. They learned the uses of wild rice, which was not a gourmet treat for them, but the storable staple, the staff of life. They learned to make and store maple sugar. Three thousand years ago, Minnesota women were cultivating the Three Sisters, maize, beans, and squash, largely in well-watered river-bottom lands.

These peoples developed the canoe, the toboggan, and the snowshoe. When the horse was reintroduced to the continent, some of them became notable horsemen.

Names and tribal affiliations begin to slowly filter into the white consciousness and onto maps as white settlement moves north and west. In the western part of the state were Cheyenne, who may have carved the later petroglyphs at the Jeffers site. Whoever used it and lived on it earlier, our land here in the Big Woods on Big Swan Lake very likely was occupied at different times by the people called the Sioux, and the people called Ojibway, or Chippewa.

Often enough, aboriginal people are stuck, not with the names they called themselves, but whatever the first European transcriber could make out of what his informant, often enough from another, maybe hostile tribe, could tell him. It is as if a Martian lexicographer landed in Belfast or London and politely asked the nearest street urchin, "What do you call those people on the other side of the channel?" Then he solemnly wrote what he heard on the map, and all his culture for the next four hundred years referred to the residents of the British isles as "Bludiprots" and the residents of France as "Frahgs."

Ojibway, or Ojibwa, or Ojibwe, or Chippewa, still an official designation on treaties and reservations, means "puckered up" and may apply either to the characteristic style of moccasins these people wore or to the fact that they sometimes immolated prisoners at the stake. In other words, they were being called "Roasters". The Chippewa have always called themselves, and today usually insist on being called, Anishinaabe, plural Anishinaabeg, which means "people, human beings."

"Sioux" comes from a French termination of a non-Sioux epithet. Daniel Greysolon, Sieur Du Luht (or Duluth), wrote, "On the 2d of July, 1679, I had the honor to plant his Majesty's arms in the great village of the Nadouecioux, called Isatyz, where never had a Frenchman been." The original name, given by tribal enemies, was likely Na-Doo-Esse, which means something like "snakes in the grass". The main part of the name, Na-Doo-Esse, was lost through usage. The French plural ending "cioux" became Sioux, pronounced Soo. "Isatyz" is a band name, later rendered "Santee". In any case, this easternmost branch of the Sioux nation has always called itself Dakota, a name shared, in slightly differing pronunciations, with its more western members, the Wahpetons, Wahpekutes, and Sissetons. It means "allies."

The Minnesota map is covered with names which are derived from Chippewa or Dakota sources, sometimes as translated through an intervening language. Minnesota, a name first applied to the Minnesota river, comes from the Dakota words "minne", water, and "sota", somewhat clouded—so, alas, despite those fetching beer commercials, it is probably not "the land of sky blue waters", but "river that looks like a cloudy sky" when the waters of the Minnesota are turbid with washed-in silt. "Mississippi", in various earlier spellings, is Missizibi, Algonquin (Chippewa) "Great River". Town names like Winona, Chaska, Minnetonka are Dakota in origin, but so are names like Blue Earth (for a mineralized soil used as face paint) and Sleepy Eye (the name of a notable chief.)

Many of our local lakes and rivers which are not named for early settlers have Chippewa names in translation. The Long Prairie River is "Gashagoshkodeia zibi", the Long-Narrow-Prairie River. Sauk Lake is "Kitchi-Osagi Sagaiigun", the great lake of the Sauks, refugees of that tribe who lived there briefly. Big Birch Lake is "Ga-wigwassensikag Sagaiigun", the Place of Little Birches Lake. Whatever it was called earlier, we know what the Chippewa called the lake we live on. It was for them what it is for us, Wabizi Sagaiigun, Big Swan Lake.

Most of my information on Minnesota names comes from Warren Upham's Minnesota Geographic Names: Their Origin and Historic Significance. Writing in 1920, Upham said about our lake name, "When the first settlers came, Minnesota had two species of swans, the whistling swan, which is yet rarely seen here, and the trumpeter swan, believed now to be extinct, like the passenger pigeon."

The trumpeter swan was the big swan. A mature male trumpeter will run up to seventy-eight inches long and have a wingspan of eight feet. Once mature, such huge creatures are susceptible to predation only by man. Between 1853 and 1877, the Hudson's Bay Company of Canada sold 17,671 skins of swans, many of them trumpeter swans, for use as plumes, powder puffs, and swansdown.

The trumpeter swan was indeed hunted to extinction in Minnesota, and almost to extinction in the lower forty-eight states. In 1933 only sixty-six examples of *olor buccinator* survived, in widely scattered lakes in the Yellowstone Park region.

But there are wild trumpeter swans in Minnesota today. Beginning in 1966, swans from Alaska were reintroduced in Minnesota, first by the Hennepin County Parks, then by the state Department of Natural Resources. There are now seven hundred resident trumpeter swans in Minnesota, twenty-five thousand in

North America. Every year the DNR cautions us to watch for migrating trumpeter swans in the expanding flocks of whistling swans, which are now called tundra swans.

I haven't seen a trumpeter swan yet, and neither species of swan nests on the lake with their aboriginal name, as they presumably once did. But the possibility exists, if not in my lifetime, then within the lifespans of my children. Something beautiful and rare which we came near losing has been brought back, gracing our spring and autumn skies with their great white V's and the music of their wings.

The oldest fossil remains of the Anatidae, the family to which ducks, geese, and swans belong, are eighty million years old. It is good to know that these survivors of the late Cretaceous have, so far, been preserved, by human means, from extinction at human hands.

WABIZI SAGAIIGUN
E.

The phrase "first white contact" is deceptive. White cultural influence in the form of kettles and blankets, machine-made beads and steel knives, firearms and gunpowder and liquor and horses, not to speak of bacteria and viruses, ran far ahead of actual white contact. There never was a single aboriginal way of life across all of North America, but if there had been, a massive process of cultural change was already well advanced before the average native ever saw a white face.

The three Native American tribes historically associated with Minnesota were the Cheyenne, the Dakota, and the Ahnishinaabe, or Chippewa. All were agriculturists when Europeans first encountered them.

Cheyenne in the eighteenth century were semi-sedentary agriculturists who made pottery and lived in earth lodges. Within fifty years they had become a typical western plains tribe, following the buffalo on horseback, living in tipis, their pottery replaced by hide containers and white trade goods.

The eastern woodland Dakota used canoes as a primary source of transportation in 1766, but by 1772 horses were common among them, and by 1796, within a generation, the horse had become their primary transportation mode.

Eastern tribes were pushed west by white settlement and pulled west by the demand for profitable furs. They pushed against more westerly peoples, who pushed on further against yet others. It was a four-century-long ripple of expansion which would extinguish many cultural groups and traditions, condense and simplify others.

So when Sieur Du Luht, the man for whom the city of Duluth, Minnesota would be named, came to the Lake Superior country in 1678, with a party of Frenchmen and three Indian slaves, it was in an attempt to make peace between the Cree and Ahnishnaabeg who were important to the French fur trade, and those pesky "Nadouecioux" out west. He also wanted to prevent Indian entrepreneurs from seeking a better price for their furs from the English.

Du Luht and others like him ushered in the age of the *voyageur*, the sturdy French-speaking canoeman, usually from Quebec, often enough with a Cree *grandmere* and an Anishinaabe wife. Intermarriage (or cohabitation) was good for business—*couriers du bois*, the actual trappers, were often one's Indian brothers-in-law or cousins.

By 1730, Grand Portage on Lake Superior was a critical link in the fur trade, because it stood at the southeast end of the portage around what the Ojibwe called *bawitig,* the falls on the Pigeon River. At this point the big canoes of trade goods were unloaded and the little ones sent west and north. Now a town of less than a hundred people, Grand Portage is also a national monument, the oldest white settlement in Minnesota. In the late 1700's it was an important rendezvous and trading post, where in July and August those who had beaver pelts to sell met with those who would buy. At the time of the Revolutionary War, it was described as the "commercial emporium" of the northwestern fur trade.

Grand Portage was the inland headquarters of the North West company, whose commercial empire stretched three thousand miles, from Montreal to the northwestern wilderness of Canada. The beaver hats of European gentlemen depended on the organizational skills, daring, and bodily strength of these wilderness entrepreneurs, and on the continuing habituation of native people to white-made goods.

"The effects of White trade were far reaching", says anthropologist Robert H. Lowie in Indians of the Plains. "Quite generally, the Indians were for the first time tempted by fur traders to kill game for gain. They adopted totally new foods and stimulants—bread, sugar, coffee, spirituous liquor. Metal utensils superseded earthenware and wooden ones, strike-a-lights provided easier means of getting fire then the drill, cloth was made into clothing with less labor than skins, steel knives cut better than flint. Thus a large portion of aboriginal culture became obsolescent, fragments being retained only for ceremonial occasions."

One small example; by the eighteenth century, the production of flaked stone tools and points in the midwest had ceased. The traditional skills which produced my beautiful quartz point had been abandoned as outmoded.

Ripples of pressure ran westward. By the 1750s, Ahnishinaabeg with gunpowder had driven the Isatys (or Santee) Dakota from the lakeside "great village" where Du Lhut planted the arms of the king of France.

Names change as power shifts. The Dakota had called that traditional place of settlement Mde Wakan, Spirit Lake. When they were driven away they retained the name. Their descendants still call themselves the Mdewakanton Dakota. To the Ahnishinaabeg occupiers the lake was Minsi Sagaiigun, Great Lake. Today's Minnesota maps have retained the French name given by the voyageurs, Mille Lacs.

By any name, Mille Lacs had prodigious beds of wild rice and enormous fish populations. After this point the Dakota were effectively shut out of northern Minnesota.

The oblong of land which is present-day Todd County is veined with small rivers and their tributary streams. The Long Prairie, the Swan, and the Sauk Rivers were all, at this time, prime habitat for beaver and other fur-bearers, but they were also highways for canoe-using people.

County historian O.B. DeLaurier, born in Todd County in 1870, remembered both a much higher water table in the days before agricultural drainage and deforestation, and two deeply worn Indian trails, described by Ojibway he knew as having been there "forever." One of them ran from the big bend of the Long Prairie River to the headwaters of the Swan, which flows out of Big Swan Lake. The other trail connected the Long Prairie to the Sauk.

The Long Prairie River flows into the Crow Wing, itself a tributary of the Mississippi. The Swan and Sauk enter the Mississippi directly. Even with today's lessened waterflow, seven central Minnesota counties are part of the watersheds of these rivers.

An amateur archaeologist we knew in the sixties told us he had located the remains of a long-term Chippewa winter encampment at the narrows of Big Swan Lake. He showed us points and pottery. Quite probably the Chippewa were not the first residents of a place with ample wood and game, and water access to the whole Crow Wing-Long Prairie-Sauk River system.

As early as 1767 or 1768, a trader named Berti set up a temporary trading post where the Crow Wing enters the Mississippi. In the winter of 1783, a trader the Ahnishinaabeg called The Blacksmith brought a company of forty men, Indian and white, to the point where the Partridge River enters the Crow Wing. Here they built a fort and temporary trading post, and spent the winter gathering furs from the area drained by the Crow Wing. The Pillager band of Ojibway came to the traders' defense when the post was attacked by a force of Dakota. Among those sheltering in the little fort was an Ojibway child named Eshkebogi-koshe (in French Guille Platte, in English Flat Mouth) who would later become a principal Pillager chief who regularly wintered his band in the Long Prairie area.

Nine years later, in 1790, Jean Baptiste Perrault and another trader named LaViolette were trading at Berti's old site, the mouth of the Crow Wing. In 1792, a sixty-man expedition led by Jean Baptiste Cadotte built a post at the confluence of the Crow Wing and the Leaf Rivers. Jean Baptiste and his brother Micheal, who was part of the expedition, were affiliated with the North West Company. During that winter they established trade relations with both Ojibway and Dakota trappers. By 1806 Alexander Henry of the North West Company kept a trader in the region of Otter Tail and Leaf Lakes, who would have gathered furs in northern Todd County.

Minnesota east of the Mississippi (including the place where John's boyhood home stands) came under the aegis of the infant United States as part of the original Northwest Territory, in 1787. Wabizi Sagaiigun and environs had to wait for the Louisiana Purchase in 1803. Zebulon Pike, then a lieutenant in the U.S. army, led a twenty-man exploring party up the Mississippi in 1805, with instructions to discover the river's source, (he got as far as Leech Lake), negotiate peace treaties with Indian tribes, and assert the legal claim of the United States to the area. He wintered on the west bank of the Mississippi, just below the rapids after which the town of Little Falls would be named.

The first permanent U.S. settlement in Minnesota was at Fort Snelling, a military outpost established in 1819, overlooking the junction of the Mississippi and Minnesota Rivers.

In the early decades of the nineteenth century, the Todd County area was generally recognized as Ahnishinaabeg territory. The treaty of Prairie du Chien, signed in 1825, codified this arrangement by establishing a boundary line between Sioux country and Ojibway country, roughly where woodland and prairie meet. It crossed the southwest corner of the county-to-be. The line was not surveyed until ten years later, and then Indians following the surveyors pulled up the stakes and ultimately slaughtered the surveyors' mules and horses.

For generations, buffalo had been finding winter shelter in the Long Prairie Valley, and Wahpeton and Sisseton Dakota had been coming to hunt them. Ojibway were equally accustomed to going out onto the prairie when and where they chose. To abandon this long-established life pattern because a few chiefs had signed a piece of paper and a few white men had stuck stakes in the ground seemed silly to most members of both tribes. Land, to the Native American way of thinking, did not belong, in the European sense, to anybody. The Spirits had made it to be shared equally by the people, the two-legged, the four-legged, and the winged.

The boundary was never fully surveyed and was obviously unenforceable, but the Dakota in particular resented it.

It was not a line on the white man's maps that kept the Dakota out of the Long Prairie valley and vicinity, but the frequent presence of Flat Mouth's Pillager band. Flat Mouth was a war chief of sufficient reputation that he was courted unsuccessfully by agents for Britain in the War of 1812.

Any modern historian looking back at these tribal rivalries and struggles can see that they were driven by competition for territory and access to resources, both shrinking as white settlement pressed closer. Just as the introduction of the horse had disrupted old migration and use patterns, the introduction of European firearms had made conflict deadlier. But these changes were hardly perceived by the men who did the fighting. They saw themselves as continuing long-established patterns of self-defense and conflict resolution.

Flat Mouth recited his exploits and those of his father Yellow Hair to Michael Cadotte's grandson, the Ojibway historian William W. Warren. Warren's account is one of avenged insults and defended honor. With minor adjustments for cultural change, these tales of largely-individual prowess could have come out of Homer or Beowulf.

There was traditional hostility between the tribes. Henry Rhodes Schoolcraft, who led a major expedition to establish the headwaters of the Mississippi in 1832, described the Crow Wing-Long Prairie system as "the war road between the Chippewas and Sioux". In his journey down the full length of the Crow Wing to the Mississippi in that year, he claimed to have seen no dwelling place, "not even a temporary wigwam".

Despite all this, there was never war, European style, with its objective of permanent conquest or extirpation. There would be an exchange of hostilities, a few scalps lifted, a few men killed, then a return on the other side, then, as often as not, a truce and the ceremonial smoking of the peace pipe. There were individual feuds and individual friendships across tribal lines. In many years there was a regular winter truce in the Long Prairie River valley between visiting Wahpeton and Sisseton Dakota and Pillager Ojibway.

During this time of *pindigodaudewin,* "entering one another's lodges", there would be exchanges of feasting and gifts. All this activity centered on the winter village of Flat Mouth's people, at the big bend of the Long Prairie River. The representatives of the North West Company or its successor, the Hudson's Bay Company, would visit these gatherings and come away with furs in their traditional ninety pound packs.

A Federal law passed in 1816 barred foreigners from Indian trade in the United States. The pelts that had gone up country through Grand Portage to Hudson's Bay now went down to Jean Baptiste Faribault's trading post at Mendota, where the Minnesota and Mississippi Rivers meet, then down river to St. Louis, quadrupling in value along the way. The canoe as transport was replaced by the two-wheel Red River cart, and, for the downriver log of the trip, the steamboat.

Red River carts were constructed entirely out of wood, secured together with wooden pins or strips of wet rawhide called shagnasty, which would dry
hard as iron.

Beginning in 1825, huge Red River caravans came down from Pembina
on the Red River of the North, bound for St. Paul. They carried furs from as far
away as the Rocky Mountains. Leaving Pembina as early in the spring as the
travelers believed there would be grass available for the animals, the Red River
carts would return laden with trade goods, which would end up in Fort Gary
(now Winnipeg) or any of the western fur trading posts.

The main Red River Trail crossed the county roughly where Interstate
Highway 94 runs today, and in the first trip of the summer of 1825, six hundred
and eighty carts made the journey. Each Red River cart, drawn by a single pony
or ox, carried a half ton of furs. Four carts were usually hitched together, in care
of a single driver who walked behind the lead cart.

The caravans, under elected "chiefs", ran with military precision, as
indeed, given the value of their cargo and their susceptibility to attack by Indians
or whites, they had to do. One thing they could not do was move silently through
the landscape. Their wagon wheels were huge ungreased discs of wood, and the
screaming sound of a Red River caravan, audible miles away, was something
observers never forgot.

Some notion of the size, wealth, and organizational scope of the fur
trade can be gained by considering the numbers of Red River carts, with their
half-ton loads of tanned pelts, which screamed down the trail in those summers,
then screamed back up with their loads of traps, rifles, powder and lead, trade
cloth and beads, cooking pots and liquor. In the first trip of 1830, eight hundred
and twenty carts. In the first trip of 1835, nine hundred and seventy. In the first
trip of 1840, one thousand two hundred and ten carts.

Most of the state was still, in Frost's phrase, "vaguely realizing west-
ward", chunks of it unmapped. There was still, very temporarily, room in it for
Flat Mouth and later Pillager chiefs named Big Dog, Bad Boy, and Hole in the
Day, and their bands, to think of this area as theirs.

The point at the big bend of the Long Prairie river where Flat Mouth's
band usually wintered became a permanent settlement with the establishment of
a reservation for Winnebago Indians.

A weary western chief once suggested that the Great White Father ought
to put wheels on his red children, so he could move them whenever he chose.
The Winnebago, a Siouan-speaking tribe which was living in permanent villages
in the Green Bay area of eastern Wisconsin when Jean Nicolet encountered them
in 1634, had begun the usual western migration in response to settlement pressure and the fur trade, and by the early 19th century they were in western
Wisconsin and the northwest corner of Illinois. Losing the Black Hawk War of
1832 sentenced them to an involuntary mobility which almost makes the commercial use of their tribal name for a recreational vehicle appropriate.

The majority of the Winnebago were moved to northeastern Iowa,
where there was considerable friction with their settler neighbors. In 1846 the

Federal government made a treaty with the Winnebagoes in which they gave up their land claims in Wisconsin and Iowa and received in exchange a tract of land in Minnesota, north of the Watab River, south of the Crow Wing, lying between the Mississippi and Long Prairie Rivers. This 800,000 acres of land, west of the Mississippi when the Mississippi was still regarded as the boundary of Indian Country, was full of swamps and impenetrable forests, and, as O.B. DeLaurier says, "supposed to be worthless to white people." It was also land that the 1825 Treaty of Prairie du Chien had given to the Ojibway, in theoretical perpetuity. (The Federal government would later carve yet another reservation out of Ojibway land, this time for the Menominee, but the Menominee never moved onto it.) After a year of government pressure and concessions, the Ojibway ceded the land in 1847, and in 1848, the Winnebago actually moved, though not with much enthusiasm.

The "Indian movers", as DeLaurier calls them, had an interesting journey north with their reluctant charges. When soldiers commanded by General Jonathan H. Fletcher put the Winnebagoes' belongings onto wagons, the Winnebagoes threw them off and declared that they would not go north. It took a detachment of troops from Fort Atkinson, combined with a "big feed", to get the tribe moving up to the Wabasha prairie in southern Minnesota.

Here the Winnebagoes refused to camp with their white "movers" and met with the Dakota chief Wabasha, who offered to sell them the land they were camping on and encouraged them to resist General Fletcher's orders. The Winnebagoes are said to have "disappeared" for three days—a neat trick, as there were over two thousand of them. More troops came down from Fort Snelling. Armed conflict was narrowly averted. Some on a steamboat going up the river, others in wagons, the Winnebago proceeded up to Fort Snelling. Back on foot and in wagons, they then went up the east bank of the Mississippi to the Sauk River crossing, where they took the old Red River trail and wound up at the big bend of the Long Prairie River, arriving in August of 1848.

Here some log buildings were erected at once, while a horse-driven saw mill produced pine boards for the rest of the construction. Provision needed to be made before the snow fell for all the Winnebago and a hundred and fifty white settlers.

Where Flat Mouth and his Pillager Ojibway were accustomed to building their wigwams, a warehouse with attached council room was constructed of both hewn and sawn lumber, strong enough to serve as a fort in case of attack. A three storied residence and office for the doctor was built on what was later known as Court House Hill. A Catholic church, a ten-roomed school, a grist mill to grind flour, and the all-important trading post rose quickly. The trading post was owned by the Chouteau Trading company of St. Louis, which had succeeded to the interests of the American Fur Company in Minnesota. There was also a hotel or boarding house, where, in 1850, forty men were housed. A three-forge blacksmith shop was presided over by David Burnham, who would later homestead on a lake known variously as Little Swan Lake and Pillsbury Lake, and give his name to the township where we live.

The house and office of the Indian agent, when completed, was said to be the finest residence west of the Mississippi in Minnesota. A later map shows an interpreter's house, a carpenter's house, and neat squared-off farm fields broken for cultivation, each with one or two little farmhouses, all very much on the white model.

In the founding and administration of the Winnebago reservation can be found a mix of good intentions and muddled execution, laced with white opportunism, Indian recalcitrance, and sheer greed.

For instance, an agency farmer was brought in, to teach the Winnebago agriculture. Winnebago women, like the women of all the eastern woodland tribes, had been farmers for centuries, growing subsistence crops of corn, squash, and beans, plus the tobacco used for religious observances. But this long feminine communal experience in agronomy was not perceived as having anything to do with "teaching the Indians how to farm".

As of a census taken in 1849, the year Minnesota gained territorial status, the Winnebago Indian Agency had 2551 Indian residents, plus white and mixed blood residents for a total population of around three thousand. This made it the largest city in the new territory, whose western boundary at that time was the Missouri river. There were around four thousand white settlers in the entire territory, most of them centered in the Fort Snelling-St. Paul area. St. Paul, the territorial capitol, had a population of seven hundred and fifty.

With this population level, there was no market for agricultural produce raised in central Minnesota, nor would there have been transportation available if such a market had existed. Thirty to forty years later, homesteading pioneers in the same area would go through the heroic labor of land clearance, then find the only product for which they had any market was railroad ties and cordwood.

Nonetheless, national policy was to make Jeffersonian yeomen out of the Winnebago and other reservation tribes. Tribal traditionalists would be described as "blanket Indians", tribal assimilationists as "farmer Indians." So land along the river was cleared and broken to the plow. Sheep were brought in, and a supply of spinning wheels provided, so the female students in the reservation school could learn to spin wool.

General Fletcher, who had managed the contentious business of transporting the Winnebagoes to Long Prairie, found his work as Indian agent for both Winnebagoes and Chippewa no easier. DeLaurier says he was able, honest, "but very firm and inflexible in all his undertakings", and that he had the confidence of his Indian charges "to a greater extent than any other agent of which we have any knowledge. While other Indian agents were becoming rich on the small salaries paid for their service, Fletcher refused absolutely to participate in any shady deals which might have benefited him financially."

This combination of honesty and inflexibility did not recommend itself to the "Politicians at Washington and St. Paul" who had secured the government contract to transport the Winnebagoes to Long Prairie at thirty dollars per head, paid on delivery. ("Other responsible parties would gladly have accomplished the removal for $10 per head.") Fletcher had kept his own tally en route and on arrival. It differed notably from that of the removal contractors. He refused to receipt for more than his own count. A new agent was promptly appointed, replacing General Fletcher. "The new agent came to Long Prairie,...signed a receipt for the number claimed by the contractors and they were paid off. Indian affairs did not prosper and soon General Fletcher was re-appointed."

Fletcher also made himself unpopular by listening to what his Indian charges wanted. The agency school was under the direction of a Presbyterian missionary named David Lowry, who had been agent for the Winnebagoes in Iowa, and had later appointed his son Sylvanus Lowry to the same position. The Christian converts among the Winnebagoes were largely Catholic. When they asked for a priest and sisters to teach in the school, the Episcopalian Fletcher listened with sympathy. With the cooperation of Washington, and of Bishop Joseph Cretin of the new diocese of St. Paul, Canon Francis di Vivaldi came to Long Prairie.

The Winnebagoes lit celebratory bonfires when they found out they were to have their own "black robe". But Fletcher had antagonized a good many whites on both religious and political grounds. It took a visit by some of the older chiefs to St. Paul, insisting to Governor Ramsey that they wanted Fletcher as their agent, to save his job.

Fletcher made a number of trips to Washington, on one accompanied by three tribal chiefs, who had been invited to meet the president. In their best broadcloth leggings and colorful blankets, with full eagle-feather head-dresses, foot long pipes, and painted faces, they toured the White House. They were particularly taken with the glass chandeliers, some of which, they suggested, would look nice in their wigwams. They shook the hand of the Great White Father. Then they traveled to Vermont, to see their agent's birthplace. The mountains of Vermont, they said, were more frightening than hostile Sioux.

It was fine for their chiefs to see "glass candles" and high mountains, and to sing and dance at the request of Franklin Pierce, but it did not make life any easier on their new reservation. Canon Vivaldi was an enthusiastic missionary ("During the first four months I baptized more than 50 small children who were brought to me by their pagan parents") but a poor book-keeper. Bishop Cretin would censure him for cost over-runs on the mission operations, and bring in a second priest to act as administrator. The Indian children would slip away from books and desks at any opportunity. (Those who would stick out a day's instruction were rewarded at the close of the school day with a few raisins.)

Their parents, many of them, would simply slip away. There was some reason for this. The 1849 census lists "137 heads of families provided by hunting", as opposed to "277 heads of families provided by agriculture". In the old way of life, villages had been places of seasonal residence. A hunter needed to go where the game was.

And a certain number of Winnebago had developed a fondness for alcohol. All reservations were legally dry, but east of the Mississippi, at settlements like Old Crow Wing and Little Falls, there was plenty of whiskey for sale. In 1849, a road from Swan River Crossing on the Mississippi to the Long Prairie Agency had been hacked out of the forest and around the swamps, paralleling the Swan River for most of its twenty-eight mile length. The project took twenty men twenty-one days. The Swan River road made transportation and communication easier for the reservation, but it also facilitated Indian exposure to white vices. Claims based on the depredations of "drunken Indians" were regularly paid by the U.S. government, out of the allotment money meant to compensate the tribes for their abandoned land claims.

At Sauk Rapids, a trader's post was turned inside out by Winnebago who wanted to see if the trader's claims that he was out of whiskey were true. An early St. Paul paper blames runaway Long Prairie Indians for horse theft within four miles of the capitol. Some homesick Winnebago managed to return to their old haunts in Wisconsin. The governor of Wisconsin demanded of Minnesota's Governor Ramsey that he keep "his Indians" out of Wisconsin.

There was on-going trouble between the Winnebago and the Ojibway, who felt they had been cheated out of their land. On at least one occasion a Winnebago hunter killed a couple of Ojibway, and a full-scale Ojibway attack on the agency was averted largely by the intervention of Canon Vivaldi and the missionary priest among the Ojibway, Father Francis Xavier Pierz.

An epidemic of smallpox visited the reservation, killing a substantial number of Winnebago. Early settler A. J. Gibson says the Indians "were superstitiously afraid of the disease and wanted to get clear out of the country."

In 1855, the grand experiment at Long Prairie was abandoned. Fletcher initially negotiated a treaty for a new reservation on the west side of the Mississippi well south of Long Prairie, near the Crow River, but the Treaty of Traverse de Sioux, signed in 1851, had opened what had been briefly Indian country to white settlement. There were already too many settlers in what would have been the new reservation, and they wanted no new Indian neighbors. Eventually a small reservation south of Mankato was set aside.

After a seven-year settlement at Long Prairie, the Winnebagoes packed up their belongings, abandoned their small farm fields and the graves of their dead, and were back in the hands of the "Indian movers", going over the Swan River Road, then heading down the great river. General Fletcher, faithful to his charge as their agent, went with them.

In 1855, the year of the Winnebago removal, Todd County was established. Like many Minnesota counties, it is named for a man whose associations with it were brief. John Blair Smith Todd, a cousin of Mary Todd Lincoln, commanded a military post called Fort Gaines, now Fort Ripley, from 1849-1854. Fort Ripley is now in Morrison County, which was separated from Todd County in 1864.

The two hundred and fifty buildings and cleared fields of the old Winnebago reservation now stood vacant, "a deserted village", as A.J. Gibson would say. He saw the empty streets and residences as a child of seven, in 1857, when his family settled there. The land had been held briefly by the federal government, then sold to the Long Prairie Land Company. Three or four other families lived in the town, most importantly the land company's agent, General Horatio P. Van Cleve.

Wandering through the empty reservation buildings one day, young Gibson stumbled upon a cache of abandoned spinning wheels, left over from the days of the Winnebago and the Indian school.

In 1858 Minnesota Territory became a state, its western boundary reduced from the Missouri River to the Red River.

At the outbreak of the Civil War, there was a scattered handful of settlers in the county. A group of land developers had platted out Kandota Townsite, in the southwest corner of the county near the old Red River Trail, but the financial slump of 1857 stopped sales, and all but one of the original investors had abandoned their holdings. The Van Cleves and the families of James Martin and W.W. Tuttle lived in Long Prairie, where the Long Prairie Land Company had found few takers for its holdings. The Gibsons and a few others lived at a settlement called Bearhead, A.H. Brower and his family at Little Sauk.

Though it took two months for the news of Fort Sumter to reach isolated places like Todd County, Minnesota was the first state to send Civil War volunteers. Among them were A.J. Gibson's father, who dyed his graying whiskers before he marched off to enlist, three of A.D. Brower's sons, "a fellow named Russell", and several others. Russell and two of the Brower boys would die in the conflict. James S. Brower somehow survived the carnage on Cemetery Ridge, during the Battle of Gettysburg, where the First Minnesota Volunteers sustained nearly two-thirds casualties in one of those fifteen-minute spasms of point-blank violence which made the Civil War so bloody.

After the departure of the Winnebago, the Pillager Ojibway began returning to their old haunts. The hereditary Pillager chief Bugonageshik (Hole-in-the-Day) was associated with the Crow Wing-Little Falls area. The chiefs Big Dog and Bad Boy returned to their old wintering grounds in the valley of the Long Prairie River.

Flat Mouth died in 1860. Born around 1774, he had lived through the coming and waning of the fur trade, through the *voyageurs* and the Red River caravans, through American annexation, into Minnesota statehood. He had seen the Winnebago establish their little town at his usual wintering site, and he had seen them leave it to a handful of white men.

Respected as a warrior, he was also formidable at the negotiation table. He was at times asked to speak by other chiefs during negotiations for the treaty of 1837, though his band did not live in the area covered by the treaty. He told the American negotiators the Chippewa were willing to sell the desired land, "but they wish to reserve the privilege of making sugar from the trees and getting their living from the lakes and rivers as they have heretofore done, and of remaining in this country." After long being regarded as extinguished, the aboriginal hunting, fishing, and gathering rights embodied in this document were ultimately upheld by the U.S. Supreme Court in 1999.

Flat Mouth was also an important participant in the treaty of 1855. He told the agents of the U.S. government as he met with them in Washington, D.C., "If we sell, we do not want to part with all...We had better not be in existence than not to have a place we can call our own...You would not think well of us if we were to jump right at your proposition without taking time to consider it."

At the time of his death, despite firearms, whiskey, and settler pressure, his people were still living to a considerable extent in their traditional, semi-nomadic way. But the veteran leader knew what was coming. "The people call me 'chief'," he said, as yet more Chippewa lands were ceded, "But I do not consider myself a chief. If I were a good chief, I would have saved my country from the predicament in which we find ourselves. I do not know where to look."

For the time being, Big Dog and Bad Boy and their people had good relations with the few white settlers. Bad Boy was particularly close to the Brower family, formally adopting A.D. Brower into his own Ojibway clan.

Things were different for the Dakota.

In the ten years preceding the Civil War, more than 150,000 white settlers had moved into country which had been lived in, cultivated, and hunted over by the Santee Dakota. Through two treaties, the woodland Dakota had been forced to surrender nine-tenths of their land and were crowded into a narrow strip along the Minnesota river. In 1862 the crops were poor, and annuity payments owed as compensation for surrendered lands were late. The consciousness that many white men were away and busy with their own war helped bring about a high state of tension among the Mdewakanton band. In the face of several thousand angry Santee demanding the goods that were due them, an Indian trader named Andrew Myrick improved on Marie Antoinette's "Let them eat cake" by saying, "If they are hungry let them eat grass or their own dung." Despite the best efforts of Mdewakanton chief Little Crow (Ta-oya-ta-duta), individual conflicts between settlers and Indians boiled up into the war which whites would call the Sioux Uprising. Myrick was one of the early victims, his killers stuffing his mouth with grass.

The Dakota Conflict, as contemporary historians call it, terrorized the newly formed state for the better part of three weeks. There was planned military action and random killing on both sides: on both sides, atrocities were committed. Nearly five hundred people, white and Indian, soldiers and civilians, died in that war. When the out-gunned and outnumbered Dakota surrendered they were treated as prisoners of war, including the women and children, who were imprisoned at Fort Snelling.

A military court of five U.S. Army officers, trying their prisoners without defense counsel since Indians had no legal rights, convicted as many as forty Indians a day of murder and other capital crimes. On December fifth, three hundred and three Santee Dakota were sentenced to death and sixteen to long prison terms. President Lincoln aroused a great deal of anger among settlers by demanding "the full and complete record of the convictions," assigning two lawyers to examine it.

Lincoln ultimately approved the hanging of thirty-nine specific prisoners. One was reprieved at the last minute. Thirty-eight men (remembered by contemporary Dakota as the Thirty-Eight Martyrs) died simultaneously on a mass scaffold on December 26, a spectator pointing out correctly that it was America's greatest mass execution. A few hours later, it was discovered that two of the hanged men had not been on Lincoln's list, and that one had saved a white woman's life during the raiding.

All Dakota treaties were abrogated. The thirteen hundred Santee prisoners were packed onto steamboats and sent down-river, via the Mississippi and Minnesota, to a reservation at Crow Creek on the Missouri. As the boats traveled the Mississippi through St. Paul on the first leg of this dismal journey, the Dakota aboard were pelted with stones and trash by settlers on the riverbank. Less than a thousand survived their first winter in their new home.

The transplanted Long Prairie Winnebago, in their southern Minnesota reservation, had taken no part in the Dakota Conflict. But to the settlers of the time, an Indian was an Indian. Terrified by the resentment of their white neighbors, they quickly agreed to accept a reservation west of the Missouri. Still later they were removed to a small reservation just north of Omaha, Nebraska. At each move, the area of land confirmed as theirs grew smaller. General Fletcher stayed with them for most of these moves.

Todd County was on the fringe of serious hostilities. As late as 1860, A.D. Brower had watched a sizable group of Dakota ride through the streets of Long Prairie in full war regalia. News of the Sioux Uprising sent most of the remaining Todd County residents fleeing for a hastily-built stockade at Sauk Centre. Able-bodied men there formed a small militia group called Ramsdell's Company. On at least one occasion a group of Dakota warriors approached the stockade, but veered off when they saw that it was defended.

Suspicious tracks and Dakota raiders were seen, or imagined, in other parts of the county. At least one settler, John H. Huffman, was killed while alone on the prairie, under circumstances which certainly suggested Sioux attack.

Several Todd County families had been warned of imminent Dakota attack by the Pillager band chief Big Dog. Brower's home was surrounded for a considerable time by a protective ring of warriors from Bad Boy's Ojibway band.

A.J. Gibson, who was a child at the time, insisted that the hereditary chief Hole in the Day was always a friend to the whites. The subsequent assassination of Hole in the Day at the hands of two fellow tribesmen was said to be retaliation for this attitude. But others believed, and told O.B. DeLaurier, that Hole in the Day and his band had intended to throw in their lot with their hereditary enemies. They were alleged to have planned an attack on Fort Ripley. With Fort Ripley secured, they would have gone down river to join the triumphant Sioux at Fort Snelling. Fifty to sixty years later, old settlers believed that Bad Boy had saved their lives by persuading Hole in the Day to call off his attack, and by warning the garrison at Fort Ripley that attack might be imminent. DeLaurier says flatly, "Bad Boy prevented....Chippewas from joining in the war and in so doing saved the lives of at least a thousand white settlers."

A good many settlers never returned to Todd County after the Dakota Conflict. In 1864, with most of the young men in the army and other potential settlers frightened off by fear of Indian attack, an election was held on the question of detaching the six easternmost townships of Todd County and attaching them to Morrison County. Needless to say, the people of western Todd County regarded this election as an unprincipled land grab. (A Morrison County historian writing in the eighteen-nineties would describe the process by which his county had enlarged itself at the expense of its neighbor as "Unedifying.") But A.D. Brower's most vigorous canvassing could turn up no more than five eligible voters in Long Prairie and three in Round Prairie, while twenty white citizens cast their votes in Little Falls for the plan of division.

The end of the Civil War brought an explosion in settlement. In 1862, Congress had passed the Homestead Act, providing 160 acres of public land free of charge, except for a small filing fee, to anyone either twenty-one years of age or head of a family, a citizen or one who had filed for citizenship, who had lived on or cultivated the land for at least five years. But Union Army veterans could, if they wished, file homestead claims on lands they had not seen, and a great many did. Early settlers in most of the county were Yankee not only in sympathy and military service, but in having New England as a place of origin.

There was also cheap land for sale, in places like Long Prairie and Kandota. And land warrants—scrip redeemable in land—had been used as soldier's bonuses in previous conflicts, as compensation for surrendered Indian lands, and as a form of financing for land grant colleges.

The old agency buildings at Long Prairie had been reduced by this point to cellar holes and the ghosts of streets. Some settlers were convinced the town had been burned by Indians, but A.D. Brower always insisted the buildings had been cannibalized for their lumber by settlers moving into the southern parts of the county. Though by 1867 there were no more than four hundred whites in the county, less than fifty of them adult men, A.D. Reichert in that year built a hotel at the site of the old agency warehouse and fort. Bad Boy contracted to provide Reichert with meat. "If he had ten deer, he would give him five; if he had one rabbit, he would give him half the rabbit." Men from his band helped finish the hotel barn.

The first day the Reichert Hotel opened, twenty-one lumberjacks showed up as guests. It was an augury for the future. By 1870 there were 2036 white residents in the county. By 1880, there were 6636.

Burnhamville Township, named for the Winnebago Agency blacksmith David Burnham who had returned as a homesteader, was organized in 1870. In agency days, two men attempting to find a route more direct than the old Red River trail had become so lost in the swampy woods between Big Swan Lake and Birch Lake that they were found nearly dead of exposure. But by 1873 there were enough settlers in the area to organize Grey Eagle township. The city of Grey Eagle was platted as a railroad village in 1882.

Bad Boy's Pillagers still came and went pretty much as they chose. DeLaurier's account is full of small instances of easy relations between Ojibway and settlers.

A woman is making corn cakes in her homestead cabin on a warm day, with the door open. The smell attracts some Ojibway hunters. She feeds them corncakes till she runs out. They depart peaceably. A few days later, an Indian arrives at the door with a *mukkuk*, the Ojibway birchbark container, full of fresh wild raspberries.

A settler is hurrying to his cabin as night falls and becomes confused. Seeing light in the distance, he walks toward it, to find himself among wigwams. The Indians gesture him in, offer him a share of the communal meal, indicate that he should sleep in the lodge. He spends an exceedingly nervous night, lying down between two men of the tribe among the buffalo robes on the floor, and is even more frightened when two of them insist on accompanying him in the morning. But it is one of the Indians who locates his cabin. His overnight hosts haul in some wood, help him get a fire going, and leave him some food, "and he could never be got to say that Indians were bad neighbors."

Bad Boy himself was fond of giving beaded moccasins to little barefoot settler children, and once brought a mess of fresh fish to the DeLaurier cabin.

For the better part of two centuries, Anishinaabeg had been welcoming white men into their communities, working with and for white men, and while there had been misunderstandings and skirmishes, there had never been a Chippewa Uprising. That redoubtable war chief Flat Mouth told the British commander who was trying to enlist him as an ally in the war of 1812, "I have never had any part in the white man's wars. For myself, I would never so much as break the window glass of a white man's house." Men like the Cadottes and Faribault had been proud of their tribal ancestry and their native wives. The myths Henry R. Schoolcraft learned from his Ojibway wife became the framework for Longfellow's familiar narrative poem, "The Song of Hiawatha".

Nevertheless, in the long run, things went no better for the peaceable and cooperative Ojibway than for the rebellious and banished Sioux. Region by region, band by band, they were pushed back onto seven reservations in the northern part of the state.

Bad Boy had displayed the foresight to buy land in Todd County, at Little Sauk, near his friend and adoptive son A.D. Brower, and expressed the wish that he could end his days there. But the "Indian movers" came all the same. On the day when the last belongings of the last Pillager Ojibway were being loaded onto boats by the U.S. Army, on their way to residence at the Leech Lake Reservation, Bad Boy's possessions included a cage containing two young pigs. He took one of the pigs from the cage and had a member of his family take it down to the boat. Then he took the cage with its remaining pig up to the Reichert Hotel and left it there. He was fulfilling his contract to provide the hotel with meat.

The reservation lands allotted to the Chippewa in Minnesota proved no safer from white exploitation than the lands granted to the Chippewa by the Treaty of Prairie du Chien. Reservation timber was illegally clear-cut, over Indian protests. Reservation lands were individually allotted, breaking the tradition of collective land ownership. Logging firms and speculators took swift advantage of these inexperienced, usually illiterate, often non-English-speaking landowners. So did "squaw men" who married Indian women, sold the land belonging to them and to their children, and left with the money. Dams built to create reservoirs for downstream use flooded traditional villages and drowned out wild rice beds.

A white friend in Todd County reported that, at ninety, Bad Boy was penniless and near starvation, having, by some subterfuge of greed or some confusion of documents, been cheated of the government allotment for the land where he once lived as chief and extended gracious aid to his white friends. As DeLaurier said, "Bad Boy...saved the lives of at least a thousand settlers....It is to be regretted that he was treated most shamefully by the government when he was old and helpless."

Between the end of the fur trade in 1848 and the turn of the century in 1900, two-thirds of the Native American population of northern Minnesota died of disease and starvation.

When not waging physical or psychological war on the people Columbus mistakenly called Indians, European-Americans have often enjoyed being sentimental about the "vanishing American." But surviving first Americans have refused to vanish. Increasingly, they are asserting their right not only to survive, but to retain their traditional value systems and ways of looking at the world. The descendants of Flat Mouth, Hole in the Day, and Little Crow are full and vigorous participants in today's Minnesota politics, and substantial contributors to its arts, culture, and commerce.

But at the moment when Bad Boy and his people climbed into their boats and headed north, a way of life established over millennia came to an end.

Writing about Eagle Creek, in northern Todd County, DeLaurier says, "When wintry winds swept the western prairies, even buffalo sought the shelter of the timberlands...As late as 1877, a band of Indians attempted to pass the winter on the Eagle and this may be noticed as the last Indian scare that disturbed the settlers in Todd County. A meeting was held at Mickey's Store at Old Hartford to take measures for protection...finding an unfriendly feeling existing among the whites, the Indians withdrew from the region....about this time another band of Indians encamped for a time at Old Hartford, about half a mile north of the store. We have been told by those living in the neighborhood, that there was no ground for apprehension of danger from this band, but that some white men actuated by a desire to show their prowess, craved action. There is also some ground for thinking that their desire for action was due to the prompting of John Barleycorn. This valiant band proceeded to the Indian encampment while the men were away hunting and drove the women and children out of the wigwams and destroyed everything. This act by a few whites did occasion fears on the part of the other whites, for the act of aggression was so uncalled for and unnecessary that they feared the Indians might retaliate. However, the Indians did not wish any trouble and left the neighborhood."

In the year that "valiant band" made its heroic assault on Indian pots and pans, the land on the shores of Wabizi Sagaiigun left the realm of the glacier and the hunter-gatherer and the fur-trapper, and came into the realm of sale and litigation. It entered the plat book.

Now, whatever else it had been or was or could be, it was real estate.

THE NORTHEAST QUARTER OF THE NORTHWEST QUAR-
TER OF SECTION TWENTY-NINE
E.

When we became owners of the land where we live, our proof of purchase included a fat wad of documents. The first of these is the deed description.

Minnesota was surveyed from south to north starting in the early 1800s.
In 1858 Mahlon Black surveyed Burnhamville Township, not long after the
Winnebago left and while the Ojibway no doubt still thought of the land as theirs,
to the extent that they thought of any land as theirs. We live on "The Northeast
Quarter of the Northwest Quarter (NE 1/4 NW 1/4) of Section 29, Township 128
North, Range 32 West of the fifth Post Meridian, according to the United States
Government survey thereof, except the following described tract..." and so on for
the better part of a closely-printed page.

Thus a part of the earth was officially delineated, without reference to
biotic communities living in, on, and under the land described, nor to migratory
species which utilize it as living space for part of the year. It is the way American
land has been described, for purposes of sale and transfer, since the National
Survey of 1785. It is the reason why great chunks of the United States, as any
air traveler can easily see, are laid out in rectangles and squares. The grid shape
is less obvious here in central Minnesota where lakes and river courses obscure
it, but farm fields are mostly still straight-edged, in tribute to those forms of
geometry with which Ptolemy and the Roman empire first began to describe the
world they were in the process of conquering.

Long as it is, the deed description fills only one page of that wad of
paper which constitutes our proof of ownership. The rest is title abstract, the
legal trail of all the official transactions our land has undergone.

Most of us have an internal picture which sums up what we mean by
"the westward movement." We see a family or families trekking west, carrying
the essential tools of wilderness taming, the ax, the long rifle, the family Bible.
Tiny and isolated against an immensity of wilderness, they turn their backs to
what they have known and light out for the territory.

This poignant image, even complicated by factors like immigration and
slavery, was the life experience of pioneers as diverse as Davy Crockett,
Abraham Lincoln, and the Ingalls family. It is the great American myth, infus-
ing our literature from Cooper and Twain, through Faulkner and Conrad Richter,
to the western movies of my childhood. As a basis for assumptions about how
society works, it underlies much American politics. The idea of pioneering,
homestead-making, was certainly in our minds, when we loaded our vehicle, our
International Scout, with household goods that California morning.

The first names to be attached to our land, once it moved from the
vagueness of wilderness and Indian territory into the precision of the plat book,
are those of Charlemagne Tower and J. Frailey Smith. But these gentlemen did
not come with rifle and ax to open our wilderness. Though two Charlemagne
Towers, father and son, are commemorated in the name of the Iron Range city of
Tower, Minnesota, it's unlikely that either our Charlemagne Tower or J. Frailey

Smith ever set foot on our land. Likely they never set eyes on it.

It is not necessary to know land, in order to buy and sell it.

On May 1, 1877, for a consideration of 100,000 dollars, the Western Railroad Company of Minnesota conveys to Messrs. Tower and Smith "all the right, title, and interest which the party of the first part now has or may hereafter have to all tracts of land granted to the territory of Minnesota, by acts of Congress, dated Mar. 3, 1857, Mar. 3, 1865, July 13, 1866, March 3, 1871 and June 23, 1874, for purpose of constructing a railroad." Charlemagne Tower and J. Frailey Smith were trustees for the St. Paul and Northern Pacific Company.

The names of railroad companies and holding companies dart through the language of our land history like sunfish through water weeds. They were parties to one of the great acts of corporate welfare in American history, the gift (as a later transaction specifies) "to aid in the construction of a railroad—ten sections of land for each mile of said railroad." This works out to twenty square miles of land granted by the U.S. government for each mile of track.

The size of that gift can be inferred from the fact that our land is over three miles from the point where the old Northern Pacific railroad line used to run through Grey Eagle.

The era of the homesteading settler, which fills so large a space in the American imagination, was a mere wink of the eye in Todd County. In addition to railroad grants, huge acreages were picked up by speculators, who bought up the land warrant scrip of discharged soldiers, Indians, and land grant colleges.

According to local historian A.H. Hendrickson, "In 1870 it was nearing the end of free homesteads. Practically all the even-numbered sections in the north half of the county were owned by lumber companies, and all the odd numbered sections by the Great Northern Railroad Company...The largest holders of the speculative land were: Farnham and Lovejoy, T.C. McClure, and N.P. Clark. Of the land acquired by N.P. Clark, 10,000 acres in the Eagle Bend country was sold to a Lord Henry Bisschoffscheim of England, who again sold it to James J. Hill and his railroad company, and when Hill and his company saw that he could not keep his land tax free, turned it over for sale to A.E. Johnson Company of St. Paul."

Our land is in the south end of the county, but our title, in an odd-numbered section, certainly moves from government to railroad to trustee to holding company to railroad, in a stately paper ballet. J. Frailey Smith dies and is replaced as a trustee by William S. Lane. The Western Railroad Company formally becomes the St. Paul and Northern Pacific Railroad Company. Messrs. Tower and Lane are successfully sued by the St. Paul and Northern Pacific and are enjoined to transfer "all the property now held by them" to the Central Trust Company of New York. Mortgages are paid off. Lands are certified as patented to the benefit of the St. Paul and Northern Pacific Railroad from the United States of America (over the signature of Theodore Roosevelt, president) and the state of Minnesota "for the use and benefit of St. Paul and Northern Pacific Railroad Company and its assigns forever."

While land titles shuffled back and forth among railroad moguls and land speculators, lumber companies and English lords, what was actually happening on and to the land?

It was probably harvested for its game. Hunting was not only a way of life for the frontier settler, it was a way of making a living. "Many of the settlers made their ready money by selling their [deer] saddles to dealers," says O.B. DeLaurier. Henry Aleshire reported that during the early eighties, on his first day's work as a market hunter, he shot ten deer, receiving 109 dollars in payment.

Only the saddles of the animals, their unsplit backs, loins, and side meat, were usually sent to market. By 1868 sled loads of slaughtered deer were being hauled into St. Cloud, for shipment to St. Paul. By 1871, four hundred saddles of venison were shipped out of St. Cloud for Pittsburgh alone. In 1872, in a ten day period, two thousand saddles of venison were shipped out of St. Cloud, with an additional thousand saddles in storage, waiting for available shipping space.

Though buffalo, elk, and pronghorn antelope had largely left the county, buffalo robes from further west still passed through St. Cloud in enormous numbers.

Waterfowl and other small game were also hunted for the market. In 1860, a St. Cloud newspaper reported "pigeons plentier than ever, sportsmen killing all they want with no trouble." These would have been the now-extinct passenger pigeon. A Todd County settler, speaking in 1878, said there had been "thousands and thousands" of pigeons in the county, especially in Burnhamville Township, going "wherever they find a supply of grain, [wild] rice, and nuts," but that they all had disappeared by 1874.

In 1862, the St. Cloud newspaper reported that "It still is no uncommon affair for forty to sixty prairie chickens to be shot by a sportsman in a single afternoon." In 1865 small game, ducks and geese were reported as "very plentiful. One nimrod killed ten ducks with one shot."

Beaver and muskrat were trapped for their fur. Wolves were hunted with hounds, a bounty being paid by the state for each wolf scalp. As late as 1887, "bears are very numerous, the roads are full of them. Thirteen carcasses were brought to market, nine in St. Cloud, five in Sauk Rapids."

Medicinal herbs and roots, particularly ginseng, were often harvested in the Big Woods. In 1859, a St. Cloud newspaper reported "hundreds of men and women" working a forty mile stretch of deciduous forest running up the west bank of the Mississippi, north of St. Cloud, making a dollar or two a day digging ginseng. An early Burtrum settler is said to have "spent the winter working in the cordwood and lumber camps...the summer he occupied his time hunting plants and roots valuable for medicinal purposes."

The chances are excellent that, in addition to being harvested for game and perhaps for medicinal plants, our acres were logged.

By the early 1870s, two saw mills were operating full-time at Lake Beauty and two others at Pillsbury Lake, within fifteen miles of Big Swan Lake. Numerous smaller, portable mills were also kept busy turning old growth trees into marketable wood product.

Most of the first logging was in the pinery which the senior of the Arnold brothers remembered as a young man. The first major lumber contracts on the upper Mississippi had already been negotiated before the Civil War and the Dakota Conflict brought commerce to a halt, the Pillager chief Hole in the Day selling off timber harvesting rights between Little Falls and the mouth of the Crow Wing River.

In 1867 there were fewer than four hundred white settlers in all of Todd County, only about fifty of them adult men. Three years later, a post-war flood of settlers had raised the population to 2036. By 1880 the population was 6636; by 1890, 12,630. By the turn of the century, Todd County would be home to 22,244 souls.

In the early years of settlement, almost every male, including farming homesteaders, worked in the timber industry. Trees were cut largely in winter, when frozen, snow-covered ground facilitated their movement, by horse or ox-drawn sleigh, to local mills.

White and red pines were cut in enormous numbers. Sylvester Thompson, an early settler, remembered in old age that he had seen the Mississippi above Little Falls so choked with logs that a man could walk across on them. Some of these logs might have been among the deadheads which John worked with in his teens.

These mature trees were also, by modern timbering standards, enormously large. During the 1880's Noah Aleshire hauled to Velie's Mill on the west bank of Lake Beauty a single pine tree which scaled 5,000 board feet, enough lumber to build a good-sized family home.

Mills followed the progress of the lumberjacks down the county. "As this mill finished up the desirable lumber in the vicinity of Mill Lake, operations began on the shores of Lake Beauty," says historian O.B. DeLaurier. "With the slacking up of lumbering at Lake Beauty, hardwood lumbering began in south Burnhamville", where we live.

The town of Hansen, which would later change its name to Burtrum, was platted in 1882 as a cordwood and railroad center. It is three miles east of us. Crews cutting oak for railroad ties and cordwood, products which were shipped west to prairie country in western Minnesota and the Dakotas, would likely have taken a first cut off our acreage at this time.

"In Reynolds township in the 70's" says DeLaurier, "One oak tree was growing on the land, which by actual measurement, was fifteen feet in circumference, a diameter of nearly five feet." Reynolds Township is a little north and west of us.

Hardwood lumbering was a commercial venture. There were small companies manufacturing "doors, windows, frames, flooring, ceiling, stair work, store fronts, interior finish or special order wood work of almost any kind" in Burtrum and Grey Eagle in 1910. But clearing away hardwood forest to bring land into cultivation, cultivation being regarded as the natural best use of land, was simply part of farming at that time. DeLaurier says, of a homestead near Bertha, "It was a difficult task at first to raise crops as a tremendous stand of timber had to be taken off or destroyed. Fine oak timber was cut down and hauled to Fischer's Mill and sawed into railroad ties, which would bring thirty-five to fifty cents apiece when hauled into Verndale. In order to clear the land he had ties made of clear white oak timber, logs over four feet in diameter...he was fortunate to have a chance to sell them for ties, as many settlers were obliged to haul the logs into piles and burn them to get them out of the way."

In 1892, a cord of good oak was worth a dollar ten cents when traded for groceries.

A local booster, touting "Agriculture in Todd County" in 1910, said flatly, "The greater part of this commercial timber has long since been cut—as an industry, logging in Todd County belongs to the past."

Grace Cottrell, born less than a mile from our land in 1907, remembers her family moving from this area up to a farm on Lake Beauty when she was ten or eleven years old "because there wasn't any more wood you could get around Grey Eagle, all the trees were cut."

In addition to being hunted and cut over, our land may very well have been farmed while it was still railroad land. O.B. DeLaurier speaks of "desirable railroad land north of Pillsbury, in Todd County...this land could be squatted on by settlers and purchased when it would come on the market."

As much as we have been interested in knowing the early large-scale history of our place, how it was shaped by natural processes, what people lived on it and when, we have been perhaps even more interested in what might be called its micro-history. Who set those fence posts, and when? Did there used to be a pasture, deep in the heart of the forty where the trees are now tall and mature? Can those really be field furrows down there, where no plow has broken ground for fifty or sixty years? And if so, who cleared that land, and when, and what did they try to grow?

In some ways, the micro-history of a place is more difficult to learn than the macro-history.

Despite a long search through available documents and the memories of people like Mrs. Cottrell, whom we had the great pleasure of interviewing in the summer of her ninetieth year, we cannot say for certain who first farmed our land.

"Agriculture in Todd County", a booklet published in 1910, presents the county as promised land and paradise to be, in the manner of booster publications through the ages. "Only 26 per cent of the land of the county is under cultivation and more than 60 per cent of the agricultural resources remain undeveloped. Thousand and thousands of acres wait the man, who is willing to invest conscientious effort and moderate capital to reap a harvest that is certain and bounteous in all years...Over practically every foot of the county, the purest water will be found at twelve to fifty feet below the soil surface...Excellent success is realized in raising...all the hardier small grains, wheat, oats, barley, flax, corn and buckwheat all producing liberally."

Use of fertilizer for this land is said to be "absolutely unnecessary", a surprise to people like us, who have plowed massive quantities of manure and mulch into our gardens over the years, and watched soil tilth and crop yield increase. The author does suggest crop rotation for wheat instead of "what was attempted in the years gone by when the farmer was satisfied to sow wheat year after year over practically all his land."

The dairying industry, the mainstay of farming when we moved here, was developing in 1910. Corn and potato acreage were increasing. There were twelve Todd County cooperative creameries in that year, including the one in Grey Eagle which still functioned in 1964. Grey Eagle itself had a population of five hundred, supported an "eight room brick graded and high school, two story brick and stone town hall, cement sidewalks on main thoroughfare, street lights", and three churches, German Lutheran, Congregational, and United Methodist. (The first Roman Catholic church in Grey Eagle, serving mostly German settlers, would be built in 1916. Vernacular parts of the service were spoken in German up to the beginning of World War II.) Fire had burned half the Grey Eagle stores in 1907, but the little town had risen from its ashes with a bank, hotel, restaurant, and weekly newspaper, the Gazette, which was still appearing in 1964.

Whether or not he had previously been squatting on the railroad land by Big Swan Lake, a man "willing to invest conscientious effort and moderate capital" became the first land-owner not connected with the railroad. On January 29, 1913, Lucious Little received from the Northern Pacific Railway Company a warranty deed to Lot Six and the Northeast Quarter of the Northwest Quarter of Section 29, Township 128, Range 32, excepting and reserving mineral rights.

The mineral rights still do not belong to us. Occasionally there is a flurry of excitement about valuable minerals or oil in central Minnesota. It is likely that current law would protect our land from the ravages of strip-mining. But where greed and need collide, bad things have happened to more unlikely landscapes. That mineral rights exclusion still makes us uncomfortable.

Lucious Little paid 675 dollars for the land, just over ten dollars an acre. "Agriculture in Todd County" speaks of "wooded farm land" for sale in 1910 at ten to twenty-five dollars per acre. Probably, for land which was partially swamp and mostly hilly, Lucious paid the going rate.

The land was in part secured by a mortgage held by the Bank of Long Prairie, signed by Lucious Little and Katherina, his wife, in the amount of four hundred and thirty dollars.

The Littles came into formal possession of the land the end of January. The probability that they had been squatting on the land is increased by the fact that they had built at least one structure. Grace Cottrell remembers, as a young woman, that "My Dad took me to see where they used to live across the road from your place...Their house was made of logs and had a slanting roof." As with much of the micro-history of our land, the location of this house remains a mystery to us.

Whatever plans Lucious and Katherina Little and their seven children had for their sixty-six acres, fate was about to intervene.

Among the copious social notes in the Grey Eagle Gazette for February 13th is "Lou Little is reported ill as of this writing." By the next issue, February 20th, it is reported that the school has been closed because of the prevalence of diphtheria.

On March 12, 1913, a second mortgage, for $122.25, is issued by the First State Bank of Burtrum to Lucious Little and Katherine [sic], his wife.

It must have been a frantic forty-eight hours in the Little home. A later announcement in the Gazette is for a hearing "In the matter of the estate of Lucious Little, Decedent. The state of Minnesota to Katherine Little, Lizzie Little, Estella Little, Bertha Little, William Little, Cora Little, James Little, Grace Little... The petition of Katherine Little having been filed in this court, representing that Lucious Little, then a resident of the County of Todd State of Minnesota, died intestate on the 13th day of March 1913, and praying that letters of administration of his estate be granted to Will Wilke..."

Just to review the dates: Lou Little, family man, probable farmer, possible squatter, secures a mortgage which will allow him to buy farmland on October 16, 1912. On January 29, 1913, the piece of paper certifying that the land is his actually comes into his hands. By February 13th, he is reported as ill. He puts his failing hand to another mortgage, perhaps to provide for the immediate needs of his family, on March 12th. The next day he dies.

On April 3, the Gazette records that "Mrs. L. Little and family have moved to this village...for the summer."

By May 22, the Gazette records among the disbursements by the County Poor Fund, "goods for Mrs. Little, audited and allowed" in the amount of eight dollars, from F.S. Fuller's Grocery. Poverty, in 1913, was a matter of public record.

The June fifth issue of the Gazette reports that "Miss Stella Little was up from Grey Eagle to visit the old home Saturday," with whatever feelings one can only imagine. On Thursday, July 16, in its Swan Lake Notes column, "G.M. Favre is making hay on the R.F. Wilke Farm, near Swan Lake," hay Lou Little might have looked forward to cutting. In the August 7th edition, funds are reported as audited and allowed from the County Poor Fund, "Dr. E.P. Storey, medical services rendered L. Little, $1.00," perhaps a final reckoning for Lou's last days.

On October 9th, 1913, the Gazette includes its first ad for an automobile, $1895 for "the original Mitchell Engineer." An ad for W.C. Barker urges, "Cold Weather Comforts for the Horse," with a sale of street, storm, and stable blankets. The Jacob Kiewel Brewing Company of Little Falls offers White Rose Beer, "as pure as the flower from which it takes its name."

Also on October 9, 1913, the Little mortgage carried by the First State Bank of Burtrum is assigned to C.E. Wilke, brother of Will Wilke, administrator of the Little estate. On October 11, a warranty deed on the Little property is transferred from Lizzie and Estella Little, the two eldest of Lucious Little's heirs, to R.F. Wilke, for "Twenty dollars and other valuable considerations."

On November 12th, "Katherine Little, widow of Lucious Little, deceased" transfers her share of her inheritance in the form of a warranty deed to R.F. Wilke for twenty dollars. In Probate Court on December 30th, the estate of Lucious Little is assigned "to Katharine Little the widow, as her homestead for and during her natural life" with "the remainder of her lands in fee simple and absolute in equal and undivided share to his children Lizzie, Estella, Bertha, William, Cora, James, and Grace." The inheritance in question had already been reduced by three parts, Katherine, Lizzie, and Stella having already sold their shares to the estate administrator, R.F. Wilke.

On February 18, 1914, in the Probate Court of Todd County, Lizzie Little is appointed legal guardian of her minor siblings, Bertha, William, James, Grace, and Cora, presumably as a result of the death or incapacity of Katherine. On March 23, she receives a license to sell the remaining undivided five eighths interest in the Big Swan land. On March 24, she sells the other heirs' remaining interest in the land to M.J. Walburn for eighty dollars.

Even the deaths of parents and the loss of Lucious's legacy does not keep the older Little daughters out of the social columns of the Gazette. On August 27, "Married at Warroad: Miss Bertha Little, daughter of the late Lucious Little, was married at Warroad, to George Hardy, on Tuesday of last week."

And on October first, 1914, "Miss Lizzie Little, daughter of the late Lucious Little, was united in marriage on Wednesday of last week to Mr. Fred Brees, of Birchdale Township, by Judge of Probate Lewis, at his office in Long Prairie."

In addition to taking on a ready-made family of four children, his wife's minor unmarried siblings, Fred Brees fathered two of his own. Writing in 1934, O.B. DeLaurier describes him as living "on his farm in Section Two of Birchdale Township, with his wife Miss Lizzie Little and two children, Chrystal and Lila May."

The land by Big Swan Lake did not go long untenanted. M.J. Walburn had purchased the last residual land shares of the Little estate from Lizzie for eighty dollars on March 24, 1914. On May fifth he sold them for a hundred dollars to R.J. Wilke, who had bought the earlier claims. On September 12th, Wilke sold the final claim to the entire land parcel to the First National Bank of Grey Eagle, for $2,202.50. On December 16, a warranty deed for the sixty six acres was sold to Orley W. Huffman, a single man, for three thousand dollars.

Note: the land originally sold to Lucious Little in January of 1913 for 675 dollars. Payments to the various Little heirs amounted to 120 dollars. Satisfaction of the mortgages cost $552.25. (It may have been that the "other valuable considerations" listed in the bill of sale by Little and Estella also included some family support.)

Even so, within a few months, the land which had been Lou Little's sole estate was resold for $2,202.50, a very tidy profit for Mr. Wilke.

And when Orley W. Huffman bought the land for three thousand dollars, he was unintentionally setting a high-water mark for land prices that would remain intact well into the 1950s.

The chronicle of Orley Huffman, bachelor farmer, can be inferred from the financial record. If the story of the Little family's land tenure is a tragedy of hopes thwarted through the death of a breadwinner, then Orley Huffman's adventures in farming are of a kind grimly familiar to many a farmer before and since.

On December 16, 1914, Mr. Huffman, son of an established Grey Eagle family—his father, James A., was the town's first postmaster—buys his sixty-six acres of lakeshore, hill slope, swamp, and some level fields for three thousand dollars. He incurs two mortgages, the first in the amount of 1,400 dollars, the second for 975 dollars.

We don't know exactly what kind of farming he did, but it is likely he was a dairyman. We can infer this because the one story we've heard about Orley Huffman's tenure on the land involved a springhouse, where milk would have been kept cold.

Two years into his proprietorship of the Big Swan lake land, on January eighth, 1916, Orley Huffman pays off his second mortgage. By June fourth of 1917, the first mortgage has been satisfied.

But on the same day, June 4, 1917, Huffman signs a mortgage for 2,300 dollars with Carl D. Knight. A second mortgage (for $62.21) is contracted through the First National Bank of Grey Eagle, on June 5, 1919.

And so it goes. Mortgages for modest sums are contracted and paid off, contracted and paid off, but always the ominous phrase "except a mortgage of $2,300 dated June 4, 1917" remains part of the legal record.

By February 15 of 1924, ten years after Orley Huffman took possession of the land on Big Swan Lake, Carl D. Knight has granted power of attorney to Louis W. Vasaly, attorney at law, to "foreclose by advertisement that certain mortgage dated June 4, 1917" on "67.50 acres more or less", "at the front door of the Court House in the Village of Long Prairie on Saturday April 12, 1924, at 10:00 A.M."

Accompanying legal papers report, "M.J. Walburn, being duly sworn, says...that on the 7th day of March 1924 and at least four weeks before the time appointed for the sale of the said land and premises pursuant to said notice, affiant attempted to make service of said notice upon the persons in possession of said land and premises and at said time and for some time prior thereto said premises were wholly vacant and unoccupied."

Lucious Little had died trying to farm this land. Orley Huffman had gone broke and abandoned his "said land and premises" after ten years of labor.

Anybody who has plowed and planted, hoed and harvested, prayed for the rains to come and the frosts to hold off, anyone who has felt the satisfying ache of labor in his bones, anyone who has risen and laid down to the sounds of his chickens and cattle knows how much of a human life went into those ten years. And at the last, it must have come down to that looming, ultimately unpayable debt, and the desertion of a place which had been home, job, and dream all in one.

The single thing remembered about Orley Huffman, failed farmer, is that once he surprised a bear in his springhouse.

This story is remarkable on two counts. The black bear was common in central Minnesota in the nineteenth century, but virtually unknown by the teens and early twenties, when Huffman was farming our land. Thus the encounter of startled farmer and cream-seeking bruin stayed in the local collective imagination.

The other remarkable thing about the story of Orley Huffman and the bear is the location in a springhouse. To make a springhouse, you need a spring. But there are no springs on this land now, nor were there any when John first saw it, in 1948.

We can speculate as to where such a spring might have been. The gully that comes down the hill behind the cabin and issues near our landing place on Big Swan Lake is, in wet years, an intermittent stream. Maybe eighty years ago, there was a spring of cold water in that place, enough to sustain a springhouse, enough to draw a bear.

It should be noted that, though the bill collector could not find Orley Huffman in the spring of 1924, O.B. DeLaurier succeeded in locating him, or in finding out his location, when he was writing his Todd County history in 1948. Orley Huffman, still single, was said to be living at that time in Bemidji, Minnesota.

When Carl D. Knight became the owner of record in 1924, the purchase price of the land is given as $2,799.76. This would have been the original mortgage price, plus interest.

We know less of Knight than of Little and Huffman. On the basis of his transactions with Huffman, it seems unlikely that he farmed the land himself. He sold the land on which he had foreclosed in 1924 on September 6, 1929, to Esther and Robert Shortridge. The agricultural depression of the twenties meant that the land for which Orley Huffman paid three thousand dollars ultimately resold for $1800, with a mortgage for $1,200.

Whoever was farming the land between the time when Orley Huffman left it and the Shortridges moved onto it, we know the Shortridges farmed it for at least eighteen years, from mid-1929 to 1948. We know they raised at least two children in a tiny, drafty house (one room up, one room down), had a small barn in a grove where we would later build a house, and a large chicken coop which was still in ramshackle existence in the summer of 1964.

Their neighbors remember that they raised Navy beans in the hill field which overlooks the lake. They raised sorghum and made and sold sorghum syrup. They were part of a small local community of Seventh Day Adventists.

We know Mrs. Shortridge loved flowers. Her lilac bushes, now mostly shaded out by taller trees, provided the starts for the lilac bushes I planted by the house in which we raised our children. Some of those same lilacs crossed the road with us, to be planted not far from Earthward, the house where we live now.

There is a grove across the road from where the Shortridge house once stood. The maples and basswoods have largely shaded out the apples and crab-apples John's mother planted there. But around their roots in early spring, the lilies of the valley planted by Mrs. Shortridge spread yards and yards of green spathes and fragrant white bells across the floor of the woods.

Some of those lilies of the valley have also crossed the road, to mix in my flowerbeds with Mother Rylander's primroses, irises, and Shasta daisies.

The Shortridges, who lived longer on this land than anybody would till we settled here, leave a very small paper trail. They did not borrow much and they paid their bills promptly.

After eighteen years' tenancy, their children raised and themselves grown old, they sold their little farm, with its marginal buildings and gorgeous lake view and beautiful but largely uncultivable lands, to a carpenter from Little Falls who liked to come fishing there, and his wife, who had always wanted a lake place.

On April 16, 1948, the name "Rylander" first enters the record in connection with the Northeast Quarter of the Northwest Quarter of Section 29. Robert and Esther Shortridge, joint tenants, sell their land by warranty deed, for a consideration of two thousand dollars, to J. Elmer Rylander and Elsie Rylander, his wife.

UPATA LAKE
E.

We always knew the cottage at Big Swan was not a permanent residence. After all, it was Mother Rylander's lake place, the land she and Elmer had bought together, the land on which he had built that cottage for their pleasure and relaxation.

It's clear that buying a piece of land essentially for recreational purposes was not something Elsie and Elmer Rylander had done without great soul-searching.

They were both the children of Swedish immigrants, all four of their parents landless peasants who had emigrated from the offshore province of Oland. Both their fathers had been laborers before they became farmers. Both their mothers had been domestics, "hired girls" in the houses of old stock Americans.

Elsie's father, John Peterson, raised three children and lost one while scratching out a living on three different small, thin-soiled, barely viable farms, like the one where John "helped out" with the hay. Elmer's father John August Rylander emigrated a little earlier and managed to acquire more and better land. Despite raising a family of four, by the late twenties John August had accumulated an impressive nest egg, five thousand dollars in a small rural bank. Unfortunately this bank was one of those ill-supervised financial institutions which collapsed in the early thirties, eating all the surplus of years of family labor and thrift.

Elmer was a carpenter, proud of having brought his wife and four children through the Depression without taking a penny of Relief. He was an avid outdoorsman, a man who could happily spend half a day rowing around Swan Lake after bass, but he was also an extremely cautious man, especially when it came to money.

Elsie had attended teacher training classes at what was then St. Cloud Teachers' College and taught in one-room country schools before she married. Later, over her husband's objections, she would return to teaching, get her B.S. from what was by then St. Cloud State College, and become a special education teacher.

But in 1948, so family tradition says, she had to "talk like a Dutch uncle" to persuade her cautious husband that they could afford a lake place.

Why or how she fell in love with this piece of land, I don't know. It's clear she did. As a widow of seventy, after a forty-five year residence in Little Falls, most of it in the same modest home right next to the Baptist Church she attended, Elsie chose to design and build her own permanent residence on the shores of Big Swan Lake, to the amazement and considerable distress of her in-town friends. In the last conscious days of her life she was asking if "the big birds"—bald eagles—had come back to the lake.

Elmer built the cottage in his spare time, thriftily, but with little elegant touches in basswood paneling and fireplace brickwork. Whatever their passion for the place, within the first year of purchase, the new buyers had sold off a choice acre of lakeside land, thereby retrieving half their purchase price. And for several years, Elsie (and, reluctantly, her three daughters) grew raspberries and strawberries on the Big Swan land. Elsie kept track in a ledger book of every penny she spent and made, as if to prove that the land was more than lovely, it was profitable. It could pay its way.

So the land was bought and the cottage built, and the Rylander family acquired "a place at the lake".

The license plates in this state say "Land of Ten Thousand Lakes". The Department of Natural Resources says that, depending on size classification, there are in fact nearer to fifteen thousand.

But lakes are more than geological oddities in the Minnesota psyche.

When Shireen was four or five and we were living near St. Cloud, her father and I were talking one day about something we had done "up at Swan Lake."

Our daughter burst into our talk correctingly. "That lake is not called Swan Lake! That lake is called Upata Lake!"

Upata Lake was where we had lived when she was a baby, when we took all those pictures. Upata Lake was where Grandma Rylander had her cottage. Upata Lake was where we went on Memorial Day, Fourth of July, Labor Day, a place for fishing and swimming and swinging with cousins in the hammock and on the rope swing. Upata Lake was Kool-Aid made with cold well water, bread raised on the warming shelf of the wood stove, Grandma stoking up the wood stove even on hot days (why use electricity when you can heat dishwater for free on the wood stove?), giggly trips to the outhouse.

Upata Lake was for her what it has been for several generations of Minnesotans, the Great Good Place.

Newcomers to this state are baffled by Minnesotans who talk about The Lake, the one they go Up To every available summer weekend. "You'd think there was only one." And for any Minnesotan fortunate enough to have known one, there is only one. It may be large or small, surrounded by pines or maples or cornfields, productive of walleyed pike or bullheads; it will be The Lake. It will linger into later memory as a place of natural beauty and childhood pleasure. Within a few feet of the chair where I write are books titled Going to The Lake; Time at the Lake; Too Hot, Went to Lake. All these books were written, published, and purchased in Minnesota. There is always some kind of lake book on the Minnesota best seller list.

One of the great pleasures of the archetypal Minnesota lake place was its simplicity. Mother Rylander's cottage, with its four rooms, plain furniture, and vinyl-covered floors needed no housekeeping beyond the occasional use of a broom and mop. To go Up to the Lake, in what now looks like the golden age of the lake cottage, was to bypass housework, lawn mowing, and social pretension. Up at the lake, the most respectable Minnesotans let their shirt-tails hang and took off their girdles. Up at the lake, the kids could always talk somebody into lighting a marshmallow-toasting fire so they could make S'mores. And if they came away with sticky hands and hair, if they stayed up till all hours, so what? You were up at the lake. Up at the lake, things were different.

116

Unfortunately the tradition of the lakeside cottage as a place deliberately separate from and unlike one's regular residence is gradually eroding. Once a lakeshore place has been gussied up to town standards, with carpeted floors and landscaped yard and a satellite dish, it ceases to be a refuge from the vacuum cleaner and the lawnmower and the TV schedule and becomes just a place, like any other place. The resale value will have increased; the spiritual value will have diminished.

Because lake property is desirable and increasingly rare, Minnesotans are loving it to death. This despite the Minnesota Shorelands Management Act, which puts quite stringent restrictions on where Minnesotans can build and how they can build, even on their own land. The impulse to "clean up the yard"—i.e., to cut down all the brush and wild plants which provide habitat for birds and small animals, and to establish a "nice lawn" of putting green quality—overwhelms nine in ten lakeshore property owners. Steve Moline, recent executive director of the Minnesota Lakes Association, points out that a handful of lawn fertilizer in a lake will produce three hundred pounds of weeds, which homeowners distressed by declining water quality often want to poison off.

Despite the growing expansion and gentrification of lakeside houses, despite declining water quality and increasing conflicts between swimmers, fishers, and users of personal watercraft, Upata Lake still haunts the Minnesota dreamtime. Memorial Day weekend still sees highways full of cars pulling motorboats, or trailers with chainsaws and garden tools in them, heading north. Those people are on their way Up to the Lake to open the cabin and put out the dock. Labor Day weekend still brings hordes of them home. An arc of natural connection with the seasons and the past, when Mom would have hung up the cabin curtains while Dad and the kids put out the dock, is thus maintained for thousands of people who otherwise live conventional urban and suburban lives.

We always knew our tenure in the cottage would not be permanent. But John knew he could have a full-time teaching job in Swanville, a town five miles from us, come fall. There was all that wood, cut into lumber by the Arnold Brothers, stacked and drying, waiting to build a home up on the hill.

Then John received almost simultaneous offers of employment from the English Departments of colleges at Spearfish, South Dakota, and St. Cloud, Minnesota.

We took a deep breath. High school teaching had its satisfactions, but it was in part the burn-out from high school teaching which had brought us here in the first place. The chance to make the jump from high school to college teaching might not come again.

The lake land would wait for us. (Mother had said she would give us a building lot.) St. Cloud was only fifty minutes away.

So we made the down payment on a small rural house near St. Cloud, packed up the household gear, loaded Peaches the Shetland pony and her foal Archimedes, and Bet Bouncer the Springer Spaniel and her five puppies into the trailer, and hit the road again.

But we did not forget our times Upata Lake. Dark water and the scent of woodsmoke would haunt our dreams.

PREMONITIONS OF EARTHWARD
J.

Finding my way earthward has been a journey of starts, stops, beginnings, surprises. On that cool lovely still-dark November morning in 1968 when I got in a boat with several friends and started down the Leech River, I wasn't expecting a mystical experience; I was only hoping for a pleasant, perhaps productive day of deer hunting.

We were going to an area only Bob had been in before. It was, he told us, low lying, mostly swamp, treeless and almost brushless, except for ridges of pine and spruce. The ridges were several hundred feet long and around a hundred feet wide. The plan was for me to find a good sitting spot on the first ridge we came to, while the other hunters crossed it and went on deeper into the swamp, to other ridges.

The morning light was coming on through the high cloud cover. Snowflakes drifted down lightly but steadily. There was no wind, so the below freezing temperature was bearable, even pleasant. I moved toward the north end of the ridge and soon found a fallen tree, a sizable old pine that had been charred in places by a fire years ago. It had a comfortable spot where I could sit and watch a couple of likely deer trails.

I sat quietly, charmed by the contrast of white snow on fire-blackened trunk, by the chatter of red squirrels, the hoarse raven croaks, and the sharp cries of Canada jays. It was lovely, haunting. The morning light filtering through snow and trees was softly luminescent, revealing and hiding at the same time.

I don't know how long I sat virtually motionless, before a pulsating, insistent awareness overtook me. I had to look down toward my feet. It came to me that they did not end where the soles of my boots touched the earth.

I knew instantly and surely that I had become part of the ridge, the log, the air. My feet had grown into the ground. They were sending down tentacles, roots, into the particles of dirt, into the very muck of the swampy earth. I was mesmerized, tingling with quiet joy and peace, at one with my immediate surroundings and the rest of creation. I was a part of, not apart from. The journey earthward was truly underway. I had been given a gift not asked for and totally unexpected. I am still grateful.

That experience has been etched in my mind so powerfully that at times, recalling it, I still tingle with delight and feel my body suffused with reverence. There is no doubt in my mind that all of us are a part of, not apart from, the stuff of the world, organic and inorganic, living and dead.

Our sense of that commonality ought to guide our actions and choices. To harm the natural world is to harm ourselves. To profess love for a Creator while behaving in our personal or professional lives in ways that abuse the Creation is to live a lie.

TRANSITIONS
E.

Our year in Mother Rylander's cottage at Big Swan Lake had helped us to clarify what we wanted out of our lives.

We wanted to provide as much as we could of our own food, warmth, and shelter. We wanted to be sure that what we ate had not been produced in ways that damaged the soil, or the lives of human producers, or the larger biotic community. We did not want the energy that warmed or cooled us to destroy watersheds or produce oil spills or generate nuclear waste. We wanted our living space to be built as much as possible of local and natural materials. We wanted it to reflect our tastes and values, not the esthetic of the mass producer and the slick magazine.

We wanted to live in a way which allowed us to share work, between ourselves and with our children. We wanted our lives to be an organic whole, not to be cut up into boxes with labels like "man's work" and "woman's work", or "work" and "leisure", or "worker" and "intellectual". We did not want to live, and to model for our children, the standard "American Way of Life", with its abstraction, its exploitation, its specialization and its consumerism. We did not want to give up any of our human potential, physical or mental, simply because the larger culture told us we were being inefficient, or "kooky", or un-American, or unproductive. We wanted to own our lives, not rent or lease them. We wanted our lives to be ours, not roles we were playing at the bidding of advertisers.

We wanted our lives to be directly connected to nature at as many points as possible. We wanted to live so that we would at all times be conscious of our place on the physical globe, of the season, of the weather, of the sky. We wanted the way we lived, day by day, hour by hour, to keep us from falling into either of the great myths of industrial man.

Like all powerful and widely-shared myths, these two are strengthened by containing a certain modicum of truth. The myth of helplessness says, "I just work here, I'm a cog in a machine, a drone in a cubicle. How I feel doesn't matter, because I can't change anything."

The myth of potency says, "I am Man. We are masters of the universe. We can do anything. The world exists for our profit and pleasure, and we can make it do what we want."

The myth of helplessness folds into the myth of potency. "Alone I'm nobody, but the market is omnipotent." The marriage of these myths produces that thundering maxim, "You can't stop progress."

What I have just written is as clear an explication as I can give of a complicated, interconnected group of ideas John and I shared then and share now. Often enough, I have wished there was a single comprehensive term, an umbrella word all these ideas would fit under. Obviously words like "environmentalism", "voluntary simplicity", "right livelihood", "sustainable agriculture" and "appropriate technology" belong somewhere in this collection of ideas, and I have the sense that perhaps they are all roots or branches of a single tree, which I have not yet the wit to name.

Most people in our position in the fall of 1965—young married couples with small children—were looking for a certain kind of real estate, safe and pleasant housing for children at not too high a price, not too distant from work. We had those needs, too, and they were partly satisfied when we moved into the little square house out on the county road across from the old quarries.

But we were still, in our deepest hearts, looking to live that way of life without a name.

In the four-room house in rural Stearns county, we could continue to do some of the things we had been doing in rural Todd County. The soil was more sandy, but we could garden, and we did. Our three and a half acres meant not only plenty of running room for the kids, but room enough for the children's pony and for the dogs. (For twenty-four years, we raised and sold English Springer Spaniel pups.) Though we could no longer walk down the hill and jump into the boat and go fishing or duck hunting, we were close to lakes and rivers. And we had easy access to the greatest swimming holes in the world.

A hundred years earlier, the land we were now living on had been oak savannah—prairie with patches of oak trees. Now most of it was farm land. Directly across the road from us were six hundred acres of land full of abandoned quarries, where Cold Spring Granite company had cut stone in the early part of the century. Thirty or forty years of disuse had let brush and grass and trees regrow. This scarf of vegetation lapped around hill-sized mounds of abandoned stone slab. Discarded booms, pulleys, and cables loomed against the sky.

Within reasonable walking distance of our house, there were maybe twenty quarry holes. Where granite had been extracted, clear cold water seeped in. When you looked into the water at the right angle, you could see forty or fifty feet straight down, see the old groove marks from the cutting and blasting.

A number of these quarry holes had names painted in large black letters along their cliff sides—BENZIE 14, HOLES 12, TREBOTOWSKI 10—designations that no doubt went back to quarrying days. Perhaps they were names of crew bosses, or foremen, who had worked here on days when it was ninety degrees, or thirty below. Back in those times the whistles blew everyday at five to four, and you would know you had five minutes to get your kids in out of the yard, before the quarrymen touched off the dynamite. Or so we were told by old Mrs. Klein, who occasionally tended our children.

When one of these veterans of the quarries died, the obituary would read, "Granite man", as if the worker had become the stubborn and lasting material of his craft.

It was a strange place, a worked-out industrial landscape containing places of haunting beauty. (Part of it is now, appropriately, a county park). On hot summer days and evenings, we took our children to swim in Benzie 14, which had a wide ledge along one side about six feet deep, before the drop-off into the really deep, dark blue water.

The house across from the quarry was ten minutes from John's job. Dan went off happily to first grade in Waite Park, a suburb of St. Cloud. The wood the Arnold brothers had milled became a living-room wing on the house, with a Franklin stove in it, so we could at least supplement our gas heat with wood heat.

Later we added a full bath on the main floor—there had been only a half-bath in the basement—and a large dormer bedroom upstairs, for John and me. By that time there were three children, Eric having been born in 1967.

Occasionally in those days, I remembered the friend who had accused us of escapism when we told her we were moving to Minnesota. Teaching college in the late sixties was not an escapist vocation. There was no way of keeping the passions of that time out of the classroom, or out of our personal lives. I remember, on the morning of Robert Kennedy's assassination, how I weeded the strawberry patch with unusual meticulousness. Then, I think, we went up to the lake. It was always the healing place.

One of the students whom John had taught at Carmel High hitch-hiked across country, stopping for a few days at our house. He had applied for conscientious objector status and been denied. He was appealing his draft status, but not very hopefully. What was he to do, surrender to a draft he thought was unjust, to fight in a war he thought was immoral? Should he go to Canada? Go underground in this country? His dad was career military. His parents, with whatever grief and distress, had stood behind him when he filed his exemption claim.

We talked about books and politics. He sat in our back yard, playing his recorder and trying to figure out his life.

John was faculty advisor to the Student Senate for 1969-70. Normally that would have been the sort of rather dull supervisory task junior faculty members get stuck with. In that year of massive student anti-war demonstrations, that year of Kent State, even the Student Senate at St. Cloud State College was an exciting place. St. Cloud State students briefly joined the nationwide student strike. A protest parade marched through the center of that stodgy, startled, Germanic town. John was one of the parade marshals.

In the spring of 1970 my father visited us. He was fifty-six years old, a strong, healthy, happy man. Since 1949 he had been a crop duster, applying agricultural chemicals in California, Oregon, Nevada, Arizona, Mexico and New Brunswick, Canada. At the time he began doing this work, compounds like DDT, parathion, aldrin and dieldrin were routinely loaded bare-handed and applied without respiratory masks. I still remember the acrid smell of the flight clothes Mom threw into the wash, and her comment that we never had the slightest trouble with bugs in the house anymore.

In the spring of 1970, my father was about to fulfill a lifelong dream and open his own flight school. He was in an exuberant mood, ready to forgive some of the roaring arguments we'd had before I left the coast, including the one about Rachel Carson's book <u>Silent</u> <u>Spring</u>. "I think the woman may be on to something," he said. "But I still don't think I killed all the salmon in the Mirimachi River, when I was on Operation Budworm in New Brunswick."

That September, after what looked like a bout with flu, he lapsed into a coma. Hospital tests showed massive tumors in two brain sites, his prostate, his spine and his lungs. He was dead within six weeks.

He had used every chemical then available, in ways the manufacturers told him were perfectly safe.

Also in 1970, the year of student protests and my father's death, the area where we lived was zoned for industrial use. Work began on a large mobile home park right down the road from us. Our quiet road carried more traffic every day. The suburbia we'd fled was galloping out to meet us.

We bought and moved into and renovated a country schoolhouse, further out of town. Again we were surrounded with green fields. But we were within earshot of a motor racing track, whose roars and screams we could hear periodically. And Dan, now in seventh grade, was not happy in his new school.

Enter a couple of old friends. Barney had taught with John in his first two years at Santa Maria High School in southern California. My son Dan and Betty's son Bryan had been born twelve hours apart, in the same hospital. When we left California for Minnesota, they left for a Greek village. Many of the same yearnings and discontents propelled us. Now they were back in the States, no happier with the major trends in American culture than they had been before.

There was something in the air back then, and I don't mean controlled substances.

A lot of American public opinion looks back now on a time which produced student protests, Earth Day, the Equal Rights Amendment, and a back to the land movement, and shakes its head. It sees a moral black hole, a time when America Went Wrong. It would like to excise all those yeasty social experiments from the collective American memory, stitching the striving fifties straight onto the go-go eighties. It may be coming close to succeeding.

My own youngest son once told me, "All the old hippies who didn't burn out on drugs are stockbrokers now." He does not believe this because he has talked to the old folks and their slightly younger friends; he believes it because powerful forces in the culture at large want him to believe it is true.

We were never hippies; we were too old, too ex-Baptist, too married, too responsible as parents. Drugs scared us; promiscuity repelled us. We were that most American phenomenon, a couple of people who wanted a better life for their children.

Yes, plenty of people got all tangled up in the variable tugs of those different, often conflicting Liberations. Yes, some of the bright young people we met back then went, in the idiom of the time, so far out that for them, there was no coming back. Yes, to believe that the world is malleable can lead to very destructive behavior.

But to have lived in a time when everything seemed possible was a great experience.

We sat around the living room of the schoolhouse where we lived, that summer of 1971, playing records by Joan Baez, Creedence Clearwater Revival, and a guitar player named Leo Kottke, who had been John's student in an English class. We talked self-sufficiency, self-expression, the ecological wastefulness of the single family home, community, connection with the earth, social change from the bottom up. We thumbed through *The Last Whole Earth Catalog* and real estate brochures. Farming was in one of its periodic horrible depressions, and land up north was cheap.

We went to see resorts. What could be better than making a living renting boats and cabins in some lovely place, then, at the end of summer, when all the vacationers went home, getting to stay in that place all winter, with not much to do but a little maintenance? One could have time to loaf and enjoy one's soul.

We wound up buying, in partnership, forty-seven acres on a beautiful little pine-fringed body of water called Howard Lake, not far from Walker, Minnesota. Cat Creek, so fast-flowing it did not freeze even in forty below, ran between the house and cabins. There was a three-bedroom house, a nifty little barn, eight cabins, a small store building, a shower house (only two of the cabins had showers), a fish-cleaning house, eight fishing boats, several old boat motors, and a more-or-less established clientele. It was a steal. At least, for people as broke as us, it was possible.

In the spring of 1972, while John finished out the term at St. Cloud State, I went up with the children to begin a year-long battle with grime at the place we christened Earthome. Shortly thereafter, Betty and Barney and their three children joined us.

We quickly discovered that there is no end to work at a small resort. Earthome absorbed all the energies of four adults and six children, with five year old Eric as greeter. There were always cabins to clean and beds to make at the end of the day. The plumbing was primitive and forever breaking down, and after a heavy rain, unpleasant-smelling seepage entered the house basement. There was never a time when at least one of the boat-motors was not in the hands of the local small engine repair man. There were bats in the wall of Cabin Eight. A skunk crawled up a drainpipe into the fish cleaning house one night, nearly scaring three Caterpillar employees from Peoria out of their wits.

The customers, many of whom had been coming for years to panfish and lounge around for a week or two, were really nice people. But the market for our bare little cabins, with their old mattresses and linoleum floors and no TV, was dwindling.

There was no way this resort was going to support two families.

Instead of spending the winter loafing and enjoying his soul, John spent the school year back in the classroom—back again in the high school classroom at Walker High School. And after a few months of shared housing, John and I and our kids moved into Cabin One. I had discovered that I was not the ever-patient, flexible Earth Mother I had believed. The nuclear family might be a hierarchical institution, but I wanted my own kids under my own roof. Territoriality might be the cause of wars, but I was territorial as hell about my domestic space. I wanted to be the boss of my own kitchen.

These were interesting new things to learn about myself. It is always useful to know one's own character better. They were not, however, the results I had expected from this particular experiment, and that was depressing.

"If I'm going to be teaching," John said late that winter, "I'd rather do it in college." (He had, fortunately, taken a leave of absence from St. Cloud State, instead of resigning.) "And I'll tell you. When I think about next year, my head's at Swan."

So we sold out to our partners, and went back to the lake where our hearts had always been.

THE MAN WHO HAD NO WASTE
J.

I first got to know Tony in the summer of 1973, when I was cutting trees to make lumber for the house we were planning to build on Big Swan Lake. I was looking for a log chain and a cant hook. I was also trying to keep a 1936 model John Deere B tractor running, so I could use it to haul the logs which would become our lumber out of the woods. I was a man with a serious need for a good second-hand dealer.

Tony's second-hand store and emporium of useful junk occupied a one-time Standard Oil gas station just across from the bank in downtown Grey Eagle. The two-room building was surrounded on all sides by old refrigerators, stoves, hot water heaters, junked farm implements, stacks of water pipe in various lengths and diameters, unidentifiable machinery and just plain stuff in various stages of dismemberment. It might look haphazard to the casual eye, but there was an order to it all.

At least there was an order to it as seen by Tony. He was a smallish man in his seventies, neatly clothed, and if you asked him where a such and such was, or where you could find a whatchamacallit, he would squint with his left eye and be on his way to fetch the desired object. Or if he didn't have it himself, he would tell you, in his pronounced German accent, where you might go to get such an object, or even if it could be found in the area.

I quickly came to rely on Tony for nuts and bolts, general advice on anything mechanical, and good humored friendship. The nuts and bolts sold in recycled motor oil cans for fifty cents a quart. The advice was free.

On one early fall day I found his good humor in disrepair. The town fathers had decided to make garbage pickup mandatory, and the cost was to become part of his yearly tax bill. Tony had gone to the Council meeting arguing that he had no garbage. Garbage was a word he didn't understand. Garbage was a commodity he didn't produce.

Tony, he was told, everyone produces garbage.

Not so, said Tony. He explained that he did not buy or accept anything made of plastic or packaged in plastic. His newspapers and other waste paper were rolled into paper logs and burned in the stove that heated his store. Any metal, including cans, he took to the salvage yard and sold. He took his food scraps to his brother's farm, where they were recycled through chickens, hogs, or dogs. I have no waste, he said. You send a garbage hauler to my house, he won't find anything to haul away.

After due consideration, affected no doubt by the fact that everybody knew Tony and Tony's business, the city government relented. Tony's tax bill would not include a charge for garbage pickup.

One day in the course of our usual discursive conversation, Tony said that he too had once built his own house. "Not a big one like you're building, but big enough for me." He had torn down an old building and recycled the old lumber. "And you know, I insulated it without buying insulation. I just saved all the insulation I took out of old refrigerators, stoves, and hot water heaters. I insulated my whole house with that stuff."

This was recycling, of course, but then, Tony had been recycling things his whole life, long before the term came into popular use, long before public opinion came to accept resource conservation as an environmental necessity. Tony hated waste. Getting the maximum use out of the material stuff of the world was an article of faith to him. It went beyond the way he made his living. It guided his every economic decision.

Tony has been dead for some years now, and his store is long gone. Nobody, as they say in central Minnesota, monkeys around with that little stuff anymore, and the remaining businesses produce the usual American complement of waste. Tony is missed for much more than the business he once ran.

LIVING OFF THE LAND
E.

So in the summer of 1973 we moved back into Mother Rylander's lake cottage again, but only for ten weeks.

Before we left Earthome, we had hired a Grey Eagle friend to build a sizable garage, in which we could stack our belongings while we built the walk-out basement of the two-story house John had designed.

We were very busy that summer, building our house, gardening, cutting the trees for next winter's heat and next summer's construction. We were up at dawn and working often into the long dusks of Minnesota days. (In June, in our latitudes, the sun rises around 5:30 Central Daylight Time, and sets around 9:00.) Most nights we fell into bed exhausted, but pleased with ourselves, indeed euphoric. We were having one of the rarest of human experiences. We were living out a dream, building it physically in block and mortar and wood framing, shaping it in garden rows and enclosures for animals and in the paths our feet made as we moved through our working days. We were doing what we had wanted to do, in the way we had wanted to do it, and it was going well.

In the first summer, we started a new garden, closer to our house site, on level well-drained ground. We built the first level of our new house and were into it within ten weeks, though it had a bare concrete floor, unpaneled block walls, and no interior doors. Much of the finish carpentry would take place over the winter.

We hauled the still-solid chicken coop John had built in 1964 up the hill to our new location, cleaned it out, and installed a flock of chickens. We bought five sheep and fenced off a pasture for them. (The fencing was inadequate. The sheep escaped, then wandered back to food and water. One had tangled with a pack of feral dogs and ultimately died of her wounds. It was a salutary demonstration of the complexity of living off the land.)

Next year came the second story of the house. It was post and beam, with a shed roof, sweeping views of lake and woods, basswood tongue-in-groove wall paneling and massive exposed ceiling beams. When completed, the house had four bedrooms, a bath and a half, a kitchen/dining room, a large living room with reading alcove upstairs, and a large rumpus/utility room downstairs. There was room for wood storage, canned good storage, manuscript storage, room to spread out the writing materials and the building materials. When we were finished we had two thousand feet of handsome, sturdy, distinctive house, built largely with wood from our own land and with our own labor. Working on this pay-as-you-go basis meant that when the house was done, it was mostly paid for. For a big chunk of our married lives, we have paid no rent and carried minimal mortgages.

Later we built a small barn, and a wood shed which would become our sugaring house when we started cooking maple syrup. We added a greenhouse to our walk-out basement. When Eric got interested in rebuilding tractors, we helped him build a shop.

Alongside this memory of when we did what, runs a long string of images, of the kind familiar to every parent remembering the growth and maturation of a family. So I see Shireen, in that first summer, her ten year old face concentrated and serious as she makes sandwiches and Kool-Aid for the construction crew. I see Dan with flecks of mortar on his blond hair and glasses, learning to balance a mortarboard, responding to the mason's cry of "Mud!" I see six-year-old Eric in his favorite bib overalls, his hand halfway up the hammer handle, learning to drive nails.

I see Shireen, in her thirteenth summer, chunking the posthole digger into hard and stony ground, with all the strength in her growing body. She has been told she can have a horse, if she digs the postholes for the corral. She kept at that work through the heat of summer, until the posts could be set and the wire strung and a handsome buckskin mare named Fern could join the other livestock.

I see Eric rushing in from school, grabbing a snack, and rushing back out, to visit his sow Miss Piggy. I see Dan driving the tractor, hauling the hay wagon, onto which his brother and sister and I hoist and stack bales, and later I see Eric driving the tractor, on his way to pick up buckets of maple sap from our tapped trees. I see all of us spreading mulch in the garden, picking rock in the fields, tending gates or grabbing sheep when the shearers came. I see Mother Rylander's flushed face, leaning over the other side of the back of a pickup truck on a bitterly-cold fall day, as we work together shoveling dry hard golden cornears out of the wagon, into the crib.

I see the five of us marching along like a small parade through early-morning mist, in spring of the American bicentennial year, planting seedling evergreen trees in woods edges and openings. Most of those pines and firs and spruces will not survive the drought of that summer. Not everything grows, not everything lives, not everything works as it was planned. But this has always been human experience, since this way of life evolved in the Neolithic.

At almost any time up to the late twentieth century, the shape of the life we were living would have been familiar. We were living off the land, the land providing us with food, shelter, and energy. We gathered berries and mushrooms. We harvested wood, maple sap, honey, ducks, deer, grouse, fish. We raised hogs, sheep, chickens, feeder calves, vegetables, herbs, and apples for our own consumption, corn and oats and hay for the animals. Our primary source of income was not agriculture, but we could live well on a modest single income because we needed to buy so little. We made modest sums selling lambs, eggs, strawberries, sweet corn, feeder pigs, butcher hogs, and firewood, mostly to people we knew. To some considerable extent, we operated outside the market.

We were doing jobs we enjoyed, our skills improving as we went along.

For most of English and American history, people who lived like us were called farmers.

As quite often in our lives, we found ourselves well outside the mainstream. We were small-scale mixed farmers, subsistence farmers, when the Secretary of Agriculture was advising farmers, "Get big or get out." All around us, farms substantially larger and better capitalized, often farms which had supported several generations, were going under the auctioneer's hammer. Even the terms "farm" and "farmer" were clearly second choices, in official pronouncements on "the farm problem" or in the glossy agriculture magazines, to the terms "agribusiness" and "agribusinessman".

People who lived as we were living were sometimes referred to as "hobby farmers", as if establishing a long-term nurturing relationship with the land we lived on was on a par with knitting. It would have been rather more accurate to say our garden, fields, coop and barn were forms of political protest, or worship.

For a time in the seventies, publications like <u>The Whole Earth Catalog</u> and *Mother Earth News* popularized an old term to apply to the way we were living. They called people like us "homesteaders". It was a name which involved a false historical analogy and a sentimentalizing of a particular period of American history, but for awhile, at least, we were part of a category. It gave us a shorthand way of describing what we were doing. But the use of that name never seemed to get much beyond the audience for what Eric called *Mother Mars News*.

By whatever name, it was a good life. It still is.

NOT QUITE OFF THE GRID
J, E

The youngest son asked me, shortly after we had installed a solar hot water heater, why not a polar power unit?

We both found the phrase amusing and had a good laugh at it. I experienced the pleased flush that comes to parents when a child has demonstrated lively intelligence and language ability.

It was also nice to see that Eric had been incorporating the family values.

Everything we've ever built has been designed not only to satisfy us and serve our needs, but also to protect the living capacity of the earth. If we couldn't quite meet Tony the Junkman's "no waste" test, we could build energy conservation and thrifty use of local resources into our house and other structures, into the bones of the way we live.

Some people living off the land talk about "living off the grid." The phrase has a general meaning, suggesting disaffection from the larger currents in society. But it also has a specific one. If you are off the grid, you are generating or trying to generate all your own power, completely cutting the umbilical cord to the electric company.

We never got quite off the grid. In part, this may have been a matter of available time and engineering skills, but there was also, probably, a slight philosophical preference involved. The magazines we were reading were full of yeasty plans for back-to-the-landers to form their own communities, for all of us right-thinking folks to get together and remake the world, and there were certainly things that needed rethinking and remaking in the world, such as the way energy is delivered to the average home. But how many ties does a person want to cut with the way most people live? There is a certain danger in pulling back from mainstream life, no matter how turbulent and polluted the mainstream is, into consciously virtuous detachment.

We were already living in an existing community, driving on its roads, depending on its public safety structure, sending our kids to its schools. It's always easier to get along in an imagined Utopian place than to meet and put up with your neighbors. But just as the time to begin social change is always "now", the place to begin is always "here"—wherever you are.

So we were never more than part way off the grid.

Eric's question about polar power would not go away. Throughout the next winter, especially on subzero days, I wondered how some of that free, nature-provided cold could be stored.

I grew up in an era when the iceman's truck was a common sight in the alleys of my home town. I remember ice blocks being delivered to our home from the ice house on the banks of the Mississippi, north of the Little Falls dam. Every winter, when the ice was two feet thick, the ice-harvesting crews would go out on the river with big specialized saws. They cut blocks of ice which were hauled up to the ice house and layered with insulating sawdust from local lumber mills.

When I was a kid, sneaking into the ice house on hot summer days was a treat. Back then, I had been enjoying the polar power my son asked about.

But how to make polar power more than a pleasant memory? Cutting ice from a local lake or river was out of the question. Probably it would have taken more of my time and energy than we would have saved on electrical bills. And there were hygiene considerations. In adult retrospect, the Mississippi river water which had cooled the iceboxes of Little Falls with its polar power probably contained substances no contemporary public health department would recommend for consumption. Cutting ice would also present a hazard to snowmobilers and winter fishermen. One would just as soon not drown one's neighbors in the search for energy efficiency.

Then I began thinking of a giant block of ice, but how to make it, where to store it? Finally it occurred to me that if we dug a hole in the ground, built a wooden box in it (maybe six feet by six feet by six feet), insulated it well and put a waterproof liner in it, we would have a container for our ice block. We could run water into it by connecting the hose in the basement, running it up the stairs, and pouring water into the unit. Probably it would freeze better if I ran in a few inches, let it freeze, then ran in a few inches more, until the unit was full. Just by extending the entry way six feet to the north, a place for the box was available.

The plan worked. The first year we had ice in the PPU (polar power unit) until late August. It was like a very large cooler, providing ample chilled space for garden vegetables, keeping containers of worms and leeches for fish bait lively, ideal for cooling watermelons and cases of beverages.

The next winter was not so cold, so the ice block was only four feet thick. Then we had a really wimpy winter and the foot or so of ice was gone by June.

Our PPU was primitive and about as low tech as one can imagine, but it also didn't cost much to build. The lumber, like all the wood we used for building, came off our own land and was sawed into boards at a local small-scale mill. The liner was blue plastic. I got it from a fellow who worked in a furniture store which sold waterbeds. An occasional waterbed would arrive in a freight-damaged condition or be returned as defective. My furniture store contact put aside a wounded waterbed or two for me, instead of tossing it into the dumpster. I paid him in home-grown chickens.

Of course, our PPU worked because the earth itself is a temperature-conserving mechanism. Six feet down, it retains a near-constant temperature of near fifty-five degrees Fahrenheit, winter or summer. Had the concept occurred to me while I was designing and building the house, I would have installed earth-tubes. These enclosed tubes, buried six feet down, can be run into a building to provide natural air conditioning in summer, and a substantial increment of heat in winter. If I had run a couple of earth tubes through our polar power unit, with a fan to move the air, we could have had temperature conditioned air at a very reasonable expense of money and energy.

Also, if we had planned to build the unit when we built the house, we could have set things up to get the water down the hole without dragging the hose up the stairs from the basement.

As it was, we had greatly expanded our cold storage space, and demonstrated that polar power is worth harvesting.

The polar power unit was our most original piece of energy-saving technology, but hardly the only one. The solar water heater, built by a local friend, was placed on the edge of the grove of trees which surrounded the house, and it faced south. Three-quarter inch copper tubing buried six inches underground carried cold water out to it and returned solar-heated water to the house. The installation of the solar power unit cut our electric bill in half.

As cold weather came on, we drained the solar power unit and shifted over to our winter hot water system, which, like the solar power system, sent preheated water into our electric water heater. The winter heater consisted of a cold water pipe, plumbed into a twenty gallon galvanized tank. Three-quarter-inch copper tubing led from the holding tank into a maze-like tubing arrangement on the firebox of our box-type basement woodstove. Once the water was hot, it moved back into the twenty-gallon tank. As we used hot water in the house, the preheated water would flow into the hot water heater, instead of the water that came out of our well at forty-seven degrees. During most of the winter heating season, the electric water heater rarely kicked on. We were generating enough hot water for domestic uses as an off-shoot of keeping ourselves warm.

Our largest energy-saving experiment was only a partial success. We built a greenhouse off the south side of our basement. Most of one spring's rock-picking in the hayfield went into the footings. The windows were scavenged, mine for hauling them away, when buildings were being retrofitted at St. Cloud State University, where I worked. There was ample space under the windows and down the middle of the building for raised greenhouse beds. At one end of the greenhouse we built a root cellar where we stored our potatoes, carrots, beets, and rutabagas. Along the back wall, where they caught sunlight through the windows, we built up a solar storage unit which consisted of five-gallon cans, filled with water, painted black. Shireen was working part time at a local restaurant which bought its cooking oil in these containers. They were her suggestion. With the owner's permission, she brought them home from work one or two at a time.

Apart from its considerable use as a passive solar unit, the greenhouse was intended to give us fresh winter vegetables. We had visions of local leaf lettuce when the snow outside was three feet deep.

Unfortunately, the trees which surrounded our house, giving us winter wind protection, summer shade, and splendid bird habitat, also gave the greenhouse too much shade. With the leaves down in winter we had thought we would get enough sun to raise lettuce. We got enough sun to get lettuce seeds to sprout and to keep lettuce alive in anemic little sprigs, but there was never enough to fill the family salad bowl.

The greenhouse did provide marvelous warm light space in which to start tender spring vegetables. For several years we started tomatoes, peppers, eggplants, tender herbs, and annual flowers down there. It was almost worth building the greenhouse, just to catch that smell of warm damp earth and growing things on cold February and March days. It boosted our human energy level. That counted for something.

LIVING WITH ANIMALS: PETS
E.

A good case can be made for our nonexistence as entities. We are not made up, as we had always supposed, of successively enriched packets of our own parts. We are shared, rented, occupied. At the interior of our cells, driving them, providing the oxidative energy that sends us out for the improvement of each shining day, are the mitochondria, and in a strict sense they are not ours. They turn out to be little separate creatures, the colonial posterity of migrant prokaryocytes, probably primitive bacteria that swam into ancestral precursors of our eukaryotic cells and stayed there. Ever since, they have maintained themselves and their own ways, replicating in their own fashion, privately, with their own DNA and RNA quite different from ours. They are as much symbionts as the rhizobial bacteria in the roots of beans. Without them, we would not move a muscle, drum a finger, think a thought.

Lewis Thomas, The Lives of a Cell, 1974.

How should we live with animals? What is the proper moral stance of *homo sapiens* in relation to other species?

We have lived intimately with animals for many years. We had the space for them. We enjoyed their company. We felt that tending them taught our children important lessons. Filling a trough with feed or a bucket with water and watching the animals dig in is the kind of work with a direct cause-and-effect relationship and an immediate payoff which even a quite small child can understand and enjoy.

The results of inattention, of not getting the chores done, are also immediately apparent. A messy room or a single lorn hamster sniffing around the cage looking for sustenance can be ignored much more easily than twenty thirsty sheep blatting at the fence.

In our animal husbandry we were guided partly by common sense (underfed hens lay few eggs) and partly by what I can only call fellow feeling. Sickness in a kennel or barn or chickenhouse involves the possibility of economic loss, of course, but it is a little more complicated and personal than suffering a loss in the value of your stock portfolio. When the steer that was kicking up his heels yesterday stands with head and tail drooping, when the hen that was scratching and clucking becomes a wretched disheveled ball of feathers, the animal tender feels distress in a way that goes beyond economics.

When we needed advice or help we turned to the neighbors more often than the vet, tapping into a centuries-old source of animal lore, which often had a strongly moral undertone. The farmer who tended his stock badly, like the man who let his fields gully and piled up trash in his yard, was held in low regard. Fellow farmers said, "It'll cost him in the milk check" or "It'll cost him at the sales barn," and this always mattered, because most farmers survive on a thin economic margin. But the clinching line of local opinion was always, "A man ought to treat his stock right. You got to take care of your animals."

"Taking care" included providing adequate food and shelter; attending to matters of health; not crowding a pen or pasture past the comfort level of the animals or the recovery-capacity of the forage; and keeping up your fences, so your animals don't wander into the neighbors' fields and destroy crops, or onto the road, to collide with cars. The old rule of "Your stock eats before you do" was still observed.

I wonder how much of this traditional code of animal care has survived and is being transmitted, in the era of giant containment-feeding operations.

I wonder, too, where the code came from. I was a regular church-attender and Bible reader in my youth, and I can tell you, there is precious little in the Bible about the ethical treatment of animals. There are instructions as to what to do to them and with them. Don't eat some of them. Don't eat them in certain combinations. Don't have sexual relations with them. But these have nothing to do with any kind of duty we owe the non-human creation. Or at least, no preacher I ever listened to addressed that topic.

When Jesus defended working on the Sabbath if the work was pulling your neighbor's donkey out of a pit, he seemed to be concerned more with the neighbor than with the donkey. The donkey was handy for the argument, like the "great fish" that swallowed Jonah, or the Gadarene swine.

Of course humankind well up to the end of the nineteenth century lived in a sea of animals. Horses and other draft animals provided traction even in the great metropolitan centers. Mixed livestock farms were right on the edge of town. The back-yard chickencoop was an institution in working-class neighborhoods. Animals came to the butcher live.

Everybody who had contact with animals—which meant, practically everybody—must have learned the unwritten animal keeper's code, about the time they learned to tie their shoes. It would have been one of the things you took for granted. It wouldn't have needed to be formalized.

Maybe it is not until we reach a point where human population dominates the earth that we begin to need an explicit and agreed-upon moral code for our relations with animals. Enormous numbers of us never have contact with animals unless we initiate that contact by buying a pet. Many of us live where we go months on end, never seeing a wild animal other than pigeons or starlings, or the odd rat or roach. A bond of fellow feeling has lapsed into disuse. At some deep level, many humans miss that contact with the live but non-human which the animals we lived among used to provide.

Most formal western religious traditions have little to say about our relations with animals. The traditions of surviving hunter-gatherer peoples, like those who preceded us on our land, often have plenty to say about how we ought to live with "the animal brothers," as the Ahnishnaabeg called them. We can learn a lot from this tradition, as from the farmer-stockman tradition of "taking care of your animals". But few Americans know these older traditions, and there are elements of them which the modern urban sensibility, honed by Disney cartoons, wants to reject.

The question of how we should live with the non-human residents of the earth is now a central ethical concern. The more we know about the complexity and interconnectedness of life, the harder it is to assume that our moral code can ignore all non-human creatures. Environmentalism, vegetarianism, the various animal liberation movements, the revival of nature-based religions, the Wise Use movement, all hinge on a central moral question; how shall we live with animals?

Of course, all human beings live intimately with animals all the time, in ways of which we are mostly unconscious. As Dr. Lewis Thomas points out, we are "shared, rented, occupied" down to the microcellular level.

Little animals whose names only the microbiologist knows swarm inside our mouths and our digestive and genito-urinary tracts. We only become conscious of these essential symbionts when their population balance gets upset. Then we get yeast infections like thrush, and really awful bellyaches.

All big animals have their internal suites of essential little animals. If you ate a hamburger yesterday, you were eating grass at two removes. Beef animals are ruminants. All ruminants eat grass, but it takes regurgitation—chewing the cud—to reduce cellulose and chlorophyll to a digestible state. At every point along the way through the four-chambered bovine stomach, micro-organisms must be present to aid the digestive process, or the transformation from grass to beef will not take place. The human stomach is simpler, but our little animal symbionts are equally necessary for the transformation of beef and bun (or broccoli and arugula) into human meat and bone.

In severe Minnesota winters, a certain number of deer invariably starve. In every such winter, both hunters and animal protectionists demand large-scale deer-feeding programs. Invariably the Minnesota Department of Natural Resources has to warn deer feeders that putting out hay for starving deer may do more harm than good. Deer are browsers. A deer that has been eating woody plants during the winter will have internal micro-organisms for the digestion of woody plants. Such a deer can die with a bellyful of compassionately-donated but indigestible hay.

Earth itself is the end result of digestive processes, many of them at the microscopic level. A complex interweaving of bacteria, worms, insects and fungi are needed to turn stone and clay, vegetable detritus and animal corpses into the fertile soil which supports forests and prairies and farm fields.

Of course, these essential creatures are not what springs most readily to mind when the word "animal" is spoken. The symbiotic life forms in our intestines, the springtails digesting dead leaves out in the woods, the scurrying small life hiding in our basements and kitchen cupboards, these are not the animals referred to in phrases like "Society for the Prevention of Cruelty to Animals" or "Friends of Animals". The Animal Liberation Front has let loose mink and lab rats, but has shown no interest in liberating or protecting cockroaches or deer ticks.

When human beings are not thinking like biologists, they tend to classify animals into four groups, classifications which have little to do with biology, much to do with human comfort and amusement. In a loose way, we think of creatures big enough to draw themselves to our attention as Pets, Stock, Critters, or Beasts.

Pets are animals we keep for our pleasure. A good many people find the word "pet" patronizing, preferring the more egalitarian "animal companion"."

The word "pet", both the noun and the verb, probably comes originally from French *petit*, little.

A companion is somebody with whom you break bread, a meal-sharer. I've known a few people who would let the cat eat from the dinner table, but not usually while they were eating, and not usually from their dish. The best medical and veterinary advice suggests that such a practice is not good for either human or animal.

I once spent time on a small island in a large, storm-prone north woods lake, with a woman who was keeping her Hungarian Shepherd dog on the same vegetarian diet she ate. Fresh broccoli had to be boated in from the mainland for her dog, which had lost a good third of its body hair. Despite this clear sign of an unhealthy condition in her animal companion, the owner had not consulted a vet; she "didn't trust vets" and "didn't really trust western science."

Her broccoli-fed canine caught me disposing of a wrapper from a ground-beef package and nearly took off my hand.

This woman shared her bedroom and her tastes with her dog. They were inseparable. I'm sure she truly loved it, even as she subjected it to severe malnutrition. To love dearly is not necessarily to love wisely, or well.

I remember an arts and crafts fair held on a very hot summer day, in Winona, Minnesota. The booth from which we sold John's woodcraft was set up on a sidewalk. The heat of the cement under our feet and the blacktop of the street in front of us poured up through our soles and into our faces.

Down the middle of the street strode two exceedingly well-muscled young men, their splendidly-developed, shaven-chested torsos on display down to the hipbones, their toned buttocks rippling their satiny shorts. They were a two-guy parade. One of them had a Malamute on a lead. The other had two leashed Rottweilers. Beautiful powerful animals, all three.

This ensemble of men and dogs made an impressive fashion statement. But the pavement which was stinging my feet through socks and shoes must have been wretched on the pads of those dogs. Dogs have rituals of male display, but this display was not one a dog would have chosen. Left to their own devices, these animal companions would surely have preferred to find some soft dirt to scratch up, some shade to lie down in, some comfortable place to sprawl and pant.

At another craft fair I caught sight of a young fellow with a carrier across his chest. The guy was narrow-eyed, buck-toothed, and shy on chin, and so was the animal companion peeking out of the carrier, though the effect was more harmonious on the small sleek beastie. The warm summer air was full of the smell of brats, popcorn, and potpourri. A strolling bagpiper and a man in a gorilla suit playing the accordion were providing music. Several thousand shoppers were in full cry. The man with the carrier had chosen to share all these sensory delights with his pet ferret.

Are dogs really interested in fashion statements? Do ferrets enjoy shopping?

Whether we call them pets, or animal companions, or Fur People, we need to remember that the creatures we keep around for amusement and company do not have the same habits, tastes, nervous systems and digestive tracts as we do. Even when we share pleasure with them, it is not the same pleasure.

When John went hunting with Bet or her successors, it was clear both striding man and bounding dogs enjoyed the brisk walk through fall fields and woods. But how differently the landscape must have registered through those differently-equipped eyes, ears, noses, and nervous systems! Man and dogs were united in the common pleasure of the hunt, but this hardly meant they shared the same experience. The goal of the hunt for the human hunter is to shoot game and bring it home and eat it. The goal for dogs like our Springers, dogs that flush and fetch, is to sniff out game, to start the pheasant or grouse from cover, to retrieve it after it has been shot, and fetch it to the hunter, preferably without tooth marks.

Our dogs loved hunting season. They would start to waggle and shudder in ecstasy when the field coat went on and the shotgun came out of the gun cabinet. But what they did in the field was not, in one sense of the word, "natural" behavior. The proto-canine ancestors of our Springers would have charged through the brush, pouncing on whatever edible small game they startled into flight and either eating it on the spot or taking it home for the pups. That is the way coyotes and foxes hunt today. It took generations of selective breeding to develop the springing behavior, which was useful to human fowlers with nets, with falcons, and ultimately with firearms. The difference between gulping a bird, and delivering it to the hunter with the desired "soft mouth" of the well-trained retriever, was equally the result of long selective breeding and of careful training. Not every Springer can learn to do these things, though the gun-shy dog or the dog who eats the pheasant instead of delivering it can still make perfectly acceptable pets.

Even the way Springers move, that quartering motion across the area in front of the hunter which is designed to cover the maximum amount of ground, checking every potential hiding place for game birds, is the result of selective breeding. (Our pups were already displaying this behavior by the time they were four to six weeks old.) Then of course there is the feathering, that plumy silky long fur on legs and belly and drooping ears, so pleasing to the human eye and hand, so effective a collection system for burrs and beggar's lice, so splendid a hiding place for wood ticks. Like virtually every animal the human race has domesticated, our hunting dogs were shaped by generations of human need and human aesthetic preference, which have produced approximately four hundred separate breeds of purebred dogs worldwide.

Every single one of those dogs, from Chihuahua to Great Dane, is genetically *canis familiaris*. We shape animals to serve our needs and affections, but they remain animals, not Fur People.

The big dogs in small apartments, the pit bulls in crack houses, the puppies and kittens that grow up to be neurotic surrogate children, are not the worst examples of things we do to our animal companions.

For awhile a whole pack of feral dogs roamed our township, their lineage traceable to unspayed and unattended farm dogs, all from one particular farm. Now and again these wild canids picked off a lamb or a calf. They certainly ran deer, and from time to time they no doubt caught one.

One summer day when Shireen was riding her buckskin mare Fern over to see a friend on another farm, the feral dogs came up and surrounded her, circling and sniffing, no single one ready to attack, but ominous in their numbers. Shireen could feel the horse tensed and trembling under her, wanting desperately to run, which would of course have brought the full pack in heel-nipping pursuit through the woods and over rough field ground.

Rini kept the frightened mare reined tight and moving at a walk while the dogs trotted along, sniffing and whining, moving in almost to biting distance, then pulling back, then coming close again. When they were close to the farm and out on the road, on even level ground, she gave Fern her head. She says it was the fastest ride she's ever had on a horse.

The dogs did not follow long; they were timid, cringing, half-starved creatures, used to being yelled at and having things thrown at them. Descendants of watch-dogs and pets, they had been made into neighborhood pests and pariahs by human inattention.

Eventually they were all shot or poisoned off, and the whole township breathed easier.

A similar fate often awaits feral cats. When John was growing up, most barns had complements of resident cats, who kept the mice down and survived on milk, scraps, and rodents. Occasionally there would be a particular named and petted favorite, but mostly, barn cats were part of the landscape of a farm, one notch more domestic than the English sparrows and barn-nesting pigeons who lived on weed seeds and spilled grain. These half-wild cats bred like a math problem demonstrating exponential numbers. (Farmers called the vet when a cow was in trouble, but only town people had their cats "fixed".) Barn cats died regularly under the wheels of tractors or cars, or were picked off by dogs, or succumbed to distemper, a barn-full at a time.

There are not so many barn cats anymore. That kind of barn, the small-scale barn where the hand-milking farmer would jet a stream of milk into the mouth of a begging cat, has also largely disappeared. There are still feral cats prowling our woods, strays picking off birds, females we didn't know were around having kittens the world doesn't need up in the sap shack. People too "tender hearted" to take animals to the shelter still dump unwanted puppies and kittens out on country roads, damning nine tenths of them to quick death and sharply impacting the local bird and small animal populations. It's estimated that an average free-ranging house cat will kill at least fifty songbirds a year.

We cannot selectively prefer one animal over others without sending out unrecognized ripples into the great sea of animal life. It is our nature to "take sides" as between the cat and the robin, the flea and the dog. We need, if we aspire to be moral animals, to be conscious when we are taking sides.

Our cat Sam used to keep an effective check on the local population of mice, gophers, squirrels and chipmunks. She was also fully capable of killing and eating a full-grown cottontail rabbit. When Sam finished with a rabbit, there was nothing left but viscera, the last joint of the hind legs, and powder-puff tail. From our human viewpoint, she was a friendly and useful animal companion. From the viewpoint of the local wild animal and bird populations, she was a dangerous and effective predator.

There are higher predators on the local food chain than *felis catus*. Cats are susceptible to predation by coyotes and the bigger owls. (We suspect this was what happened to our cat Broccoli, who went off for her usual woods stroll one night and never came home.) And judging by our local roadsides, only skunks and raccoons suffer more automotive collision fatalities. (We know this is what happened to Sam, because we found her body afterwards.)

In A Place in Space, poet and essayist Gary Snyder says, "On a deep level I do not think I can approve of the domestication of birds and animals; too much is taken out of their self-sufficient wild natures." After a lifetime of living with animals, with dogs, cats, sheep, chickens, calves, pigs, geese, after delivering their young and tending their wounds and sometimes speeding them out of this world, after seeing the cruelties humans inflict even on creatures they claim to love, I understand what Snyder is saying.

We can wish *homo sapiens* had never made that first step, never thrown a bone to the wolfling at the edge of the firelight, never left meat scraps as a thank-offering for the wild mouse-catcher who keeps the grain-store free from vermin. But that is like wishing Eve had ignored the snake, Adam refused the apple, that humans had never learned to knap stone and tame fire. We are curious, sociable animals. Unless we are starving or frightened, lost weanlings and nestlings must always have brought out our nurturing instinct. We tamed animals because we enjoyed their company. No doubt they let themselves be tamed because they enjoyed ours.

The human-animal partnership, inevitably one-sided (since we are bigger than most of our animal companions, smarter in many though not all ways, and longer lived) is too old to dissolve. We cannot un-wish our history because parts of it embarrass us. To attempt to do so is to lie about the kind of animal we are.

But Snyder's phrase "self-sufficient wild nature" is worth remembering. We talk about "animal companions" as if our domestic familiars could drive, use credit cards, and vote, but too often we treat them as "fur people", the stuffed toys of childhood miraculously come to life. Our relationships with them are happier for both parties when we keep in mind the dogginess of the dog, the cattiness of the cat, the essential *otherness* of the beasts we live with.

I remember the first time Bet went swimming. At the time we were given Bet Bouncer, she had lived her whole life first in a kennel, then in a fenced yard in Carmel. Her owners, people who had named her for an allusion in an eighteenth century comedy, gave her to us because they knew we would be living out in the woods, and they could not keep their dog in the yard. She kept escaping. Sooner or later, a car would pick her off.

She had been with us maybe ten days when we went down to the dock on Big Swan Lake in our bathing suits.

Ten days is not long, but she had decided we were her people. She came when called, wagged her tail when we petted her, barked when strangers approached the cabin.

Back in Carmel she might have been walked along the beach, but a lake was a different body of water. When we started wading out into that strange water, when we took the children out into the water, she did not like it. She paced back and forth on the end of the dock, nervously whimpering, then barking, a sharp warning tone.

Finally, convinced that drastic methods were called for, she leaped into the lake. I could swear her original thought was to drag the little ones to safety.

But at the point where she hit the water, her entire body tone changed. It was like that moment in cartoons when the giant light bulb comes on over the head. She bobbed to the surface dog-paddling and panting with entire natural-ness and delight. "Oh," she seemed to be saying, "Now I get it!"

Nascent in that moment were all the hours she would spend with John in the duck boat, all the enthusiastic leaps into cold fall water to fetch back game, all the waterfowling dogs in her lineage and among her descendants. This poten-tial pleasure had been part of her nature all along. It was a delight to her human friends, to share a moment in which she discovered one of the things she was really good at. It is what we all want out of life, whatever kind of animal we are.

A GAY WAY OF GOING
E.

It was a mid-morning in February. I was going to take the dogs for a run.

From 1973, when we built the big house at Big Swan Lake, to 1987, when we moved across the road, there were always Springers in the four kennels built across the end of the garage. Usually we had two or three breeding bitches and a stud.

The normal household routine was for John to let the dogs out of their kennels briefly and give them water before he drove off down the road to his job at St. Cloud State University. I would come out later, sometime between ten and eleven, depending on how bad the weather was, how energetic I felt, how much else I had to do that day. I would visit the other animals, picking eggs, dispensing food and water, checking gates and fences and doors. I would take the dogs for a walk. Our mail arrived in the RFD box at the end of the long driveway, around 11:15. By that time I would be done with the winter morning animal chores and could see how many brown envelopes full of rejected manuscripts I had gotten back that day.

We had the usual amount of lousy weather that winter. The snow was only calf-high, except in the bigger drifts, but everything was skinned with ice, especially the cleared-out area in front of the kennels. All these years in Minnesota have not habituated me to walking on icy surfaces.

I had attended to the animals properly, but the walks I had taken with the dogs had been brief. And their runs needed cleaning badly.

Today, I thought, I would give all the runs a good cleaning, and take the dogs for the walk they deserved.

The three younger dogs shot out of their kennels as they always did, their liver and white or black and white coats shaggy with winter. They ran out in a long barking oval, bouncing over each other, giving each other play nips, sometimes plunging into and out of a snowdrift in a great "foof!" of glitter. They would swing back, either to return to their kennels, or to go further afield, if a human would take them.

Bessie was in the end kennel. She was black and white, just slightly under the American Kennel Club breed standard for size, a sweet-natured animal who had taken easily to the obedience training we gave all our dogs. On her AKC registration blank she was Quarry's Queen Bess, out of Bet Bouncer by Quarry's Black Jack, the well-loved pick of Bet's second litter.

She had known no human care but ours, since she was whelped in the end of the garage, next to the house across from the quarries. She had been with us when we lived in the school house, gone with us to Earthome, watched from this run as we built our house. She was older than Eric and had been around for most of the other kids' lives.

Her name was part of the pedigree of each of the younger dogs in our kennels, repeated so many times over the years in our breeding records book that John had stopped writing it out in full and taken just to scrawling, "QQB". At fourteen years old, she was out of the breeding rotation now.

Till quite recently, no dog had responded with more enthusiasm to the gun coming out of the cabinet and the donning of the hunting jacket. She had never been quite as good a duck dog as her mother, or her older half-sister Kate—she would hesitate, as they did not, before leaping into water with ice on it—but as a grouse dog, she was without peer. She was, as they said in the hunting magazines, "birdy". She would bust brush for you all day long. John could tell you impressive tales of her prowess afield, and I have heard him do just that, spend time with other gun dog owners telling Bet stories, Kate stories, Bessie stories. It is part of the pleasure of hunting, the retrospective re-creation of fall sky and leaf smell, abrupt roar of wings, gun-roar and tumble of falling bird, and amazing retrieves in dense cover. Reeds, cornfields, dog-hair aspen, thorny plum brush, prickly ash, Bessie would do it for you, Bessie would bring back the bird.

The kennels were large fenced cemented runs, each accessing a nest box built into the end of the garage. Bessie was out in her run, wagging her tail at the sound of my voice. But though I opened the door and called, she would not come out of the run.

In fact, when I thought back, I could not remember that she had come out of the run any morning recently. I had been going out with the other dogs, but she had been staying back at the kennel. How long? I couldn't say exactly how long.

I went into the kennel to look more closely at her. She not only wouldn't come outside; she wouldn't come out into the middle of the run, away from the fence. It was as if the space frightened her.

When I poured water into her drinking bowl, she bumped it with nose and foot, spilling half its contents when she reached to drink.

I knelt down next to her, distressed at this odd behavior, angry at myself for not having paid attention before. Was she hurt? Was she sick? What was going on?

Her nose was cold, her coat thick. She moved a little stiffly, like a cautious old lady—like me on ice—but she wasn't limping, there was no blood on her coat or other evidence of wounds, nor could I feel any lumps, like those tumors Kate had, before we took her to the vet and had him give her the injection. Bessie didn't look or act sick, she just acted cautious and clumsy.

Then, noticing the angle of her head, the way she looked at me, but not at quite the normal angle, I thought, with a great rush of shame, she's gone blind. She must have been developing cataracts and now she can't see!

Animals cannot tell you what they want and need. They cannot tell you their symptoms. Caring for animals forces you to assume a level of near-absolute responsibility.

There was essentially nothing I could have done about her declining eyesight. Still, I ought to have noticed, I ought to have known.

Outside the kennel, her younger relatives were wagging and whining and eager to go.

I took her by the collar. "Come on, Bessie, good girl, that's a *good* dog—"

I nudged and pulled her out of the run, down the slick cemented area in front of the kennels, out onto the snow, where the footing was easier. It was strange to feel timidity and caution in that body which had joyously put in miles through heavy brush in the hunting field.

A free-running Springer does not trot at your heel. It races back and forth in windshield-wiper sweeps, intersecting your path, keeping track of where you are, ready to come at a call, but on its own.

Away from the buildings, Bessie began to move more freely. Perhaps the smells were less confused and it was therefore easier for her to keep track of where she was. She didn't join the great racing swings of the younger dogs, but it would have been possible, watching her, not to know that anything was wrong. For a few minutes she lost that old-lady-on-ice gait and moved as the AKC breed standard said she should; "A gay way of going."

I don't know how long I had the dogs out—ten minutes? fifteen? As I put her back into the kennel, I was stroking her, telling her we would do more tomorrow, apologizing for not having noticed her condition.

She seemed perkier, even though she had bumped the door frame as she went through. She drank a lot of water.

I gave her a last pat after I cleaned the pens, hauling away frozen dung.

That night, I mentioned Bessie's condition to John. He agreed with me; he had noticed her vision problems. He just had not said anything about it, because what was the point? She was fourteen, already older than most of the dogs we'd owned. But she'd eaten well. It was good to have gotten her out.

The next morning, he found her dead in the kennel.

LIVING WITH ANIMALS: STOCK
E.

I think I could turn and live with animals, they are so
                        placid and self-contain'd,
I stand and look at them long and long.

They do not sweat and whine about their condition,
They do not lie awake in the dark and weep for their sins,
They do not make me sick discussing their duty to God,
Not one is dissatisfied, not one is demented with the mania
                        of owning things,
Not one kneels to another, nor to his kind that lived
                        thousands of years ago,
Not one is respectable or unhappy over the whole earth.

Walt Whitman, from Section 32, "Song of Myself", Leaves of Grass, 1855

Animals are Other.

If there is anything I have learned as an egg picker, chicken gutter and plucker, hog tender, dog walker, and lamb midwife, it is just that; animals are Not Us. They are not necessarily made happy by what would make us happy, nor made miserable by what would make us miserable.

In the pre-dawn hours of April 5, 1999, a group of people in ski-masks broke into two University of Minnesota buildings, where research was being conducted on Alzheimer's disease, brain cancers, Parkinson's disease, and child-hood heart disease. The anonymous invaders filmed themselves smashing computers and lab equipment and leaving open the doors on freezers which contained brain tissue samples, donated by relatives of deceased Alzheimer's victims. The vandals did more than 1.5 million dollars worth of damage. Researchers said their projects had been set back by months or years.

A group called the Animal Liberation Front sent E-mail messages that afternoon to other animal rights' groups, claming credit for the vandalism and for "rescuing" twenty-seven pigeons, forty-eight mice, thirty-six rats and five sala-manders which had been used as research subjects. Among the mice were animals bred over generations to develop Alzheimer's symptoms.

Fourteen of the banded pigeons used in memory research were later recaptured, one with a broken leg. Eight of the white rats were later found on the shoulder of a rural road and in a nearby field. (Asked how he was sure they were the right rats, University research animal supervisor Ed Craig said, "How many albino rats do you see around?") Four of the rats had died of hypothermia. (Nightly Minnesota temperatures that week were in the thirties.) Another had been partially eaten.

Asked whether it was a real kindness to turn loose animals who have spent their whole lives in labs, ALF spokesperson Kevin Kjonaas told the Minneapolis Star-Tribune, "A chance at freedom is better than certain death at the hands of those animal researchers."

"Live free or die" is a profoundly significant political sentiment, for humans. As a human, I endorse it. Whether it ought to apply to lab-bred rats—whether rats could make any sense of it—seems dubious.

Spending a lot of time with animals does not necessarily give the animal tender any special moral vision. I know animals are good company. I have spent many Whitmanian moments checking out a new litter of puppies, easing the hot egg out from under the hot feathers of a hen on a below-freezing day, scratching behind the ears of Eric's beloved sow, Miss Piggy. I believe that hanging out with animals, being responsible for the food and the water and the crap and the corpses, is good for the human soul.

Experience with animals is sometimes helpful in predicting how they may behave. All my experience never gave me the slightest belief that I could read animal minds, or that their tastes and moral sensitivities were at all like mine.

When, in a consideration of human/animal relations, one gets outside the category of pets and animal companions into the category of livestock, popular opinion often holds that those animals have no brains worth bothering about. Probably my best known poems are a sequence called "Lambing". I don't know how many times people whose only contacts with sheep have been stained-glass windows and lamb chops have looked at me wisely and said, "Sheep are really dumb, aren't they?"

I always want to say, "What do you mean, dumb?"

It's true that sheep, unlike dogs and cats, are largely unresponsive to human emotional expressions. A sheep will not cringe and whimper if you yell at it, nor will it come up and rub against your legs if you call it. Knock you aside to get at the grain, yes. Sheep are herd animals (as if humans are not!) but this hardly argues stupidity. The sheep in the middle of the flock is the sheep most safe from predators.

Sheep are smart enough to survive and procreate. They belong to a family of animals, the Bovoidae, which began in the Miocene and has survived to the present. They have been living with humans as domestic animals for at least seven thousand years.

Certainly, sheep are smart enough to know when they need help. The same ewe that will cut like a tailback to escape being grabbed by the shearer will also, when in labor, allow a human being to slide a hand up inside the birth canal.

I was the lamb midwife because, John said, I had smaller hands than he did, but I suspect also that he thought I would have more feeling, in every sense of that word, for the cramped hot interior world of a pregnant female creature. I don't know how many times I knelt in cold, sheep-smelling straw, usually in the middle of the night, my hand up in birth-spasmed darkness. I had spent a lot of time reading about birth presentations in The Small Farmer's Guide to Raising Livestock and Poultry, and looking at little line drawing illustrations. Head only, legs back; head and one leg; hind legs presented; breech presentation; entangled twins. All the complicated ways a lamb could exit the mother and enter the barn.

The critical moment, always, was making the translation from what the book said to what my hand felt.

Sometimes I failed. I remember the enormous lamb, caught at the shoulders, born dead; the pair of twins, of which both were delivered, but one never breathed; the ewe with the massive uterine prolapse, who took a day to die.

Ah, but when I succeeded, then all that careful pulling and shifting brought a sudden loosening. What was intended to be easy suddenly became easy. There would be a slithering sound as the lamb emerged from the birth canal. Sometimes the little new one would bleat from inside its birth-sack and the mother would respond with a soft mutter, before she licked and tore the membrane away. Neither animal ever made exactly those sounds at any other time.

At such moments, whatever the human news, the world seemed a comprehensible and straightforward place in which my skills had made a difference.

I have gained some deeply resonant experiences from living with animals. These experiences do not seem to have very much to do with the intelligence of animals, or their economic value. They grow out of a biotic stratum of experience, the animal past all living things share, even when they sit upright and wear clothing, vote in elections, pay taxes, and operate computers. Hearing the tiny "beep-beep" sounds from the not-yet-cracked eggs under a brooding goose, then hearing the goose respond, was such an experience. Helping ewes lamb was another. I feel I am a different and better person, for being involved with all that wool and blood and manure.

Among things I learned in the barn is that sheep accept and reject their young for reasons obscure to the shepherd. Sometimes a ewe, having delivered successfully, would look back over her shoulder at what E.B. White called "her little tomato surprise" and simply stroll off, showing no further interest.

Sometimes, says The Small Farmer's Guide, a ewe's milk will not be "in" when she delivers. In this case the suckling reflex will not exist and the ewe will reject her young. Sometimes the lamb does not have sufficient strength and coordination to assume the proper nursing position. Lambs nurse with their front legs kneeling, their rear ends in the air. They have to reach down and under the skirt of grimy wool, then up to grab one of the two fat little teats on the round firm udder. Once they have learned how to do this, they hang on for dear life, nursing so vigorously that if a ewe is feeding twins, their combined attack on her udder will lift her hind legs off the ground in regular nursing pulsations.

Not all lambs can do this immediately. Sometimes the female is impatient with the lamb's weakness or clumsiness. (I spent an awful lot of time scuffling around on my knees, trying to bring weakling lamb and twitchy ewe together.) Sometimes the lamb is so weak that the teat simply slides out of the mouth. Without that first vital nourishment, the lamb brought into the world with such struggle can exit it within an hour or two.

Sometimes a ewe will reject her lamb on one breeding cycle, only to mother successfully the next. Sometimes she will nurse a couple of times, then reject the lamb. Sometimes a ewe will accept one lamb from a pair of twins, while rejecting the other. And while rejection may mean no more than walking away from the little rusty puddle in the birth sack, it can also mean swinging the head around and under and up in the full butt that sends the rejected progeny flying into the barn wall with a bone-rattling slam. Get the hell away from me, you little woolly nuisance!

As I said; animals are Other.

It is possible, with persistence, small nursing bottles, and commercial lamb milk replacer, which comes like powdered milk in big bags, to bring "orphan" or "bummer" lambs to healthy adulthood. Tradition and my own experience suggest that they are never as thrifty and fast-growing as lambs nursed by the ewe, but with enough help from a human nurturer, they make it.

One year I had no less than six orphan lambs down in the house basement. (They were born in March of a very cold winter.) They had to be fed every three or four hours. Their frantic blatting would rouse me from sleep upstairs, and I have rarely felt so essential and so exploited as when I stumbled down the night stairs. My little flock, penned in a child's old wooden playpen, all came lunging at me at once. I would have a bottle in each hand and reserve bottles at the ready. The hungriest got fed first, tails twirling, while their pen-mates blatted and butted and tried to extract nourishment from the folds of my bathrobe and the fuzz on my slippers.

All the other members of my household slept through the whole performance, night after night.

When lambing season was well past and the new grass was up, we used to move our sheep across the road, into pasturage in the forty. We loaded them into a drag we could pull behind the tractor. (I have to admit we called this primitive bit of home-made sheep-hauling technology the ewe-boat.)

When the ewes hopped out of the ewe-boat onto the fresh grass, they always did something very interesting. They spread themselves out at uniform distances, no sheep directly behind another. I don't know what this grazing interval was, exactly, but the sheep did. Even lambs observed this instinctive protocol.

There was nothing very obscure about this behavior. Sheep like to eat clean grass, grass which other sheep have not peed or pooped on. On pasture they spread themselves out so they never come in contact with each other's waste.

If sheep do this as a matter of instinct, why should it be so difficult for the dominant species to manage?

We began raising sheep because they were cheap, because we had appropriate pasture for them, and because they didn't require twice a day milking. We started raising pigs partly for literary reasons.

I don't know how much the porcine portion of our lives was inspired by copies of *Farm Journal*, and how much by Laura Ingalls Wilder's biographical novel Farmer Boy. All our children read all the Wilder books, as I did. Eric was particularly partial to Farmer Boy, which is Mrs. Wilder's account of her husband Almanzo's childhood on a New England farm.

The senior Wilders were thrifty folk. In one section of the book, Manzo goes to the county fair with his town cousins, who are spending freely on cotton candy and lemonade. Father Wilder gives him fifty cents, along with a cautionary lecture about making the best use of it.

Young Manzo walks the whole fair, sniffing the root beer, listening to the carousel music and the pitches of the carnies, inspecting every available buyable pleasure.

Then he invests his fifty cents in a weanling gilt with breeder potential.

A thrifty eleven-year-old farm kid can accumulate a tidy sum of money. Eric came to us in April of 1978 with a business proposition. He would spend his money on a feeder pig, donating his labor as feeder and shovel wielder. We would buy the feed. At the end of the summer, we would purchase our winter supply of pork from Eric at below supermarket prices.

So a healthy forty-pound Duroc-cross gilt, pink with black spots, came to live in one end of our small barn. Almanzo Wilder named his pig Lucy. Eric named his for that irresistible Sesame Street porker, Miss Piggy. His parents had always insisted previously that animals intended for the table or the shipper's truck that would take them to the meat packing plant be given names like "Chops" or "Proteina". But it was Eric's pig.

With a large pen all to herself, a pig-tender who had invested his life savings in her welfare, and four other interested humans looking in on her from time to time, Miss Piggy quickly demonstrated that pigs are intelligent, sociable animals. She discovered the pleasures of galloping around her pen, bouncing off the rails and kicking her heels up in the air. She found out that if she put her front trotters up on the rails and said "hoink, hoink" when there were humans in the barn, she would get scratched behind the ears. When spoken to, she would respond with a whole repertoire of vocalizations. She was the most conversable animal I've ever known.

She was also a clean animal, as pigs will be if they have sufficient space and attention. Pigs need to be kept cool (they have no sweat glands) and this is why they will wallow, but they would rather be clean than dirty. And unless they are ill or in too small a space, they will pick out a bathroom area of the pen (what The Small Farmer's Guide calls a dunging area) and use it consistently.

By fall she was up over two hundred pounds. Shipping weight. But she was also a fine healthy young sow. It was not an unreasonable idea to have her bred. And of course, it put off some hard choices.

Most sows want to be left alone when they are farrowing. Miss Piggy's successors wouldn't let anybody near them at this time. Miss Piggy was so accustomed to our company, she seemed to enjoy having Eric crouched behind her, clean towel in hand, as the piglets emerged. He had no difficulty wiping them off and putting them in their warming box till she was finished farrowing and ready to nurse.

A healthy new-born pig is an amazing creature. Lambs and calves and foals come into the world limp. It takes time for them to lift their heads, get their legs under them, find their mother's nipples. Piglets are all muscle. Their eyes pop open as soon as they hit the light. You can see them peering at you through the birth membrane. They not infrequently use their own snouts and front legs to rip themselves free, and then go trotting up beside the great continent of the maternal flank to find nourishment.

This combination of small size and precocity is comic, though it does present a danger to the piglets, who can easily be crushed by their much larger mother. Commercial farrowing operations restrain the mother in a farrowing crate, or "creep", so that the little pigs are not in danger of being rolled on. We transferred our newborn pigs into a large cardboard box under a heat lamp, (little pigs needs to keep very warm those first few days) where they could get out, but the mother could not get in.

To hold a little pig is to hold pure energy. Their skin, not yet bristled, feels like slick felt. They are hot as stoves, hard as athletes, full of wiggles and bounces and curiosity. A little pig in the hand is a sovereign antidote to despair.

This is pure guesswork on my part, but the precocity and independence of the newborn pig may have had something to do with those cultures and religions which view the animal as ritually unclean. Any creature so full of life and so energetic at birth may have seemed uncanny, even devilish.

Pigs of any age love to play, with each other, or with any object like a feed pan that they can knock around the pen. Our little pigs quickly learned the pleasures of what John called "porcine pinball". They would race across the pen, bounce off each other, tumble and roll and get back on their trotters and have another go.

Miss Piggy was a prolific breeder and a good mother. She presented Eric with four large healthy litters, at a time when forty pound feeder pigs brought up to fifty dollars each. (In the fall of 1998, we could have bought a two hundred pound butcher hog for twenty five dollars.)

Miss Piggy also continued to grow. Unlike humans, domestic pigs grow all their lives, in all their dimensions. By the summer of 1980, two year old Miss Piggy weighed well over six hundred pounds. When she put her front trotters up on the rail, which she still loved to do, she looked down at most of our visitors. We had to reach up to scratch behind her ears.

Eric had said a number of times, "I'm never going to ship Miss Piggy out. I'll keep her for the rest of her natural life, and when she dies I'll have her taxidermied and put her in my room." But he was beginning to realize that so huge an animal would leave no room for Eric. He was beginning to say, "Maybe I'll just have her head stuffed, to remember her by."

With her fourth litter, Miss Piggy was in trouble. Her labor was long and difficult. We had never had to call the vet before; now we did. "You're lucky it's not hot," he said. "If the temperature was in the eighties or nineties, this would kill her."

The litter, when it finally came, was as healthy and vigorous as usual. But for a day or two after farrowing, Miss Piggy hardly moved. We had to shove her into position by brute force, no easy task with such a large animal, so the little ones could nurse. The vet said another litter would kill her.

What do you do with a six hundred and fifty pound sow who eats plenty of pig rations, takes up a large space in a small barn, and needs to be shoveled out after, when she can produce no further young? Eric's fantasy of feeding and housing and cleaning up after her for the rest of her natural life, as if she were a retired Kentucky Derby winner, might have been feasible if we were millionaires with a big estate. Paul McCartney could have done it. (But why would a vegetarian buy a meat hog?)

154

We had other uses for that money, that space, that labor.

There was no argument. None of us were happy. But even Eric knew what we had to do.

When the truck arrived from the local stock hauler, the driver opened the barn door, took one look at Miss Piggy with her trotters on the rail, and exclaimed, "I'm not goin' in there with a hog that size!"

John grabbed an ear of corn, called, "Here, Piggy, here, Piggy", and opened the gate. She followed him docilely up the ramp, into the darkness of the truck, and was driven away without trouble. He said he felt like Judas.

Eric promptly bought two replacement sows, but they had not been socialized like Miss Piggy. They produced good litters for us. But they never learned to request an ear-scratching, and if you had to go into the pen with them when they had little pigs, you needed to be able to vault out over the railing fast.

They were good pigs, as livestock. They provided Eric with a steady supply of funds for all the things young men need to spend money on. They were not Miss Piggy. When Eric went out into the world to seek his fortune at eighteen, he left some bristles from Miss Piggy stuck to the wall in his room. I have them still.

Recently I saw an exchange of letters in one of the major syndicated advice columns. A woman was furious with her husband. She had asked him to throw a dead squirrel out of the yard, before the children saw it. Instead of using a shovel, he had used her mother's antique sterling silver sugar tongs. She soaked the tongs in bleach and then ran them through the dishwasher several times, but she still could not bring herself to use them. Just looking at them turned her stomach.

The letter elicited much responsive mail. Most of the commentary focused on the husband, and the sterling silver sugar tongs, and all that ritualistic cleansing.

Nobody but me seemed to ask, Why didn't she take care of the squirrel herself?

Or, why was it okay to throw the squirrel into the neighbor's yard, instead of burying it in hers?

Or, most importantly, why didn't she want the children to see a dead squirrel?

When you live with animals, death and the evidences of death are never far from you.

Junebugs thump against the windows and plop onto the porch. In some seasons, windrows of dead insects drift in the lake shallows. Birds fly into our windows, through errors of navigation or, in breeding season, to attack the reflected interloper perceived as invading their territory. Most of them, having bounced off the glass, shake their heads and fly up into the trees and recover. (Certainly more live to survive than when we had cats, who regarded stunned birds as nice snacks.)

Twice, male ruffed grouse have smashed with maximum velocity into our living room window. Male grouse in the fall of the year take to the air and fly as hard and fast as they can, as far as they can get from their natal place, till they drop from the sky with exhaustion. Sometimes they drop from the sky into some place entirely unsuitable for grouse, like a major city, or the middle of a lake. Not infrequently they collide with objects, like trees or tall buildings or our window. Ornithologists call this activity "the fall shuffle" or "crazy flight". It serves the sound biological purpose of mixing and dispersing the gene pool. Fatalities are high, but from a biological point of view, the loss of a few young males is probably advantageous.

I used to think of crazy flight often during our sons' adolescence, especially when they were out cruising with their friends.

Incidentally, we did not dispose of those suicidal grouse with a sterling silver sugar tongs, or even with a shovel. I brought them in and dressed them and roasted them with mushrooms. Why should we leave them for the skunks and raccoons and burying beetles? There are very few North American herbivores we have not eaten, from beaver to squirrel.

You cannot go far in biologically-healthy country without finding feathers or bones, many of them the end product of somebody's meal. In fifth grade, Eric found a gopher skull in the garden and strung it on a cord and wore it around his neck to school. He wears it in his school picture from that year. One of his female classmates examined it with interest. "Hey, Eric, is that a gopher skull?" It's hard to gross out country girls, even in the fifth grade.

Among the totemic objects in my writing corner is the blade-bone of a deer's shoulder. It came from a deer that died in late fall, maybe a hundred yards from the corner of our garden. In the following spring almost the entire articulated skeleton remained, and a few strands of hair. Otherwise, all of the deer had been absorbed into the fabric of the woods around it. It had run off in the bodies of other animals, or been sucked up by the roots of plants.

Deer shoulder bones were used as hoes by Native American agriculturists. Hoes made of blade-bone scraped up the dirt which made the effigy and burial mounds of the Mississippian culture.

I look at my blade-bone, this retrieved chunk of corpse. I see it first as *memento mori*; as this animal is, so I will be. I see it as part of the structure of a living creature, the lever of those great soaring leaps deer make, the way they flow and float and are gone, before the watcher can say more than "Ah!" I see it also as tool, instrument, useful extension of the human hand.

The little knob at the base fits my hand neatly. A straight stick to use as a handle, a piece of thong (or the cord Anishinaabe women made from the inner bark of basswood) to tie handle and head together, maybe a little sharpening of the blade end, and this deer shoulder-bone would be a very serviceable tool. I could use it to prepare garden soil, to dig the hole into which I would drop the corn, to chop out weeds. I could use it to loosen and excavate the earth, out of which I and my people would form funerary mounds for our dead, and effigy mounds, to commemorate our gods.

If I thought about animals as my early human predecessors on this land thought about animals, I would imagine the deer had grown the blade-bone for me. I mean, look at the shape of the thing. Having used it herself as long as she needed it, the deer had given me this handy tool by dying in a convenient place. I would be grateful. I would sing a praise-song to the spirit of the deer as I made the hoe, and every time I use it.

I make such a praise song now, looking up at the blade-bone where it lies on top of the speaker that came with my new computer package, just above the letters that say, "Power Woofer."

You cannot keep animals without mortality, although mortality is always greater among wild animals. A sow will roll on a piglet or two in most litters. An occasional lamb or puppy will miss a feeding and be found limp, ignored in the hay of the barn or pushed to the back of the nest box. I know chimpanzees mourn over the bodies of their dead, that elephants will sometimes lift the limp limbs and try to make the dead walk, but most animals, even if they have been attentive mothers, treat the bodies of their dead young like any other inanimate object.

We buried or composted small corpses or hauled them out into the woods for natural reprocessing, like that deer. For larger animals, we called the local rendering plant. The dump truck which picked up animal dead had one of those plastic name plaques across the front of the hood. It said, "Black Vulture."

One day a sheep which had dropped dead in the pasture without previous symptoms of disease, a thing sheep will do from time to time, was lying next to the fence, waiting for the Black Vulture to pick it up. A couple of the other sheep squeezed their necks through the fence, pulled tufts of wool from the body of their dead sister, and ate them.

Animals are Other.

A two-year-old steer named Star, for the white spot on his black face, fell over one day in the barn, with what appeared to be a stroke. We had bought him out of the sales barn in his first or second day of life, as we did other calves at other times. I had fed him calf milk replacer from a quart-size nursing bottle for his first couple of weeks.

Now he could not stand, though he kept trying. He lay on one side, scrambling with his good legs, trying to get up, able only to grind himself around and around in the straw. If I put feed into his mouth he would attempt to chew on one side, but the hay or grain would slide out the other. I gave him water from a watering can with a long spout, since a bucket was impossible. Even when I got the spout almost into his throat, the water continued to run out.

The vet said there wasn't a thing he could do for the stricken animal. Star might regain some use of his injured side spontaneously, but probably not. The vet also said something about an illness cattle may contract, if they are housed where sheep have been housed. If this was a diseased animal, we did not want the meat to go into the family larder.

I called the Black Vulture. The young guy who drove chewed me out for not having killed the steer before he got there, even as he took his shotgun from the cab.

He put a chain around Star's neck and hauled him out of the barn, out where he could conveniently hoist him into the truck. Star's limp body jerked along over the ground. His eye rolled back as he tried to figure out what was going on. He made no sound. He had been unable to low or bellow since the stroke.

I followed. When you have held the nursing bottle to the avid mouth, you are committed to the rest of the journey.

Finding a killing place that satisfied him, the driver from the rendering plant took aim at the back of the head, between the ears, from a distance of about a foot. The noise was less than you might expect. A little jet of blood, maybe four inches high, shot up from the wound, falling back like the dying plume of a fountain that has been turned off. That was all, except there was no more of that horrible grinding futile effort to rise. I thought of all the deaths by gunshot I had seen in the movies and on TV, and how different this was.

The Black Vulture driver used his hoist to haul Star up into the back of the truck, where I could see and smell the rest of his day's take. A couple of sheep, a pig, anonymous tangled stiff legs. Then off down the driveway and the county road, where his cargo would be made into fertilizer and whatever else they make in a plant where the sign out front says, "Bi-Products".

Some of the mortality of a farm is, of course, planned for from the moment you buy the calf or turn the ram in with the ewes. Our litters of feeder pigs went off to the sales barn alive, but for the sheep, we brought in a custom slaughterer, an old Norwegian with a fondness for coffee and cookies and an assortment of very sharp knives on his belt. He would come up quietly behind a lamb with its mouth in a pan of feed, straddle the animal, pull its head back, say, "Have a good journey," and cut the throat with a single deft slash.

At intervals during the summer, chickens met the traditional fate on the chopping block, usually in groups, so that plucking and gutting and cutting up for the freezer could be done a number at a time. Some friends came to visit us on a day when this pen-to-freezer processing was going on. Their four-year-old daughter watched solemnly as the kids and I plunged just-beheaded chickens into scalding water and stripped off handfuls of wet feathers.

After awhile she said, "My Mama's chickens never were alive. They just always were in a little box in the store."

Producing the death of any living thing is serious business. Much necessary killing takes place at the periphery of our attention, and most of us like it that way. When the doctor prescribes an antibiotic, we do not mentally translate "antibiotic" into "anti-life agent." Humankind in all its varied cultures has rightly seen that the act of killing is at the nexus of a whole knot of ethical questions.

Most cultures have rituals governing the taking and processing of flesh. One of the packing houses in Long Prairie keeps rabbis on staff as kosher slaughterers. In some cultures, to be a slaughterer or a leather-worker is to belong to a ritually unclean caste.

Many aboriginal peoples required prayer and abstinence before the hunt, ritual praise afterwards. But they did not always make the distinctions among food and energy sources that modern western culture makes. If the deer was thanked, as it was, for giving its body to the hunter, the wild rice plant was equally thanked for giving its seed, the maple tree for the gift of its sap, the birch tree for yielding its skin. The people who were here before us, the ones with the blade-bone hoes, did not see themselves as exploiting food and energy sources. They saw themselves as maintaining a spiritual relationship with the stuff of the world.

I have seen hunters like John mark the face of a novice with the blood of his first kill. It was a gesture learned from other hunters. It seems like a very old ritual.

A question which often crossed my mind when I was picking eggs or slopping the hogs or waiting on a ewe in labor was, If the vegetarians win, what will happen to animals like these?

When I say, "vegetarians", I do not mean to pick a fight with those who practice one or another form of dietary restriction as part of a body of religious belief and practice. I am in favor of any religious practice, social teaching, or political movement that strives to make humans more consciously aware of their connection to the non-human world, less inclined simply to accept what shows up in little boxes at the store.

I am thinking about the people who write earnest letters, with acreage figures in them, about how we could cure world hunger if we all gave up animal exploitation and flesh food.

When the whole human race lives on tofurkey and soy-milk, when we all dress in psuedo-leather and faux fur made out of wood pulp or petroleum distillates, what will become of all the creatures which once provided us with meat, leather, eggs, milk, cheese, and yogurt? If we no longer consume animals and the products produced by animals, what are we to do with the animals we no longer choose to consume?

Once upon a time, our sheep had wild ancestors. (Give them a hole in the fence, and they will imitate their bighorn cousins.) So, for that matter, did every other domestic animal we ever had on the place.

But none of them, sheep, pigs, calves, geese, chickens, the Nubian milk goat we owned briefly, were wild creatures. All had been bred over many generations to thrive in captivity. If sheep are, as people say, dumb, it is because human beings over time have preferred herdable, biddable sheep. It is selective breeding by our species which has produced the meaty-hammed hog, the tranquil Holstein who pumps out eighty to a hundred pounds of milk a day, the chicken breeds which can lay three hundred eggs a year and never go broody, the broadbreasted meat chickens which reach slaughter-weight in nine to eleven weeks.

Once these animals were wild boars, the aurochs portrayed on cave walls, lean speedy stringy jungle fowl. But that was a very long time ago.

Even those vegetarians who countenance animal products like milk, wool, and eggs, would have no room in an all-vegetarian world for our pigs. And our Suffolk-cross sheep were a meat breed, their wool comparatively coarse and short. Most of the years we kept sheep, the price of wool was so low that we wound up paying the shearer for his services and throwing in the wool gratis.

For thousands of years humans have bred animals to fill our needs. If we now decide that human-animal partnership was exploitative and immoral, something we humans have outgrown, what are we to do with these creatures we created?

Turning these animals loose—"liberating" them, like the Animal Liberation Front turning loose those rats and pigeons—would be impossible. The Encyclopedia Britannica estimates that there are more than one billion domestic sheep in the world presently. Some other researcher will have to find the numbers for cattle, hogs, goats, chickens, domestic ducks and geese and rabbits, water buffalo, yaks, camels, llamas, emus, ostriches, and other domestic creatures humans currently use for food and animal by-products.

Certainly, there is no niche in nature for them. Finding sufficient survival room for wolves, elephants, ibexes, prairie dogs and black footed ferrets is difficult enough. Everywhere in the world, the most pressing problem for wild animal and bird populations is the destruction of habitat.

Turn loose a dairy herd, a bunch of hogs, a flock of sheep, and as with fur-farm mink or lab rats, most of the bewildered "liberated" beasts will not survive. Most, in fact, will not go far. On the occasions when our animals escaped, they were nearly always back outside the fence at feeding time, hollering for food. A good many of those "rescued" University of Minnesota lab pigeons were found fluttering around in the lab.

Domestic animals which do survive without human attention in a feral state become major environmental threats, like the wild goats which have denuded Caribbean islands, or the razorback hogs of the American south, which are descended from domestic hogs gone wild.

A world-wide acceptance of the vegetarian philosophy would lead inevitably to a holocaust of the animals humans would no longer need.

I suppose it would be a gradual holocaust, one farmer after another liquidating his stock for as long as there was any kind of market. Then a lot of shoot and shovel. It would largely take place out of the sight and thought of the idea trend-setters who had brought it about. Like the eighteenth century wearers of beaver hats in Europe, they would have only the faintest idea of the enormous social and ecological changes they were unleashing on the world.

I suppose here and there, a few animals of the smaller domestic breeds might survive in petting zoos, with explanatory placards. "We used to raise these animals so we could eat them. We have now decided this is immoral. So we don't raise these animals any more." Such displays would serve much the same purpose as the old-fashioned museum illustrations of primitive man. They would assure viewers (and their children) that they had progressed morally. "We used to be dumb and primitive, now we are smart and good," is always a winning message.

It seems a shabby and ungrateful way to end a long partnership.

Of course, this is how we have always treated animals, isn't it? I don't mean "we", the individual pet-owner or stock-breeder, but the group "we", the economist's and historian's "we". When we as a species wanted animals, when we found them useful or pretty or tasty, we encouraged their breeding, and when, for whatever reason, we no longer wanted them, we walked away from the problem. (People who run animal shelters shudder every time a big animal movie comes out. They know that, predictably, a certain percentage of the viewing audience will fall in love with the screen Dalmatian or Saint Bernard or pigmy goat, and that a few months later, their shelters will be swamped with throw-away animals, who were a lot more work at home than on screen, and not near so cute.)

It just seems strange and rather horrible that we are being pushed in this direction by people who genuinely want to improve the lot of animals, who would tell you that they love animals. That they act out of love, in wanting all the animals to die free.

THE BATTLE OF THE BUDWORM
E.

This is the enemy—a spruce budworm feeding on the tender green spring growth of a New Brunswick balsam fir...There is no known way of stopping a budworm epidemic. The budworm can only destroy himself—by destroying the forest on which he feeds.

...this year the budworm was checked...This is a battle report in the war between the forces of modern forest management and the budworm..

Pamphlet, "The Battle of the Budworm, An Experiment in Forest Management," New Brunswick International Paper Company, 1952.

Dad brought the pamphlet home with him from New Brunswick, Canada, after the '53 forest spray season. On its front cover is a photograph of a crop-dusting biplane flying at tree-top level. A scrolling vapor trail pours out behind the plane, DDT in an oil solution. My father piloted planes like that. From 1949 to 1963 he was a cropduster. From 1953 to 1961, he was part of what pilots called "Operation Budworm."

People are always distressed to see plants die, and the bigger the plants are, the more distress they feel. Most home owners are distressed if a single tree dies in their yards. A defoliated forest is a depressing sight, especially if you are a manager of a paper company viewing those trees as potential pulpwood.

Cultivators and foresters have practiced techniques to control plant pests from time immemorial.

First generation pesticides were simple preparations made of ashes, sulfur, arsenic compounds, ground tobacco, or hydrogen cyanide. Before 1940 there were a few dozen of them on the market. The chemical compound dichloro-diphenyl-trichloro-ethane was synthesized by a German chemist in 1874. In 1939, the Swiss chemist Paul Muller discovered its insecticidal properties.

DDT was effective and cheap. It increased crop yields and promised an end to insect-born diseases. In 1944, Muller was awarded a Nobel prize for his discovery.

DDT was the first of a whole group of related substances, the chlorinated hydrocarbons, second generation pesticides like chlordane, heptachlor, dieldrin, aldrin, and endrin. Later came the third generation pesticides, the alkyl or organic phosphates, like parathion and malathion, and the herbicides, like pentachlorophenol, 2,4D, and 2,4,5T. These amazing new chemicals promised swift victory in "the battle of the budworm" and other conflicts with pests.

By the end of World War II, some twenty-three per cent of Europe's farmland was out of production. Many millions of Europeans were homeless. The pre-war transportation system was in ruins. Large parts of Asia were equally devastated. Feeding the hungry was a first priority. The new pesticides, with their promise of improved crop production, seemed miraculous.

Equally products of the war were large numbers of surplus military aircraft now available for civilian use, and lots of young men who had learned to

163

fly, and wanted to keep flying. The aerial application of pesticide over large areas became feasible. The cropduster entered agriculture and forestry.

My Dad had the misfortune of having to pay for his flight training. Indeed, he was tempted, before America entered the war, to join the Canadian RAF during the Battle of Britain. His family had been Canadian and he wanted to defend the Mother Country, but also, they would have taught him to fly, which he wanted to do more than anything in the world. But he was supporting a wife, two daughters, and a mother with heart trouble, and besides, he had just achieved his American citizenship, which he would have had to renounce.

So he spent the war riveting planes which had been shot up in places like Guadalcanal, but in 1945 he resumed the flight training he had begun in 1940, and by 1947 he had his instructor's rating. He had been a laborer, a miner, an industrial worker. Now and for the rest of his life, he would always proudly describe himself as a professional.

And he loved what he did, loved the feel of a light plane under him, would say, truthfully, "I have a good wife, but aviation is my mistress."

Of course, right after World War II, he was competing for piloting jobs with men who had flown multi-engine planes, on instruments, across oceans and under fire. These competitors were quickly joined by young men who spent their GI benefits getting pilot licenses. (His Log Book 2 notes, on September 15, 1946, "G. I. program #1 started.")

He always said that if he could make a living entirely by flight instruction, he would do so. And of course he would have loved to be an airline pilot, but it was impossible, with his meager self-bought hours, to compete with the returned pilot GI's.

Crop-dusting, for all its well-known dangers, was an obvious career option. Besides, he liked the idea that he was fighting world hunger, protecting living things. He loved nature, loved open space, loved stretches of country where the human presence was absent or unobtrusive. His favorite family trips were to the ocean at Santa Cruz, or up to the trees at Big Basin Redwoods State Park. He was deeply concerned with issues like over-population and soil erosion.

It pleased him to think his work as a cropduster was making the world a better place.

You can tell a good duster, he used to say, by how close he flies to the ground. If he is dusting or spraying an agricultural crop, his wheels ought to be just above the tips of the plants. For forest spray, you need to be fifty to a hundred and fifty feet above the treetops. The best hours for dust and spray work are early morning and late evening, when the wind is less likely to be gusty. Wind both makes the flying dangerous, and causes wastage of the dust and spray, which winds up on non-target crops.

Your enemies, the obstacles that can bring you down, are powerlines, irrigation standpipes, the tree you didn't see in time, unanticipated turbulence, engine or mechanical failure, inattention, over-confidence, and that great catch-all cause of most plane crashes, "pilot error." His attitude was that he did not and would not make errors. He was fond of quoting the maxim, "There are old pilots, and there are bold pilots, but there are no old bold pilots."

So far as I can tell from his log books, carefully kept in his tiny meticulous writing, he began his career as a crop-duster on April 29, 1949, flying a World War II military plane, a PT-17, fitted up with the necessary tank and nozzle, out of Lovelock, Nevada. But for most of his crop-dusting career he flew the plane most dusters of the time preferred, a Stearman biplane with a 450 Pratt and Whitney engine, what they called a "bull" Stearman. Stearman aircraft had been pre-World War II army trainers. They were good aerobatic planes, which meant they had lots of power and excellent climbing ability.

He dusted and sprayed out of Lovelock in the spring and summer of 1949, noting the hours and minutes he spent crop dusting at the end of his log book: "Total dust and spray, season 1949, 241:30; 2,4D 187:30; dust 54." He was back at Lovelock in the spring and summer of 1950, for part of that time doing forest spray for budworm control out of Joseph, Oregon. In the summer of '51, he was spraying for budworms out of Big Rock Flat, Oregon. (Seventeen airplanes and seven pilots were lost in spraying operations in the Pacific Northwest that year.)

Later in '51, he did agricultural spraying and aerial cotton defoliation in places like Calexico, Blythe, and Parker, California; and Roa and Chepultapec, Mexico. The end of that log book lists, "Dust and spray season, '50, 164:55 total; spray, 2,4D, 86.20; spray, 71:15; dust 4:20; forest spray, 60:00. Dust and spray season, '51, Forest, 19:35; dust, 37:00; total, 116:35"

Up in New Brunswick, they were gearing up for Operation Budworm.

"During the summer of 1949," says the IPC pamphlet, "Foresters confirmed an alarming increase in the population of spruce budworms in the balsam-spruce forests of the Upsalquitch watershed in northern New Brunswick. In 1950 some 200 square miles were stripped of new foliage and in 1951 some 2,300 square miles were severely attacked.'"

"Late in the summer of 1951, Dr. R. E. Balch, head of the Dominion Entomological Laboratory in Fredericton, reported that if the epidemic ran its normal course, widespread tree mortality was probable on a heavily-infested area of crown forest included in the limits of New Brunswick International Paper Company."

"The area involved was part of a valuable timber reserve backing up the company's newsprint mill at Dalhousie. Officials of the paper company and the government of New Brunswick decided that the threat justified a bold move, and plans were drawn up to spray by air some 200,000 acres of heavily infested forest...Never before in Canada had a forest-spraying operation of this magnitude been attempted."

"The budworm is vulnerable to forest spraying only during a brief period in early June when it is feeding. Eight months remained in which to prepare. An airport had to be carved out of the wilderness, quarters for 150 men constructed, every ton of spray, fuel and equipment hauled over frozen roads and stored before the spring breakup, airplanes and pilots found and engaged, and a precise plan of operations drawn up."

"...On November 24th, ground was broken for the airport in the middle of the spray area, deep in the forest of the Upsalquitch watershed. The Battle of the Budworm was joined."

In 1952, Dad was part of an American budworm-control operation, spraying Douglas fir in Oregon and northern Idaho. From June 6th to July 8th, he was "chief pilot, Mount Hood Unit, NAAC, spruce budworm operation." Later that summer, he did local dust and spray in the San Jose area. He was flying a Piper JC3, the ubiquitous and reliable Cub, which he had always thought was an ideal trainer and excellent beginner's plane—"a real forgiving airplane"—but with a Lycoming 125 engine it was underpowered for dusting. His log book neatly lists, "aircraft extensively damaged while crop dusting". He clipped a powerline with his wing and "augured in", as the pilot's phrase went, crashing nose first. But the cockpit remained intact and he came out of this, his only serious aircraft accident, with two sprained ankles and a broken nose.

The San Jose Mercury-Herald covered that crash under the headline, "Duster Bites Dust." I think the headline hurt him more than the physical injuries of the crash. He hated anything which made aviation seem dangerous.

He is not one of the men pictured in the IP pamphlet, which he nonetheless brought home as a treasured souvenir. On the page captioned, "These were the men: combat veterans from Europe and the Pacific, ex-barnstormers, racers and carnival stunters—cool, skilled pilots, eager to tackle the biggest single forest-spraying job ever attempted in Canada" is an autograph from Dale Kaponen of Seattle, Washington, with the motto "To Budworm Success." The other photographs would apply to Dad's experiences there, too, and it is hard not to look for him in them, though I know he was not there yet, not singing (which he loved to do) to the fiddle and the guitar, not eating at the big mess hall table, not having his hair cut outdoors, in an impromptu fresh air barber shop. In '53, when he was there, as in '52, men waited for good weather, checking out their planes. And the huge drums of chemicals would have been the same.

And no doubt, the martial tone of the pamphlet was at least in part the tone of the men's conversations.

When Dad went to New Brunswick in '53, it was as a chief pilot. There were six airstrips by then, and a work force of eighty pilots, instead of the single air strip called Budworm City and the twenty pilots of the first year.

Dad's "Battle of the Budworm" pamphlet is autographed like a school yearbook. "Keep 'em flying Charlie—C. A. 'Chuck' Tackett, Aurora, Colo." "Jake Flynn, radio operator, Yarmouth, Nova Scotia." "Happy Landings, Bob King, Yakima, Washington." "Good luck from Bob Bowman, Lipan, Texas." "W. L. Johnson, Cape Breton, New Brunswick." "John Stuart, Conchatta, Louisiana." "Aw—just one more load, Charlie, puh-leeze? Ray A. Berry, Beaver, Oklahoma." "We never had it so good—back in '54—Deane Brandon, Central Point, Oregon."

I knew Deane and his wife. I met other dusters, knew still others by reputation. There are names I have forgotten, and Dad has not been around to ask since 1970. Men would almost literally drop out of the sky to visit, wearing leather bomber jackets and coveralls that smelled faintly of benzene hexachloride, talking about jobs spraying trees in Idaho, dusting melons in Mexico, seeding wheat in the valley of the Ganges. Sometimes they called in the middle of the night, drunk and grieving, to share the news that good old Beebe, remember him from Operation Budworm?, yeah, well he augured in, he bought the farm—

In the pictures they are dashing men, good at a difficult and dangerous job, come from all over the world to defend the forest, to fight The Battle of the Budworm.

It was Dad's pride that, when they were under his direction, they fought it safely. A press clipping from the Mercury-News for May 15 of 1955 pictures Dad standing next to the two-seater tandem Aeronca monoplane we rebuilt in our single-car garage. (We called it Pogo.)

VETERAN SUNNYVALE PILOT TO FIGHT FOREST PARASITES, says the headline. He was going off for his third year as a chief pilot, one of twelve by now, who sprayed 2,000,000 acres during that phase of the Battle. "In the three years I have been supervising in Canada, there have been no pilots lost."

Sure as the robins came north, Dad would fly to Canada every spring, from 1953 through '58 and again in '60 and '61. Among his effects is a graph he made, captioned, "Budworm Project, New Brunswick—Quebec", which tracks numbers of aircraft, gallons of DDT, acres sprayed, accidents and fatalities from '52 to '58. According to his records, Operation Budworm peaked in 1957, when two hundred aircraft sprayed three million gallons of DDT-solution over six million acres of forest. From '52 through '59, he lists 30 accidents, two fatalities.

Those fatalities would, of course, have been the immediate effect of the aircraft accidents. Plenty of dusters "bought the farm" in crashes.

I don't know if anybody has done a longitudinal survey of non-accident deaths among crop dusters.

Such a study would be difficult, for dust and spray men moved around, going where the work was. In addition to his work in Canada, Dad dusted and sprayed and seeded and slug-baited and fungicided by air, all over northern and southern California and southern Arizona. He was working on contract, spreading the substances the farmers and ranchers had been sold on. He kept track in a general way of how many hours he was spending cropdusting, and he invariably noted the places where he had worked, but he kept no track of the specific substances used till he was near the end of his work as a dust and spray pilot.

"How many budworms did we kill?" asks that International Paper pamphlet, at the end of the first year of Operation Budworm. "We killed almost all of them," Dr. Balch said. "Our observations since the spraying show that between 99.8 and 100 per cent of the budworms on our plots at the time were killed."

Such mortality, using the grand-daddy of the broad spectrum insecticides, would have extended to most of the other insects in those woods, and other forms of life as well.

By 1947, eight years after the introduction of DDT, genetic resistance to DDT was being reported by Italian researchers. If you kill off all but one per cent of an insect population, the surviving one per cent will likely have survived because they are naturally immune to the insecticides you have been using. The immune survivors multiply and increase. By 1960, 137 DDT-resistant insect species had been identified, creatures that could crawl through DDT, absorb DDT, eat and digest DDT, without damage.

Broad-spectrum insecticides not only foster immunity in target species, they sometimes turn minor pests into major pests. In 1956, the U.S. Forest Service sprayed 885,000 acres of forested lands in Montana and Idaho with DDT, to control spruce budworm. The following summer, most of the sprayed area suffered a spectacular and destructive infestation of spider mites, a tiny, chlorophyll-sucking arthropod. The insecticide applied to kill budworms had also killed the predator species, such as ladybugs, gall midges, and predacious mites, which had kept the spider mite in check. The spider mite has now become a worldwide pest, along with numerous previously-innocuous insects whose numbers exploded after insecticides killed off their natural controls.

It also became clear over time that the second generation insecticides, like DDT, persist for long periods in the earth—aldrin for four years, heptachlor for at least nine, toxaphene for ten, benzene hexachloride at least eleven, chlordane for twelve. Repeated spraying builds up soil concentrations. They also persist in the bodies of creatures sprayed, tending to concentrate in the reproductive organs. And they move up the food chain, from earthworm to robin, from aquatic insect to fish to eagle.

As DDT proved ineffective, it was first sprayed more often and in stronger concentrations, then replaced by newer pesticides. I know Dad and the other dusters of his generation regularly used aldrin, dieldrin, chlordane, heptachlor, endrin, myrex, toxaphene, lindane, phosdrin, metaphos, diazinon, malathion, parathion, and carbaryl, also called Sevin. Most of those pesticides are now banned in the United States, but are still widely used in other countries.

The promise of a pest-free world was running up against the limitations of nature. Rachel Carson observed in 1962, writing about Operation Budworm, "The budworm is a native insect that attacks several kinds of evergreens. In eastern Canada it seems to become extraordinarily abundant about every 35 years." In her discussion of Operation Budworm, she focuses on the Miramichi river, which is south of the Upsalquitch watershed, but was part of the 1954 spray area. It was also a splendid salmon stream. "The Fisheries Research Board of Canada had been conducting a salmon study on the Northwest Miramichi since 1950. Each year it made a census of the fish living in this stream. The records of the biologists covered the number of adult salmon ascending to spawn, the number of young of each age group present in the stream, and the normal population not only of salmon but of other species of fish inhabiting the stream. With this complete record of prespraying conditions, it was possible to measure the damage done by the spraying with an accuracy that has seldom been matched elsewhere."

Carson's account of what happened to the Miramichi is a classic passage in a classic book, Silent Spring, which was published in 1962. Carson had written the book in part because the magazines of the time would not publish her articles, for fear they would lose advertising. My father and I had a furious argument about Silent Spring shortly before I left California. He thought it had to be wildly exaggerated. He did not want what this experienced field biologist wrote to be true. (Shortly before his death, he did say, "I think there's something to it.")

"Soon after the spraying had ended," she wrote, "there were unmistakable signs that all was not well. Within two days dead and dying fish, including many young salmon, were found along the banks of the stream. Brook trout also appeared among the dead fish, and along the roads and in the woods birds were dying. All the life of the stream was stilled. Before the spraying there had been a rich assortment of the water life that forms the food of salmon and trout—caddis fly larvae, living in loosely fitting protective cases of leaves, stems, or gravel cemented together with saliva, stonefly nymphs clinging to rocks in the swirling currents, and the wormlike larvae of blackflies edging the stones under riffles or where the stream spills over steeply slanting rocks. But now the stream insects were dead, killed by the DDT, and there was nothing for a young salmon to eat."

"Amid such a picture of death and destruction, the young salmon themselves could hardly have been expected to escape, and they did not. By August not one young salmon that had emerged from the gravel beds that spring remained. A whole year's spawning had come to nothing. The older young, those hatched a year or more earlier, fared only slightly better. For every six young of the 1953 hatch that had foraged in the stream as the planes approached, only one remained. Young salmon of the 1952 hatch, almost ready to go to sea, lost a third of their numbers..."

"...Repeated sprayings have now altered the stream environment, and the aquatic insects that are the food of salmon and trout have been killed. A great deal of time is required, even after a single spraying, for most of these insects to build up sufficient numbers to support a normal salmon population—time measured in years rather than months..."

"...The budworm populations, instead of dwindling as expected, have proved refractory...there is no evidence anywhere that chemical spraying for budworm control is more than a stopgap measure.."

As of 1999, the Canadian Forestry Service supports Rachel Carson's point of view. Its Internet website says, "Spruce budworm have a major impact on forests although the extent of the area defoliated has declined in recent years. In 1994, control of the pest consisted mostly of salvage of damaged stands. The large scale operational spray programs of previous decades are now replaced by limited programs for foliage protection in areas of high population or special value." The recommended control is *baccillus thuringiensis,* a natural bacillus which affects only plant-eating insects, or Sevin, an insecticide that breaks down within a few days. (Still a nerve poison, and nasty stuff.)

Put another way, the deaths of trees, even in very large numbers, are part of the self-perpetuating life-cycle of the forest. There is no real way, on any large scale, to stop them.

Operation Budworm was far from the only heroic effort to eliminate a pest which failed of its objective. From 1956 through 1961, massive DDT spraying in Pennsylvania, New Jersey, Michigan and New York was part of a program for the eradication of the gypsy moth. The Canadian spray program had used an application of a half pound of DDT per acre, in an oil solution, cutting back to a quarter pound per acre in 1960, but the standard American application was a pound to the acre. Birds, fish, crabs, and non-target insects were killed in massive numbers. Unsuspecting suburbanites and children at play were sprayed. Dairy herds turned up with fourteen parts per million of DDT in their milk. One bee-keeper lost eight hundred colonies of honeybees. He and fourteen other bee-keepers sued New York State. A group of enraged Long Island citizens took a suit all the way to the Supreme Court. By 1961, the spraying had been severely cut back, partly because the moth had rebounded in the original spray area, Long Island.

In 1958, the Department of Agriculture started a program to eradicate the fire ant in Texas, Louisiana, Alabama, Georgia, and Florida, with planes spraying the much more toxic dieldrin and heptachlor. Massive deaths occurred among raccoons, armadillos, bobwhite quail, and wild turkeys, with almost one hundred per cent loss of songbirds and fish in some areas, and numerous reported losses among pets and livestock. In 1959, the Food and Drug Administration banned residues of heptachlor or its breakdown product, heptachlor epoxide, on food. The Department of Agriculture in that year offered the chemicals free to Texas landowners who would sign a release absolving federal, state, and local governments from responsibility for damage, and the state of Alabama refused to appropriate any more funds for the project. By 1962, the director of entomology research at the Louisiana State University Agricultural Experiment Station, Dr. I.D. Newsom, declared, "There are more infested acres in Louisiana now than when the program began." Florida officials said the same thing. The fire ant eradication program, like the gypsy moth eradication program and the budworm eradication program, had clearly done more harm than good.

It had always been possible to treat the fire ant by applying insecticide directly to fire ant mounds when they occurred in nuisance places, such as playgrounds and lawns. It just wasn't as grand a goal as "eradication." You cannot write heroically about going out in the yard and squirting the ant mound, the way that International Paper pamphleteer did, in writing about The Battle of the Budworm.

When Dad began as a cropduster, both the pilot and the swamper, who loaded the dust or spray into the plane's spreader, worked bare-handed and bare-faced. By the time he stopped dusting in 1963, gloves and respirator masks were in general use.

I know that on one occasion, when he was loading either aldrin or dieldrin in the Salinas Valley of California, a tank of the insecticide spilled on him. By the time he arrived in the emergency room, he was in severe respiratory distress. The doctor took one look at his pin-point eye pupils and began questioning him about drug use, but then realized he was a cropduster. After that he was given atropine to carry in his pocket, to use in case of another exposure. Probably that incident had something to do with his getting out of cropdusting.

My father finally got financial backing to open his own flight school in the spring of 1970. In the summer of that year, he passed the rigorous annual physical mandated by the Federal Aviation Administration for holders of commercial pilot's licenses. Six weeks later he was in the hospital, in a coma. Six weeks after that he was dead.

It would be interesting to know how many cropdusters, those fellow veterans of the Battle of the Budworm, died as he did, of fast-moving, rapidly-metastasizing cancer, in robust middle age. Being an excellent pilot, recording a total of 21,706 hours and fifty minutes of flight time over thirty years with only one accident, was not enough to save him from buying the farm.

LIVING WITH ANIMALS: CRITTERS, VARMINTS, VERMIN, PESTS
E.

Language changes over time, the change in words reflecting changes in attitude, the currents of thought carrying tone and word-choice along with them.

It's strange to read that International Paper Company pamphlet from 1952. Written today, a pamphlet like that would surely still focus on protecting the forest, and "protecting the forest" would still mean the same thing—keeping pulpwood moving into the papermills, keeping profit moving into the company coffers, keeping the shareholders happy.

Most of the pamphlet is pictures, and today, the pictures would be different. There would be fewer pictures of bulldozers ripping out roads, no picture of those acres and acres of chemical drums. Definitely no pictures of chemical drums. A moose, a bear, no, three bears, Mom with cubs. A healthy-looking salmon leaping upstream. That is how the forest protection message would be conveyed today.

The text would still talk about protection. It probably wouldn't talk about war.

However, everybody who has ever tried to make a crop, whether that crop is pulpwood or hay, corn or roses, has had times when metaphors of war, or, at least, defense, sprang naturally to mind. Confronted by riddled leaves, plants chewed to sticks, the unmistakable droop of dying foliage, the most conscientious and animal-loving of organic gardeners will feel a great rush of righteous wrath, and wish, if not for a lethal weapon, at least for those force-fields which surround space ships in popular fiction. Shields up! Phasers on stun!

If you are a farmer or gardener, the things you want to grow struggle for space and sunlight with other living organisms, some as obvious as thistles or deer, some so small you don't even know they are present. Plant competition has to be weeded out, either directly, with hands and hoe and cultivator-blade, or indirectly, with pesticide sprays. Insects and birds and those animals we think of as critters (or varmints, or vermin, or pests) are always happy to harvest our crop before we get to it.

Among the animals with whom we have to fight every year to put our beans and corn and lettuce on the table are rabbits, deer, gophers, woodchucks, and raccoons.

Wild rabbit populations are cyclic. In some years there seem to be hardly any. In others, to walk out the door is to startle a rabbit. In winter, rabbits eat the bark off trees and shrubs, sometimes girdling and killing them. In summers with a heavy rabbit population, our lettuce and carrot-tops have been mowed down to ground level and our peas reduced to leafless spikes.

Deer are also partial to peas. One June day, I came out the back door of Earthward at ten in the morning. A hundred feet away, a doe was proceeding down my pea-row, where the plants were just at the point of blossoming. She was methodically eating off the top of every plant, taking with her every potential pea-pod. I shouted, "Get out of there, you damned animal!" and waved my arms. A futile gesture; this deer merely lifted her head and looked at me, flipping her ears. I had to run at her, shouting anti-Bambian imprecations, before she would vacate the premises, and then she never startled, never threw up the white warning flag of her tail, merely loped off into the woods.

Deer are fond of corn, too, both the growing tips of the plants, which they will eat as that doe was eating my pea-vines, and the ears. They also like apple trees, not only the fruit, but the leaves and the tender new growth of wood. A deer standing on its hind legs and stretching its neck can reach and eat everything up to an eight foot level, and they do. This will not destroy a mature apple tree, but it will certainly decimate the crop. And if you live where you have both deer and rabbits around, keeping your fruit trees alive the first few years, while the rabbits eat off the bark and the deer nip off the new branches, is a major undertaking, a running battle requiring constant vigilance.

The woodchuck, that humorous hero of the popular tongue-twister (how much wood would a woodchuck chuck) is an impressive consumer of plants. A woodchuck will enthusiastically wipe out big patches of the alfalfa the farmer had expected to harvest as hay. Woodchucks, which have two to nine hungry young annually, are also partial to corn, beans, melons, strawberries, beets, and lettuce. A mature woodchuck may, at one feeding, consume food plants equal to a third of its nine or ten pound weight. It will eat favorite foods, like blackberries or apples, till its stomach is visibly distended. (The Audubon Wildlife Encyclopedia says "Comically distended," but if those are your blackberries or apples, that fat old chuck may not seem so funny.)

Pocket gophers eat the roots off plants. You notice that the plant is looking droopy, you give it a little tug, and it comes away in your hand, detached and dead. We have lost any number of asparagus plantings and probably half of a thousand tree evergreen planting to pocket gophers.

Everyone knows about raccoons and their affinity for corn. The worst part of getting raccoons into your corn patch is that, like deer and woodchucks, they are samplers. They yank down an ear. Half the time, this breaks the corn stalk, ruining other potential ears. They take a bite or two. They drop the first ear and grab another one. They tend to do this just a day or two before the corn is perfect for human consumption.

Other critters are interested in crops after they are gathered. The human race probably became domestically associated with cats because human crop storage attracts mice. The mice that infested Egyptian grain-stores drew wild cats in from the desert, and cats have been hanging around humans ever since.

Every year in the fall, when the weather gets cold and food gets harder to find, we have to repel an invasion of mice in the house. In addition to the standard all-gray house mouse which our European ancestors brought along involuntarily in their ships, we are patronized by the native white-footed mouse, also known as the deer mouse. Deer mice are beautiful animals. They look like a creature drawn by Beatrix Potter and animated by Walt Disney, fine-limbed, big-eyed little charmers in opera gloves. They can wiggle through a three-eighths inch opening. They also carry hanta virus.

Now and then our traps also yield meadow voles, and I have found insectivorous shrews dead in the front porch of Earthward, and, when we lived across the road, in the greenhouse. Shrews have the highest metabolic rate of all mammals and can die within a few hours if deprived of food. Presumably these shrews had run through the in-house supplies of sowbugs, crickets, and small beetles.

When we kept dogs, our dog food supply had to be secured from chipmunks and squirrels. John once diagnosed a baffling automotive problem when he discovered that the muffler of our pickup was packed tight with dry dog food, probably the food store of an ambitious chipmunk.

One day, going out to pick eggs, I went past the front of the chickenhouse, with its little slit window up under the roof. Suddenly there was a shape in that window. A fierce-eyed, hook-beaked, desperate hawk face flashed into the opening. When I opened the chicken-house door, the hawk, probably a Cooper's or sharp shinned hawk, shot out past my head.

We never lost a chicken in that pen to predation, but this hawk must have swooped very low to follow one in the ground-level door. Once in the pen, it clearly lost all interest in chicken dinner and began bashing itself against the high window, the source of light, trying to get out.

Where there are humans and grain, there will be rats. We hadn't actually seen a rat when we found a single rat hole in the chicken house floor. By the time we were done with our extermination campaign, we had poisoned no less than twelve rats.

We try to deal with these interesting, often beautiful, occasionally pestiferous Animal Brothers as non-violently as we can. Every spring and every fall I carry a certain number of bewildered garter and ribbon snakes out of Earthward. We have scooped up invading bats in landing nets, releasing them outside unharmed. I once dipped a near-drowned bat out of the rain barrel. After drying off in the sun, it flew away, no doubt to return to its anti-mosquito patrol.

With sprays made of rotenone and hot peppers and *bacillus thuringiensis*, with whirling toy windmills in the garden beds, with dog excrement and human urine to mark garden borders, with hungry cats as companion animals, with electric fencing, with a radio in the corn patch during raccoon season, we have sometimes, to some extent, been able to keep our crops and shelter for ourselves.

All of these non-violent methods for keeping pests out work sometimes, to some extent. We have also had to resort to traps of the lethal variety, to poison, to pellet guns and John's shotgun.

The one thing we have not tried is the live-trap which lets you dump your problem on somebody else's property. If a woodchuck is destroying our garden, would it be kind to encourage it to eat our neighbor's garden? Most animal shelters will not accept wild animals, which do not make good pets. Moving wild animals from their natural habitat, unless they are members of some rare and endangered species and the habitat is about to be destroyed, is almost always problematic. Many die of shock. The rest, dumped into strange environments, have to scuffle for survival and sustenance with the animals already present. The process just spreads the death and environmental destruction around.

No decent, healthy human being enjoys inflicting pain. It is entirely natural, in a world where every newscast brings us images of our fellow human beings inflicting pain and death on each other and on other creatures in the most wholesale and ingenious manner, to say to ourselves, "I will not inflict pain. I will not kill. I will do no harm."

But in the natural world, of which we are inescapably a part, almost nothing but human beings dies what human beings call "a natural death", meaning a peaceful painless cessation of the life process. The deer not shot by the hunter will, in a natural world, have its neck broken by a mountain lion, or be run down by wolves or dogs, hamstrung, and eviscerated. Or, in a hard winter, it will succumb to malnutrition and internal parasites. If there are too many deer and not enough predators, the deer herd will overgraze its range, producing a population crash in which most of the deer will starve. Old deer outwear their teeth and starve with plenty of browse around.

It is problematic which death is more painful, but all are natural. This is the way everybody but human beings and the occasional beloved pet dies. This is the structure of nature.

Human beings are good at distancing mechanisms, both physical and psychic, so that we can keep the unpleasant things we sometimes have to do for our survival and comfort at a distance from ourselves. We put the handle on the fly-swatter. We use the spray-gun, instead of stomping on the bug, because it is so unpleasant to feel the bug squish or crunch under the shoe. (Also sometimes our aim is off, and we do not quite kill the bug, but leave it writhing and dribbling away, which is both disgusting and depressing.)

A live-trap is a distancing mechanism, like the extermination service or the crop duster's plane, which allows human beings to kill creatures without seeing them die or admitting what is going on.

It is true, of course, that the paper company executives and New Brunswick forestry employees and crop dusters who planned and executed Operation Budworm had not the slightest interest in killing ladybugs and caddis flies, wood thrushes and salmon. They only wanted to kill budworms. (Though they must have known about the ladybugs and caddis flies.) All the other creatures they killed (and kept on killing, after the initial applications were over) represented, as Defense Department spokesmen characteristically put it, "collateral damage."

We have tried to face up to what we are doing, not to produce any more collateral damage than we must to survive, but to admit it when we do. We know that merely by being living creatures, biological competitors in the dense and death-rich dance of nature, we have blood on our hands. Death at two removes, or ten, is still death. Death by indirection, death by environmental change, is still death.

We don't spray in the house, so we have to keep it pretty clean, and, sometimes, we have to stomp on bugs. We use snap traps for mice, so we have to throw the mournful little corpses out into the woods, where the burying beetles will enjoy them if the owls don't get them first. It seems to us to be morally appropriate, when we have to kill something, to do so as directly as possible, and to acknowledge the death by dealing with the corpse.

Sometimes we shoot persistent and undiscourageable critters. Mostly, when we have shot them, we eat them. We try not to waste what has been given us.

One of the reasons we have such open and obvious conflicts with the Animal Brothers is that we live in a comparatively healthy and diverse environment. There is a lot of different kinds of life around, and some of it makes its way into our garden and our house. Surrounding our cultivated spaces are woods, hayfields, and undrained wetlands where wild creatures can live more or less natural lives.

Most areas of large-scale agriculture are not like that. Modern American agricultural practices encourage, even demand, monocultures. Here in the Midwest, this means miles of corn and soybeans, where once there would have been a diverse mix of grasses, herbs, and forbs, interspersed with groves of trees. Through the central valley of California or the Salinas valley, where my father used to dust and spray for the biggest lettuce grower in the United States, one sees environments where virtually nothing grows unless there is a market for it. Such a landscape may be green, but it is in no way natural; it is an industrial landscape. On roads in such areas, the only road kill you will ever see is domestic, the stray dog or wandering cat. No skunks, no squirrels, not even a flattened snake or frog. Where would it come from? How would it live?

In these places of intensive agriculture, these American bread and fruit and vegetable baskets, there are no deer or raccoons, gophers or woodchucks or turtles or lizards or bats, and precious few birds of any kind. Their habitat has been cut down, leveled, drained, poisoned, eliminated. Entire ecosystems, with every animal form from the bacteria in the soil to the eagle in the sky, have been destroyed. You could probably go for days or weeks in a place like that without having to consciously kill anything.

Your work as a food consumer has been done for you.

Putting it another way, that land has been brought into full agricultural production by the best modern methods. Most of the vegetables, fruits, and grains in supermarkets and on the restaurant salad bar come from such cultivated lands.

The fact is, even if you are not personally killing animals, nor eating the products produced by animals, animals are being killed to produce the products you eat. Modern agriculture lives by killing the creatures, the critters, varmints, vermin, pests, which compete for soil nutriment and sunshine with the crops of the agriculturist.

Agriculture has always done this, but now the killing is distanced and easy to ignore. Fewer and fewer of us anymore remember a grandma who chopped the head off the chicken we were going to eat for Sunday dinner while we watched, a grandma who chopped cutworms in two and squished potato bugs. Fewer and fewer of us have a grandpa who went out after deer when the corn was picked, and brought along venison sausage when he visited. For most of us, food comes in those little boxes in the store. We not only don't have to think about the processes which brought it to us, it is extraordinarily difficult to figure them out.

It is not uncommon to see opinion pieces and letters to the editor which offer vegetarianism as a solution to the problem of world hunger. Commonly the writers estimate the number of acres devoted to raising grain which is fed to animals, then suggest that, without human use of "flesh food", that acreage could grow food that went directly onto the tables of the hungry.

There is one obvious snag to this argument. Cattle and sheep are grazing animals, and pigs can live on almost anything. If they are raised (or more frequently "finished off") on diets with a heavy grain component, it is because grass-fed meat is tougher (though more flavorful) than grain-fed meat. One restaurant in St. Paul has for generations advertised "the silver butterknife steak". It takes intensive graining of the beef animal to produce steaks that tender.

So many of those acres of grain that go into animal feed could perfectly well go into human feed, if human tastes and marketing practices changed.

Grazing and browsing animals can grow healthy and fat on grass. Humans cannot digest grass directly. The vegetable and grain crops humans can eat need agriculture to produce them. This means breaking land to the plow, to feed the current (and still growing) human population.

Where is that land to come from? Most of the earth's "undeveloped" areas are covered with forest, wetlands, deserts, or icecaps, and the day is long past when we could assume that these ecosystems were mere "wasteland". They have their own embattled native ecosystems, and their own indigenous populations, trying to survive.

Modern field agriculture, the kind of agriculture encouraged by the U.S. Department of Agriculture, the big grain, seed, and chemical companies, and lending agencies, is tremendously hard on the soil. The USDA Economic Research Service estimates that for every ton of corn currently produced in the United States, at least five tons of topsoil are lost, blown or washed away.

Very large areas of the earth now in some kind of agricultural production should never have been broken to the plow. In some ways, the most ecologically sustainable use of much of the American great plains occurred at the time when the buffalo ate the grass, and the humans ate the buffalo.

How many more acres would need to be brought under cultivation to feed the human race, if the human race abandoned animal-based food?

I have no idea. But I think the people who suggest this change in diet should and could come up with some numbers. Figure out how many calories of vegetable food it would take to adequately nourish six billion people. How many acres under cultivation would it take to grow that much food? Are there that many potential acres available? How much jungle, forest, swamp and grassland would have to be destroyed, in order to grow grains and vegetables on that land?

I do have some idea of how much more land John and I would have had to bring into cultivation, if we had wanted to feed ourselves entirely on non-animal-based food.

We have raised much of what we ate for the last thirty-eight years. John has periodically floated the possibility of raising everything, every bite, for a whole year. I always balked at giving up lettuce in winter, occasional white sugar, coffee, cheese, and other little pleasures.

Of course a person could substitute honey or maple sugar for white sugar, and our land does sustain both honeybees and maple trees. We didn't grow our own wheat (for flour), oats, or barley, but we could have. We did grind our own cornmeal. We usually bought milk, butter, and cheese, but we could, if we were willing to buy a cow or goat and commit ourselves to the two-a-day necessity of milking, have produced all those products ourselves. (We did make wonderful yogurt and cottage cheese during the two months we owned our Nubian goat.)

But of course if we were committing to complete vegetarianism, we would have had not only no meat, but also no milk, no yogurt, no eggs, no cheese.

At our peak garden size, when we were not only raising our own vegetables but also selling sweet corn, cabbages, and strawberries, we had about an acre and a half of garden land. We also had around twelve breeding ewes and a ram, whose lambs we would slaughter or sell at the end of the summer. We would have a litter or two of pigs a year, most of which we sold, and a feeder calf, which we would slaughter when it was two. We would start the summer with a hundred baby chicks. By wintertime, we would be down to about twenty laying hens, the other chickens having gone into the freezer. The laying hens provided all the eggs we wanted most of the time, and sometimes I had some extra for sale. Old laying hens were canned for soup stock.

These animals were fed largely off pasturage, which they enriched with their manure and which we were careful not to overgraze, five acres of field corn and five acres of hay, plus some bought feed.

If we had committed ourselves to complete self-feeding, producing enough calories from vegetables, grains, and legumes to feed five people, how many more acres would we have needed to cultivate?

As anybody who has ever been on a diet knows, meat, eggs, and dairy products are nutrient dense. Human beings can be adequately nourished on an all-vegetarian diet, but it takes a greater volume of food to sustain them. Far more Americans worry about eating too much than about eating too little, but something like a third of the world's population routinely consumes too few calories for maximum health.

I would guess that we would have needed to triple or quadruple our cultivated land, if we had been feeding ourselves an all-vegetable diet. We would have had to make another ten or fifteen acres into plowed ground, clearing trees and brush, eliminating the complex plant and animal communities that live there. The nutrients we had been drawing indirectly from pasturage and woods, in the form of lamb, beef, grouse, and venison, would have dropped out of our personal energy equations. Ten to fifteen more acres of Big Woods would have been lost to the world.

And we would have needed to apply chemical fertilizer, instead of the tons of animal manure we plowed into our garden over the years.

I doubt if it would be physically possible, given human numbers and current available acreages of agricultural land, to feed the human race this way.

It could not be done without massive ecological destruction.

And what would be the point? We would be doing it essentially to distance ourselves from the direct knowledge that we were killing other forms of life.

I don't know how many vegetarians have gone beyond revulsion at the chopping block and the packing house, to trying to imagine a world in which the relationship between man and animals has entirely altered, a world without domestic animals.

Yet we are rapidly moving toward a world in which the only animals most people (certainly most people in industrially-developed countries) ever see are either pets, or animals in zoos, or the lovely wild images of the nature documentaries.

John and I and our children have had the great privilege of living intimately with animals in a way that hardly anybody does, anymore, and which both economic trends and intellectual sentiment are making more and more difficult.

We did not have the kind of farm the USDA and current market patterns encourage, but with our barn and chickenhouse full, our farm assumed a shape familiar to any reader of nursery rhymes and childhood tales.

The small, self-sufficient agricultural entity, adapted to local soil and weather conditions, has a history that goes all the way back into the Neolithic. The life-patterns of such a farm go beyond Old MacDonald, and those patterns are not random.

Where modern agribusiness is likely to specialize in one crop, the old-fashioned mixed farm used nearly every available ecological niche. Cattle ate the fine grass. Sheep and goats ate grass and brush cattle wouldn't touch. Pigs scavenged grain left by the cattle and cleaned up the human food scraps. Chickens ate spilled feed, weed seeds, and bugs. These animals fed the humans and their manure was cycled back through the soil of garden and fields.

Crops could be closely adapted to soil types. The Todd County *Country Courier* for October first, 1999, commemorates a Century Farm, a farm which has been in the same family for a hundred years. This farm has been under cultivation and in the same family since at least 1882. Currently, it's a dairy farm, which means the proprietor's primary cash crop is milk. Such a farm will raise cattle, with corn and alfalfa as feed crops, and now and again some oats, as a nurse crop for a new field of alfalfa.

But as a Century Farm, it has at various times, sometimes simultaneously, produced rye, barley, wheat, buckwheat and millet as field crops, in addition to the present crops, and oxen, horses, sheep, turkeys, chickens, geese, ducks, and pigs, in addition to cattle. (Wool from the sheep was spun into yarn by the women of the household, providing socks, mittens, and sweaters.) Honey, firewood, maple syrup, and ice (cut from a nearby lake) were gathered and used on the farm. The family also ran the neighborhood sorghum mill. Neighbors who grew sorghum cane brought it for crushing, boiled it down on the premises, and paid a percentage of the sorghum syrup for using the mill, the horses that powered it, and the cooker. The sorghum, like the maple syrup and the honey, would be used in cooking as a substitute for store-bought sugar.

All of these uses were remembered as occurring within the lifetimes of the present owners.

When we moved here, in 1964, the subsistence farm was clearly on the way out. More and more farms were specializing in dairy production. But the tradition of raising a few pigs ("mortgage lifters") and a feeder calf or two, and running a flock of chickens in the yard, was still vigorous. Our neighbors never thought we were crazy. A little eccentric (especially me, since I was a Californian and a "town girl"), but not crazy.

The pressure was on to "get big or get out", but fifteen to thirty cow dairy herds were common. An eighty-cow farm was a big farm. Farm auction bills characteristically listed the sale animals not only by breed, weight, age, milk and calf production and gestational status, but by name.

From the point of view of the farm economist, the small mixed farm is obsolete, though, by every possible ecological measure, such farms were much easier on the land than the farms that have replaced them. I recently heard a Minnesota expert on these matters tell a gathering of farmers distressed about milk prices that, to be properly competitive, a Minnesota dairy farm should milk eight hundred cows.

An eight-hundred-cow farm is a milk factory. Its animals spend their whole lives in confinement. They are continuously medicated and often treated with hormones to increase their milk production. As soon as their production slips, they are shipped to the packing plant. No single family can possibly run such a farm with its own members. An eight-hundred-cow dairy farm uses enormous quantities of feed, probably all grown somewhere else, on another kind of specialized farm. It produces equally enormous quantities of animal waste, with inevitable impacts on local air and water quality. You would not want to live downwind from it, and if you lived anywhere near it, you would need to test your well water often to make sure it was not contaminated.

Such a farm produces lots and lots of cheap food, a small number of low-paid jobs, and enormous pollution. It also produces a kind of slow, continuous social disruption, as it gradually and remorselessly drives smaller farms out of existence. The big thriving industries in our county now are huge farms that grow potatoes for fast-food French fries, huge confinement barns for turkeys, and meat-packing houses. Many of my neighbors, whose fathers and grandfathers tilled their own land, now make a living on jobs with names like Live Poultry Hanger, Gizzard Cutter, and Lung Sucker. These human lives, too, are by-products of the industrial farm.

No human-constructed biome, not the best-balanced and husbanded of mixed farms, is ever as stable and diverse as a natural biome. But small mixed farms provided a decent, independent living for the majority of the human race, for most of its history. And though there were undoubtedly times when animals were badly used in such circumstances, they were at least known individuals, Bossies and Dobbins, not the biotic machines of the eight hundred cow industrial farm.

At their best, these farms provided a space where humans and animals could interact companionably.

The industrial-model farm regards humans, animals, and soil not as biological entities, but as production units. This is an outrageously over-simplified model of the way in which living creatures should share the world. All the economic and most of the political pressures in our culture are pushing in this direction.

We have lived many years with animals, lots of different kinds of animals, pets, livestock, critters. We are fortunate to have had the chance. We live in a world in which that sort of relation is becoming more and more difficult to sustain.

HUNTING

J.

In late April or early May, when the soil is not too wet and cold, I start up the tractor and go down to our large garden area.

First I hook up the disc and use it to cut up the vegetative residue from last year's garden, so it won't clog the plow. Plowing follows, turning last year's leaves and roots and stems under, where this dead matter will quickly rot and release its mineral content, improving the tilth of the soil. I disc a second time to break the clods down. Finally I hook up the many-toothed drag to smooth and level the soil, creating a good seed bed.

When conditions are right—again, that phrase of gardener's art—we plant the cold-tolerant vegetables: potatoes, peas, onions, lettuce, cabbage, broccoli, kohlrabi, parsnips, parsley, dill. As the season advances, so do plantings: carrots, beets, beans, rutabagas, corn. Past the date of possible late frost, the tender things go in—tomatoes, eggplant, peppers, cucumbers, squash, melons, sweet basil. We take a deep breath. By the time the last plantings are in, the first plantings need to be weeded. As soon as plants are big enough to reach above it, we lay down a thick coating of mulch.

Somewhere in planting time, the tracks appear, the little double-pointed deer tracks. I think, do they know we've planted? Are they hunting for the first tender shoots of peas, and later of corn? I unroll the chicken wire to protect what I can. When the sweet corn ears are developing, the entire corn patch will be surrounded by electric fence.

We manage to save most of what we plant for our own consumption, but we know we will always lose some. We are invading their territory. You can't blame them for hunting a meal.

One November morning, when the harvest is in freezer bags and jars and the root cellar, when killing frost has taken out this year's plants and I have disced the residue down, I put on orange outer clothing. As the shapes of the leafless trees begin to show in the dark, above the leaf-strewn ground which may be lightly covered in snow, I walk as quietly as I can down the hill from our house. I climb onto a platform eight feet up in a clump of basswood trees.

Here, as the winter sun flushes tree trunks, I wait for our summer garden to walk by in its animal form.

One has to be patient, as in waiting for seeds to sprout. Most winters, we go into the deep cold with a shelf or two in the freezer full of venison. Peas and corn and cabbage and rutabagas taste incredibly good in that four-legged form.

We bless the deer. We invite the Animal Brothers to make tracks in our garden for many years to come.

LIVING WITH ANIMALS: BEASTS
E., J.

Some of the earliest human images of animals are also among the most magnificent. They are the bison and boars, horses and hinds, of Altamira, the aurochs, oxen, horses, and swimming stags of Lascaux.

These were animals as our remote ancestors saw them—huge, beautiful, strong, worthy of awe, worthy of worship. Nobody knows exactly what rituals accompanied the making of these great cave paintings, what stories and ideas were associated with them, but that there was ritual and myth is almost certain.

One thing we can say about these animals of the painted caves. They are not pets, animals kept for human pleasure. They are not livestock, animals kept for food and traction, though our horses and pigs and, perhaps, our domestic cattle are their remote descendants. Nor are they mere varmints, animal competitors, though humans must often have feared them, for good reason. These are beasts, the animals we revere.

In modern terms, the nearest equivalent of the cave beasts are the charismatic megafauna of conservation movements, the whales, tigers, wolves, elephants, bears and eagles whose posters we hang on our walls.

It is worth remembering that, at least in recent history, many of these animals were regarded as pests to be exterminated. Most of Europe wiped out all its wolves and bears so long ago that they exist only in fairy tales. The African farmer whose crop represents not mortgage payments or tax money, but literal physical survival, has a very different view of the elephant trampling that crop than the well-fed viewer of the TV special on endangered species.

Wolves were deliberately exterminated from almost all of the continental United States, mostly by "wolfers", who killed predators to collect a bounty, using poisons, bullets, and traps, digging pups from their dens. In 1924 alone, more than 3.5 million strychnine baits were placed to kill western predators.

Up until the passage of the Endangered Species Act in 1973, the Federal government was the primary killer of wolves, but it was carrying out an extremely popular policy. Any animal that competes with humans for space, kills their livestock and frightens them, is likely to be perceived as a menace and a threat, better off eliminated. The fear of such beasts need not even be based on any real danger. Consider the irrational terror many otherwise reasonable human beings display, in the presence of snakes or bats. A great many people who regard hunting as an irrational and bloodthirsty exercise will immediately call the extermination service at the first flutter of a bat in their houses.

Wolf poisoning began in the Yellowstone area in 1870 and continued until 1926, when the last wolf was killed. As late as 1958, wolf controllers were poisoning wolves in Mexico, to keep them out of New Mexico.

In the lower forty-eight states, Minnesota alone retained a viable breeding wolf population when the Endangered Species Act was passed. This was largely the result of its northern location, relatively small population, and large areas of wilderness and tax-forfeit, logged-over land. Minnesota was still paying a state bounty to hunters who killed wolves when we moved here in 1964. A friend of ours financed his college education partly through collecting wolf bounties.

People travel to Minnesota's Boundary Waters Canoe Area Wilderness today in part on the hope that they can hear wolves howling. But there are still Minnesotans who regard wolves as varmints at best, blood-thirsty menaces at worst. Wolf management can still be a hot topic, an issue on which local elections are won and lost, especially now that a recovering wolf population is spreading out of the north, down into one-time habitats long since turned to farmland and suburbs

We are back with the same old question; how are we to live with animals? Do we have any sort of moral contract with them, by virtue of sharing the same biome? What does the Biblical injunction to "have dominion over them" mean? Does it mean we have not only Adam's right to name, but the right to judge and to eliminate, on the basis of current economic utility, esthetic pleasure, or perceived threat? Are animals Darwinian rivals over which we have triumphed? Are they mere "resources", like ore and soil and plants?

There is a large traditional body of literature which tells us how to live with animals. I thought of this when I was brooding on the phrase "animal companion". It struck me that the true realm of the animal companion, the friendly and helpful beast, is in myth and literature.

The wolves in Kipling's The Jungle Book, the clever cat in "Puss in Boots", are not only companions of humans, like Lassie and Flipper and Gentle Ben on TV. They are social equals, sometimes social superiors. Mowgli has to prove that he is worthy of the attention he gets from Baloo and Bagheera. Animals in these tales are mentors and models. Puss is not only smarter than his nominal master, he is smarter than all the humans in the story.

Folklore is full of wise and helpful animals. The sure mark of the hero is that he is the one who pays attention to these potential guides and helpers. He hears the birds cry warnings, pays attention to what the ants whisper in the wall, will not leave the faithful hound unfed. The animal helper runs through all literatures, all mythologies.

What does all this mean, if we look at it through modern eyes? It means animals, in their full observed complexity, have something to tell us.

Of course, to see animals in their full complexity, we need to see them in a natural state. The bear on a bicycle, the zoo coyote endlessly pacing, the trained seal doing a hula, these are animals shaped by human contact and desire. They tell us more about ourselves than about the nature of the other beasts.

If we want to see animals as animals, we need to preserve the environments in which they naturally live. So living with animals ultimately means preserving healthy animal environments.

Writing in the early eighteen fifties, Henry David Thoreau sounded one of the great rallying cries of wilderness preservationists ever since. "I wish to speak a word for Nature, for absolute freedom and wildness, as contrasted with a freedom and culture merely civil—to regard man as an inhabitant, or a part and parcel of Nature, rather than a member of society....in Wildness is the preservation of the world."

Notice that Thoreau says, "Wildness", not "wilderness." Clearly he is talking about both the physical benefits of wild places, their constant regeneration of soil, and the equally important spiritual benefits of the wild, as food for the human imagination. "A town is saved, not more by the righteous men in it then by the woods and swamps that surround it. A township where one primitive forest waves above while another primitive forest rots below—such a town is fitted to raise not only corn and potatoes, but poets and philosophers for the coming ages..."

One of the odd disadvantages of writing as powerfully as Thoreau does, is that it is possible to read the work only as evocative metaphor, and not as literal fact. As literal fact, what Thoreau the surveyor and naturalist observed has been confirmed by the advancing science of ecology. Writing a little over ninety years after Thoreau wrote "Walking", Aldo Leopold, in <u>Sand County Almanac</u>, observed, "The most important characteristic of an organism is that capacity for internal self-renewal known as health."

Leopold calls for a rethinking of man's relationship to nature in his justly famous essay, "The Land Ethic." In his career as a professional forester and teacher, Leopold observed widespread loss of soil fertility and water quality, and the breakdown of inter-related natural systems. "...The disappearance of plants and animal species without visible cause, despite efforts to protect them, and the irruption of others as pests despite efforts to control them, must, in the absence of simpler explanations, be regarded as symptoms of sickness in the land organism. Both are occurring too frequently to be dismissed as ordinary evolutionary events."

Before we can know what constitutes health in the "land organism", Leopold says, we need a "a base datum of normality, a picture of how healthy land maintains itself as an organism."

"The most perfect norm is wilderness. Paleontology offers abundant evidence that wilderness maintained itself for immensely long periods; that its component species were rarely lost, neither did they get out of hand; that weather and water built soil as fast or faster than it was carried away. Wilderness, then, assumes unexpected importance as a laboratory for the study of land-health."

In his call for a land ethic, Leopold calls for accepting that we humans are indeed "part and parcel of Nature", part of the "land organism" ourselves. Soils, waters, plants, and animals have the same right to continued existence that humans do, and, "at least in spots, their continued existence in a natural state....In short, a land ethic changes the role of *homo sapiens* from conqueror of the land to plain member and citizen of it. It implies respect for his fellow members, and also for the community as such."

<u>Sand County Almanac</u> was published in 1949, the year I graduated from the eighth grade, the year my father began cropdusting. Despite those amazing photographs of the earth from space, despite Earth Day, despite the Endangered Species Act and other environmental protections, we still have no land ethic. All the environmentally-destructive trends Leopold outlines are continuing on a global basis, plus acid rain and global warming. We are in the middle of the

greatest mass extinction since the Cretaceous, and there is no mystery as to the reason. The human race is simply crowding everybody else out.

This is one of the reasons why I get so exasperated with the mouse-rescuers and meat denouncers. They seem to me to be fighting tiny, peripheral battles, while a war for the survival of the earth in any livable form, and quite possibly for human survival, is raging. We are not going to heal and sustain the green earth one mouse and pork chop at a time.

I get angry with these people because I assume that environmentalists, like John and me, share common goals with animal preservationists. Since we are on the same side, I feel this gives me a right to criticize their tactics.

But perhaps I'm wrong about this. Perhaps our goals are entirely different.

Minneapolis and environs is lucky enough to have a great deal of park land, largely because its nineteenth-century developers may well have read Thoreau. There is a substantial urban deer herd in the Twin Cities metropolitan area. How local humans are to live with these large wild animals is a question which comes up every few years. The public discussion of this question has by now become as stylized as a Noh drama.

In a natural forest, a continuing balance is maintained between deer and the wolves and mountain lions which prey on them. But there are no non-human predators large enough to kill more than an occasional deer in the metro area. Periodically the deer population explodes.

Commenting on what happened to wild western lands when the last of the wolves were gone, Leopold says, "I have watched the face of many a newly wolfless mountain, and seen the south-facing slopes wrinkle with a maze of new deer trails. I have seen every edible bush and seedling browsed, first to anemic desuetude, and then to death. I have seen every edible tree defoliated to the height of a saddlehorn. Such a mountain looks as if someone had given God a new pruning shears, and forbidden Him all other exercise. In the end the starved bones of the hoped-for deer herd, dead of its own too-much, bleach with the bones of the dead sage, or molder under the high-lined junipers."

"...while a buck pulled down by wolves can be replaced in two or three years, a range pulled down by too many deer may fail of replacement in many decades."

Urban deer herds never get to this condition, at least not in Minnesota. Long before the parkland becomes seriously over-grazed, the state Department of Natural Resources announces a special hunt, usually with bow and arrows only, to reduce the deer population.

This invariably produces a blizzard of call-in show complaints and letters to the editor. The deer are beautiful! (Certainly true.) The deer are innocent! (What could deer be guilty of? Behaving like deer. Overgrazing their range, if their numbers are not reduced, till they die of starvation.) It is shameful for humans to kill something beautiful and innocent. (Does nature kill only the ugly and wicked?)

I always hope for the letter suggesting that re-introducing wolves to Carver Park Reserve and Fort Snelling National Cemetery would bring the deer back into balance with its available food sources quite nicely. I have a friend buried in Fort Snelling who would enjoy wolves running over his grave.

Of course, wolves re-establishing a natural balance would be observed killing deer. They would leave kill sites where ordinary urban Americans could see them. They might vary their diets with occasional free-running dogs, too. And a certain number of kindergartners, and rather more mothers, would have Red Riding Hood nightmares. So this eminently natural, ecologically-sound solution to the deer overpopulation program has never even been suggested.

If we are talking about natural predators, humans have been among the natural predators for deer in Minnesota for ten to twelve thousand years. Granted, aboriginal hunters did not have firearms or modern high-tech bows, but they were far more experienced than any modern hunter, and they hunted year round.

A second wave of response follows the animal protectionist letters. These communications are from people whose rose bushes and bulb beds have been devoured for several years running, from people who have narrowly missed deer crossing busy highways, from people whose cars have collided with deer, with bad effects on themselves, the deer, and their insurance rates.

Then follow more pro-deer letters, and demonstrations by people in Bambi suits, and probably a law suit. If the deer population has to be thinned, why not trap and transport them?

The DNR points out that deer are susceptible to shock, that darting and netting deer causes mortality of up to forty per cent, and that the deer habitat in the rest of Minnesota (and most of the rest of the United States) has its own healthy deer population. There is really no place for those deer to go.

All right, then, comes the animal protectionist response, if they can't be moved, why not birth control for the deer?

I believe that there are, in fact, scientists working on a contraceptive dart for deer. But at this point in the discussion, I always lose patience. *Dama virginiana*, the common eastern white-tailed deer, is in no danger of extinction. Many other animals are, however, in nearly all cases because their habitat is being destroyed by humans. Surely in a world with an exploding human population, a world where access to safe, inexpensive contraception is far from universal, it would make more sense, if one wants to protect animals, to concentrate on birth control for humans.

Environmentalists want, insofar as this is possible, the restoration of that wildness which is the salvation of the world. Probably most animal protectionists would at least say they are working for the same goal.

But I suspect what they really want, at least on the evidence of the fights they pick, is a world in which nothing kills anything and nothing dies.

Perhaps many of them have simply not thought through these matters. They see animals being killed, they feel bad about it, they want to stop it.

After all, what could be so bad about trying to make the world a better place?

The human race has dammed rivers, cleared forests, plowed prairies and drained wetlands in the pursuit of profit. But equally, and often just about as destructively, it has destroyed native ecosystems in an attempt to make the world cozier, more familiar, prettier and more convenient. All the municipal lakes in Minneapolis were dredged in the nineteenth century, eliminating the reedy, waterfowl-harboring borders that ringed them. This "improvement" process turned a certain number of marshes and swamps into salable real estate. But equally, it was an esthetic choice. The nineteenth century saw nothing wrong with destroying a whole natural landscape, with all its resident organisms, in order to fit human ideas of natural beauty. Humans by and large like banks they can walk on without wetting their feet, and swimmable waters lapping at clean sand beaches.

It is entirely possible to mess up the world out of love, by trying to make it nicer.

To restore the world to as near a natural state as possible, to bring human beings into the proper balance with their fellow biotic citizens, will be an incredibly difficult task. We do, however, know such a world existed once, and there are still shrinking patches where it exists today.

But a world without death and pain is not a natural world. I once heard a sermon in which the pastor referred to death as "the great obscenity." Presumably he was speaking in theological terms. Certainly he was not thinking in natural ones. Thoreau's "primitive forest waving above while another primitive forest rots below", Leopold's "capacity for internal self-renewal known as health," all depend on death.

This is one of the lessons we learn from animals, from the vole we trapped in our storage space this morning, from the male grouse who crash in crazy flight, from the eight-point buck who materialized in front of John's shotgun yesterday morning, whose tenderloin we ate last night. Everything dies. Everything eats everything else. That is the way the great harmony of the earth continues.

This is a point of view which would not have seemed strange to the people who lived here before us. They would also have nodded over all of those traditional animal tales, as I have seen contemporary Native Americans nod at careful ecological explanations of natural balance. "We have always known that," they say. "It is what the old ones taught us."

It is a very long time since those European old ones made the paintings in the caves. Contemporary western culture wants either to use animals, or to rescue them. Simply to co-exist with them, as fellow citizens in Aldo Leopold's ethical democracy of life forms, is something we can only imagine.

In Kipling's great beast tale, when Mowgli becomes a young man, he must leave the jungle, leave Grey Brother and the Four, leave Baloo and Bagheera, and become Nathoo, the Indian village boy. This seemed right to me, as a near-adolescent, just as it seemed right when Christopher Robin left the Hundred Acre Wood, though both made me cry.

Of course, Piglet and Pooh and Tigger were toys, the Hundred Acre Wood an imagined place, and Christopher Robin must leave them because he is growing up. But the Indian jungle, whatever actual contact Rudyard Kipling had with it, was a real place, with real animals in it.

Mowgli has to become Nathoo because Rudyard Kipling had to become a *sahib* and a Victorian gentleman. Both have to take their places in their respective caste systems, leaving the democracy of the wild, in which, as Aldo Leopold says, we are all equally citizens.

I wonder what Flat Mouth or Bad Boy would have made out of the ending to <u>The Jungle Book</u>. Up to that last chapter, I think they would have found it a fine story. The stories they often told were full of talking animals, helpful and not so helpful, shape changing animals, animals at once numinous and comic. Bagheera and Baloo would seem not too different from Manobozho the hare, the animal-trickster-God, the thief of fire, who would have been Raven further north, Coyote or Fox out west. For them, learning from animals was not something that stopped when you became an adult. Every one of their people knew which *do daim* he belonged to, whether they were bear people, loon people, turtle people, fisher people. The *do daim*, a word nineteenth century anthropologists recorded as "totem", was both clan lineage, and the revered animal companion/ancestor associated with that clan lineage.

Their naming ceremonies and those of their mothers, sisters, and wives all involved special connection with an animal companion. The dreams they sought in their vision quests, the dreams their sisters sought in their puberty huts, often involved animals.

So, I imagine some perceptive Ahnishinaabe asking Rudyard Kipling, Why did Mowgli leave the animals? They were good helpful friends.

In the story, Mowgli must leave because he is Man, i.e. European, capitalist, nature-taming man. "He must leave because he is Man," says Kipling.

The aboriginal questioner shrugs. "I'm a Bear clan man myself," he says.

How are we to live with animals? We have lost the awe of the painted caves. We have lost that old brotherhood. Important parts of our religious tradition tell many of us that we are a special creation, that our animal nature is something to outgrow, to leave behind, to lose. When we speak of someone who has committed an outrageous crime, we say, "He's an animal."

Yet many Americans, even the grumpiest upholders of the Man-the-Conqueror tradition, have an itchy place in their souls when they think about their relationship to the natural world. We look at our infinitely expanding suburbs and freeways, we look down from the jet and see the continuous smog-envelope curling around the earth, and we think, There's got to be a better way.

In one version of the Ahnishinaabe after-life, the person making the journey to the Place of Good Hunting must first swim through the Churning Water. If the Animal Brothers had reason to be angry with him, they would keep the water churning, making his trip long and difficult.

They would be angry if he had not treated them appropriately. But what does that mean? It was appropriate under the right circumstances to eat, to wear, to sleep under the skins of the Animal Brothers, as it was appropriate for them, under the right circumstances, to eat you.

Here is a story about inappropriate behavior and its punishment.

A man marries a beaver. She is sleek and handsome and the beaver family accepts him into their lodge. All is well for a time. He lives happily eating roots and bark. Then he begins to notice how pretty his sister-in-law is.

He sleeps with his sister-in-law, without asking his wife for permission. Worse than that, he kills and eats his lover. He admits his bad behavior to his father-in-law, who sends him to find all the bones of his paramour-dinner and put them back in the water where she used to swim. He is remorseful, but the job takes a long time. When he has found all but a few tiny foot bones, he throws them all in.

His lover returns to life in her beaver form, but she is lame in one foot. Like Mowgli, the impatient bone-collector is cast out of the community of animals.

He will have a very hard time in the Churning Water.

To be an ethical being is to be responsible. It is not to pretend to a non-existent purity. We all do harm. We all eat each other. We all have blood on our hands. To be responsible is to admit this.

We need to say, "Have a good journey" as we cut the throat of the lamb we will eat for Christmas dinner. We need to put all the bones into the water, every single one.

We have largely designed a culture which makes this right relation to the Animal Brothers difficult. Get that damned squirrel out of the yard, but don't use Mother's tongs!

We need, in our relations with the Animal Brothers, to get through our own version of the Churning Water.

BUILDING EARTHWARD
J.,E.

Some university colleagues visited us in 1975, after we were moved into our mostly-completed home on Big Swan Lake.

In the summer of 1973 we had completed a walk-out basement, which we lived in during that fall and winter. Much of the interior was unfinished when we moved in, but it was weather tight, comfortable, and large enough for the five of us. During the summer and fall I cut down the trees which would provide the upstairs portion of the house. That lumber was stacked to dry in our front yard in several piles, perhaps ten thousand board feet in all.

During the late fall and winter months when outside work was unpleasant, the downstairs was finished off, and the following summer, all that stacked wood was converted into our top story. It was a large, pleasant, and even modestly elegant home into which we welcomed our friends in the summer of 1975.

They knew this history. They had just bought some rural property, on which they were planning to build. They were very interested in what we had done.

At the end of an afternoon of looking and questioning, over the remains of a home-grown leg of lamb, my friend Don the dean made a trenchant comment: "If a damn English teacher can build a house, so can I!"

Quite a few other people have indicated their amazement at our willingness to tackle building projects. No doubt my early experiences following my father around as he did carpentry, learning while working with him, had something to do with my confidence level. Spending summers on a small mixed farm where almost everything was done from scratch also helped form my attitudes. Our era tends to turn everything from exercise to sex to cooking into a complex mystery, solvable only with the help of experts. This pads the pocketbooks of certified experts and leaves the average citizen feeling helpless.

I believe that anyone in decent physical health who can read should be able to build a house. That has been our experience. In addition to books on basic carpentry, the essential tools are few: a hammer, square, level, and saw. A willingness to seek advice and help when problems are encountered is also valuable.

The house on the hill overlooking Big Swan Lake provided us with fifteen years of good living. Its glorious sunset views, its ornate kitchen wood stove, the interesting knots and grainy swirls in the wood which let us see a mermaid on the living room wall, a dragon on the beam over the dining room table, would not be easy to leave.

But like all builders, I did occasionally think of other ways I might have done things. Or might do them, if I were to build again. The technologies of energy conservation continued to expand and improve after we drove the last nail on that house. I was particularly interested in the prospects of earth-sheltered building. Our house had an earth-sheltered basement, of course, but would it be possible to build a completely earth-sheltered house, an underground house, which was light and comfortable and esthetically pleasing? I started reading about stackwood masonry, a technique which provided great strength and energy conservation at small expense.

By June of 1985, our children had scattered to college and jobs. They kept close and affectionate ties with us, but they were occasional guests, not residents. The two thousand square feet of house, which had been full of rock and roll and "Hogan's Heroes", adolescent drama and "Monty Python's Flying Circus", just-remembered homework assignments and impromptu late-night Risk tournaments, suddenly contained only two middle-aged people. We did not need all that space, but we still had to heat it, clean it, and pay taxes on it.

By this time I had been teaching, first high school and then college, for over thirty years. I still enjoyed classroom teaching, but the work on various academic committees was beginning to wear on me. I had always been good at dropping the hassles of the workplace as I walked through the door at home; now they began to bleed into my married life and my free time. At one point, I realized that on a particular issue of academic politics, I was fighting the same battle that I had fought in the early seventies. Perhaps this is part of the nature of organizational life, that some issues are never entirely settled, but must be reconsidered and re-argued every fifteen years or so. In any case, I felt that once had been enough and twice was more than enough. Let somebody else fight the good fight from now on.

Taking early retirement looked more and more appealing.

The sixty-six acres which had been the old Shortridge place, later the Rylander place, was divided by a county road into twenty-six acres of lakeshore, and a wooded, rolling forty acres on the other side of the road. We had purchased five acres on the lake side of the road from my mother, and on this land we had built. Later we bought the forty. My mother continued to use her lake cabin often, sometimes complaining about having to go back into town. On one occasion Eric said, "Why don't you just build a house out here, Grandma?" At age seventy, over the dire warnings of some of her friends, she did just that, building up the hill from us, at a distance that allowed us to visit easily, but also to live separate lives.

She had been the best of neighbors, a well of gardening and canning lore, a close and dear part of her grandchildren's lives. But she was gone, now, and the division of her estate with my sisters meant the sale of her house and the lakeside cottage in which we had made our first experiments in Minnesota living. Her section of the lakeside land had never been ours on the county Register of Deeds, but it had felt like ours. It was not ours anymore.

We didn't need all the space we had. If we built a new place, a two-person house rather than a family-with-kids house, there would be all these new interesting techniques to try. Now she didn't have the kids to look after, Edie could help more with the construction. Laying the mortar for cordwood masonry looked easy enough for a complete amateur to try.

And then there was the prospect of early retirement. If we sold the big house and built a small house over in the forty on a pay-as-you-go basis, we ought to wind up with a decent nest-egg, to supplement my modest teaching pension.

We talked through all these factors. Without perhaps being fully conscious of it, I had already looked over the forty and picked a general building area, thinking to myself, "You know, that looks like the kind of hillside where a person could build an earth-sheltered house." Now, within a few days of the winter solstice in 1985, we crossed the road and walked through the snow, finding a site with some level land suitable for a garage, shop, and shed. Behind this area was a hillside with several large red oaks. Further to the north was a fairly level space, suitable for a large garden.

It was not happenstance that we chose our building site near the time of the winter solstice. I had been sketching and planning. Our house plan called for a structure backed up into the hill, built on a shallow curve, with windows to catch as much winter light and warmth from solar gain as possible. The center section of the house, the kitchen section, would face due south, with the bedroom end and living room end facing in at slight angles. We wanted the kitchen to get morning sun. We staked out our building site, aiming it toward the sun on the shortest day of the year.

We followed the same building schedule with the new house as with the old one, beginning by building a garage. Edie's journal entries catch some of the feeling of that time.

June 4: "John has been building footing forms. Helped him hold and level things—harder work than it sounds." June 5: "Helped John fill in a lot of the form with rocks. God knows we have lots of rocks." June 6: "Dan (up from his job in Minneapolis) and his friends Cleo (male) and Terry (female) up to help with footings. I shoveled sand and dumped it into the cement mixer. It took about three hours to pour the footings for the west wall." June 9: "John and I poured the east footing, together. Mostly I shoveled sand (six small buckets to a load of cement) till my back felt permanently bent. By God, I can *work* when I put my mind to it." June 11: "Yesterday's rain filled the north and south footings, so Kevin came up with his Ditch Witch and put in some drainage ditches. By today everything was drained out."

This is the way construction goes. Something goes wrong. (Something will always go wrong.) There are exclamations of distress. If the builders are wise, they will avoid second-guessing ("You ought to have been able to see...") and recriminations ("Didn't I tell you?") at this point.

Mishaps are part of the adventure of self-building. Solutions will be found for the problem. The process of finding a solution is, in itself, enjoyable. The builders will take a deep breath, get a good night's sleep and go back to work.

Much of the experience of self-building is captured in the June 12th journal entry: "John and I poured the north and south footings. The work goes easier now we know what we are doing."

By June 14, with Dan's help, I had raised the north, south, and west walls. A local carpenter hung the double garage doors. By June 19, the garage was roofed with galvanized steel.

By this time I had read extensively about cordwood masonry building, which is the setting of wood (rather than stone or block) in mason's mortar. I had looked carefully at all the pictures and diagrams in the books. But we had not actually seen any construction done that way. So we decided to make the east wall of the garage, the back end, a first experiment in cordwood masonry.

The wall we built was fourteen inches thick. We experimented with various mortar mixes. (July 7: "In the first lot we used dry shavings rather than wet sawdust and it came out lumpy and crumbly.") We set our peeled log sections in more or less haphazard sizes and without great concern for establishing a pattern. We made plenty of mistakes. (July 17: "I've been filling out less far and less far with each lot of mortar as the wall got higher. I wondered why all those log ends were sticking out. If I keep up like this I will end up with lots of bare wood and two inches of mortar under the ceiling. I took all the excess mortar which falls—which is a lot if a person is doing the work properly—and am using it to stuff places I didn't do before.")

When we were finished, we had a serviceable wall. But we immediately decided that when we built the house, we would use wider mortar separations between log ends to better frame the wood and enhance structural strength.

We were glad we had experimented. Otherwise, our cordwood masonry house would have a very different appearance.

While Edie finished the cordwood masonry wall on the garage, I had been dropping trees to form the beams of the house. We had decided to call the house "Earthward", taking the name from a favorite Robert Frost poem.

I had also bought two thousand board feet of lumber from a man who had torn down an old house, planning to use the lumber himself, then decided he did not have time for the project. He had dimension lumber and boards of clear pine, and fir flooring. These would go into the second phase of our building plans.

Earthward would definitely be a house for two. But we wanted to provide space for visiting children or other guests. We were planning to build a simple structure with no indoor plumbing, one which we could shut up when we had no guests. We had no idea how long it would take to sell our present house, but we wanted to make sure, if it sold quickly, that we had someplace to live. So the guest shelter would come next.

By July thirtieth, Eric (home for a week from his job in Florida) was helping me with footings, with Edie back shoveling sand. We also had considerable help from Dan, who chose a name for the place. I had been calling it "the convent" and "the think tank." Edie had suggested "the Scholary", a name she picked from an Ursula LeGuin novel. Dan took a look at the trees around the building site and said, "Why not Birch House?"

Birch House can sleep five. It has a sizable main room, a bedroom, and an entry porch which includes a composting toilet.

Upstairs from the entry porch, accessible only by ladder, is Edie's poetry tower, a small room with great views in all four directions, a number of low-brow paperback books, and a built-in desk. It exists because on the morning I went over to begin framing the entry, I leaned the two by fours I had picked out of the pile of used lumber against the wall of the cabin. The two by fours were fourteen feet long. They reached well above the already framed wall. It seemed a shame to cut them. How often does a builder encounter fourteen-foot-long two by fours?

The notion of a two-story entry porch came to me, the second story accessible only through a two foot hole in the corner of the room. The materials were on hand. I let whimsy control the building process. The result has amused adults and fascinated children.

Less elegant than William Butler Yeats' writing tower—it is more tree fort than castle, and has never been completely finished on the inside—it is still a valued retreat.

Even as we completed work on the cabin, I was dropping trees and getting lumber sawed at a local mill, for next year's construction on Earthward. Some of the lumber came from our land, but our rafters and some beams were cut on a farm several miles away. The farmer had fifteen large straight oaks out in a pasture, which he was willing to trade for two cuttings of hay from our five acre field.

By fall of '86, our garage and Birch House were complete and the excavation for Earthward had been made. Lumber cut for the framing was stacked and curing.

I had spent hours of time designing and planning for this house. One of the smarter things I did was build a scale model of our house-to-be, on a scale of one inch to one foot. It helped me to visualize the slanting roof lines, the unconventional crescent shape, and the utilization of space in that structure.

I know builders can do fancy planning with blueprints, and even fancier planning with computers, but there is nothing like being able to put your hands on things and move them around in three dimensions.

In the early spring of 1987, we hired a young man to peel the aspen, oak, red elm, birch, and basswood logs which I had cut. After I had bucked them to twenty inch length, he stacked them to dry. These would become stackwood for our south-facing, exterior walls. The ends which would be visible on the exterior walls of the house were dipped in used motor oil and a wood preservative.

In mid-May of 1987, as the academic year at the college drew to a close, I wrote a letter of resignation. I was still not sure whether I would submit it. A few days after writing it, I went to the President's Office. I sat down in the waiting area for a few minutes, considering. Then I walked out.

In the hallway, the thought of where I wanted to be in September insinuated itself strongly, demanding an answer. I turned around, went back to the president's office, gave the secretary my letter, and walked out smiling.

On June first, 1987, a local crew came in to pour our footings. Later they poured the slab for the floor. I did the post and beam framing carpentry. Edie and I laid up the cordwood masonry front wall, a section at a time. Into the center of the wall, between the outer layers of stiff masonry and around the logs, we poured cellulose insulation. Our walls are twenty inches thick. In addition to the beauty of sanded and sealed log ends, the walls are punctuated by decorative bottles and stones. We would later paint the mortar around the stones ivory, to set off the colors of the wood.

The walls are sturdy and distinctive. They show wood grain, the pressure of the mason's trowel, fingermarks. It occurs to me that when we are gone, the marks of our fingers will remain in the front wall. Few houses register the touch of their builders that personally.

For most of the summer, we had a couple of recent high school graduates working for us. Mike and Chris were familiar with most carpentry tools; otherwise they were unskilled, but willing. They did most of the heavy lifting and "gophering"—go for this, go for that. We contracted out the wiring, plumbing, and blockwork on our curved back wall. (Know your limitations.) The blocklayer commented that he had never built a curved wall before.

By summer's end, we had a tight and livable, if not entirely finished, house. When our home across the road sold unexpectedly, we were far enough along to move in. On October 25, 1987, we watched the Minnesota Twins win their first World Series and then crawled into bed for our first night in Earthward.

There was more work to do, of course. We sanded and sealed log ends. I paneled walls with homemade paneling. I built the floor to ceiling bookcases which cover twelve feet of back living room wall. With help from a local carpenter, I built a wardrobe and a china cupboard. I built shadow boxes to fill all the odd spaces which are the result of building non-square rooms with slanting ceilings. We discovered that the shadow boxes were wonderful display spaces for the paintings, vases, statuary, and souvenirs we'd accumulated over the years. And we both did a lot of finishing, painting, and touching up.

Earthward nestles into a hillside, facing out toward an irregular patch of lawn and naturalized flowers which runs on out into woods. We grow less lawn, more flowers and herbs, every year. Two-thirds of the house is dug into a natural hill. The bedroom end of the house is bermed. In our first fall here, concerned that the raw dirt of the berm would erode, we covered it with aspen logs, laid up from the ground toward the top. That end of the house looked like the world's biggest beaver lodge. Over the years the aspens have decayed, leaving only faint shadows of shape to tell where they were. That hillside is covered now with the same dense sod as the rest of the roof and with wild raspberry and elderberry bushes.

The sod roof, over its layers of gravel, insulating membrane, insulation and wood, is green in summer, white in winter. Approached from the rear, the house could be mistaken for a grassy knoll, except for the clotheslines, the back door (opening out of a hillside as if opening out of a mine) and the chimney on top. It is perfectly safe to walk on. (Our first fall, we woke up one night to strange thumping sounds. Stray cattle were on the roof. They did not damage anything.)

The house itself has a walk-in entry porch, its Plexiglas roof providing added solar gain, one large bedroom, a modest galley-style kitchen, a pantry, a living room, a bathroom which is also a laundry room, and a utility room. Behind the utility room, a short tunnel we call the Trollway provides wood storage space, room for a root storage cupboard, and access to the back door, the clotheslines and the garden.

Down the hill and around the corner from Earthward, Birch House lifts its tower. Up hill are the garage and tractor shed. We have also added a sap shack, for our maple syruping, which additionally provides storage space for some of the stuff two people will accumulate in forty-plus years of marriage.

Earthward provides approximately eight hundred and seventy five feet of interior space, which we built, in 1987, at a cost of twenty dollars per square foot.

It is not everybody's house. The walls are not blank spaces, waiting to be given a room treatment or to be used as hanging space. (Before we hang up anything, we ask ourselves, Is it better looking that the natural wood and finger-marked mortar it will obscure?) Most of it is not square. It is full of odd angles. Some guests have said, "It must be like living inside a sculpture."

A few visitors are acutely uncomfortable. Their eyes shift around, trying to come to terms with this place, with its exposed beams and the Mother Post in the center of the living room and the House Spirit peering out from the stone wall behind the decorative woodstove. It just doesn't fit their preconceptions of houseness.

Occasional delivery persons have been found knocking on the door of Birch House, or the garage. They just can't believe people live in a place whose back side is a hill and whose front side looks, with its whitewashed masonry walls and log ends, like a frontier fort.

It is light and bright and comfortable, warm in winter, cool in summer. It reflects our tastes and desires and what we think is important in life. We hope to live here for many more years.

THE PLACE
E.

I see against the sky the place
Where the old barn stood,
Though nothing is left but two stacks of salvaged wood,
And corner holes. And the collective ghosts
Of animals housed and work done there.

We threw it up fast, using old power poles
For framing, and rough-hewn green basswood
For facing boards. It was not one of those barns
They picture in slick magazines;
Just a dirt-floored shed for ten years' assorted animals.

For Fern the mare, when our daughter was horse age;
For our son's sows when his dreams
Ran to fields instead of cars. For a transient goat.
For breeding ewes. For calves
I bottle-fed up to steerhood and hamburger status.

For laying hens. For guineas with voices like drills.
For beautiful raucous geese. For steel-blue swallows
Hovering over gaping young
In their plastered nests.
For the sparrows' tangles of hay and string. At the last

It was miscellaneous storage. Old buckets. Onions
Hung to dry. Doors and windows for the new place.
Tools. Shreds of plastic from the balling gun
We broke forcing a worming capsule
Over the stubborn teeth of a ram named Henry.

A saggy, leaking old shed
With tufts of wool and feathers
On its hand and beast-worn wood,
And stratum after stratum of straw, spilled feed,
And peaty manure,
Where the stock had stood.

The kids are grown. These days I herd
Words, which do not bleat or bolt.
The house is sold.
The barn-full of time is down.

A few framing branches.
A sky full of stars.

A WALK WITH MAX

J.

The botanist Max Partch and I are strolling in the woods of our forty acres. It is late May. Every direction we look reflects back to us subtle shades of Minnesota spring.

Max has volunteered to make a plant inventory of our woods. Plant inventories are a way of measuring the healthiness of a wild environment. A diverse plant community will provide numerous living spaces for other life-forms, like the spring birds chorusing around us.

I see the trees and shrubs and other vegetation I have learned to name; Max, who is busily annotating the vegetation on a sheet of paper entitled "John Rylander's woods", is steadily commenting on what he sees. Occasionally, he bends down to look more closely. Much of what he says is the Latin of Linnaeus, followed by the common name in English.

Some of the trees he identifies are large enough to be cut for timber. Some of the flowers, in this time of woods bloom, are lovely enough to catch the eye of the non-botanist. But most of what we are walking through, the compli-cated community Max is recording plant by plant, is what the average real estate buyer would classify as "brush". Most of it would be "cleaned up" if this was the average building lot.

We move slowly, erratically. Max is obviously pleased with the diver-sity he's finding, the overall health of the plant community. We move down the slope toward the swampy area. Max touches and smells and tastes. He's a man in his element, professionally and personally.

The dinner bell rings. We haven't gone a hundred and fifty yards from the house. We haven't come close to the swamp, with its myriad vegetative forms, many of them entirely different from upland vegetation. We return to Earthward and dinner. Max is charmed by what he has seen, and so am I. But I'm also critically aware of how little I know, how much there is to learn, about the place I live.

These woods are not wilderness. They have been cut over and pas-tured. Parts of them, on the less steep slopes, have been broken to the plow, only to regrow into what Max tells us is "sugar maple-basswood, or Southern Dry Mesic community." Until recently, patches of woods like this survived as wood-lots and because the soil was too poor and the hillsides too steep to turn them into farm fields. They had no value except to the hunter and logger. They stood on the tax rolls as "unimproved land."

The amazing profusion of life which Max is recording, Latin name by Latin name, is the result of nature's capacity to hang on and heal over, in the face of human abuse and indifference.

Looking again at Max's plant inventory, I am reminded of these gaps in my botanical knowledge. I have known this place intimately for a good part of my life. But Max asks me questions to which I don't have answers.

Max, I know we have wood onion and wood anemone. I'm not sure about the other plants.

MAX'S LIST
E.

This is Max Partch's plant inventory, copied down as he wrote it. Where we customarily use a different common name for a plant, that name is listed in brackets.

Apart from the sheer number and variety of plant species listed here, I am knocked out by the names. Hog peanut. Bittersweet. Enchanter's nightshade. Honewort. (Was it once used to hone knives?) Fleabane, bedstraw, touch-me-not, which is also jewelweed and impatiens. Ironwood, trembling aspen, carrion flower, motherwort.

I am tempted to simply list the names as a poem, for their beauty and imbedded human history, and ignore their importance as a biotic inventory, listing the green residents of one small part of the earth.

Date: June 9, 1988
Location: Rylander's woods, Todd County, 3.4 miles north of Grey Eagle

1. Box elder, Acer negundo
2. Sugar maple, Acer saccharum
3. Hog peanut, Amphicarpa bracteata
4. Columbine, Aquilegia canadensis
5. Sarsaparilla, Aralia nudicaulis
6. Spikenard, Aralia racemosa
7. Jack-in-the-pulpit, Arisaema triphyllum
8. Wild ginger, Asarum canadense
9. (Forest) milkweed, poke milkweed, Asclepias exaltata
10. Large-leaved aster, Aster macrophyllus
11. Lady fern, Athyrium filix-femina
12. Paper birch, Betula papyrifera
13. Rattlesnake fern, Botrychium virginianum
14. (Interrupted) sedge, Carex rosea
15. Blue beech [American hornbeam], Carpinus caroliniana
16. Blue cohosh, Caulophyllum thalictroides
17. Bittersweet, Celastrus scandens
18. Enchanter's nightshade, Circaea lutetiana
19. Pagoda dogwood, Cornus alternifolia
20. Gray dogwood, Cornus racemosa
21. Red-osier dogwood, Cornus stolonifera
22. Hazel, Corylus americana
23. Honewort, Cryptotaenia canadensis
24. Pointed-leaved tick trefoil, Desmodium glutinosum
25. Leatherwood, Dirca palustris
26. Canada fleabane, horseweed, or mulestail, Conyza canadensis
27. (Obtuse) fescue-grass, Festuca obtusa

28. Strawberry, Fragaria virginiana
29. Black ash, Fraxinus nigra
30. Green ash, Fraxinus pennsylvanica
31. Cleavers, Galium aparine
32. Sweet-scented bedstraw, Galium triflorum
33. Wild geranium, Geranium maculatum
34. White avens, Geum canadense
35. Hepatica, liverleaf, Hepatica americana
36. Bottlebrush grass, Elymus hystrix
37. Touch-me-not; Jewelweed, Impatiens capensis
38. False lily-of-the-valley, [Canada mayflower], Maianthemum canadense
39. Sweet Cicely (fuzzy), Osmorhiza claytoni
40. Anise-root (smooth sweet Cicely), Osmorhisa longistylis
41. Ironwood, Ostrya virginiana
42. Five-leaf ivy, woodbine, Parthenocissus inserta
43. Lopseed, Phryma leptostachya
44. Hairy Solomon's Seal, Polygonatum pubescens
45. Trembling aspen, Populus tremuloides
46. Black cherry, Prunus serotina
47. Red oak, Quercus borealis
48. Bur oak, Quercus macrocarpa
49. Poison ivy, Rhus radicans
50. Prickly gooseberry, Ribes cynobasti
51. Red elderberry, Sambucus pubens
52. Bloodroot, Sanguinaria canadensis
53. Black snakeroot, Sanicula marilandica
54. False spikenard; (forest) False Solomon's Seal,   Smilacina racemosa
55. Smilax (no tendrils), Smilax ecirrata
56. Carrion-flower, Smilax herbacea
57. Zig-zag goldenrod, Solidago flexicaulis
58. Dandelion, Taraxacum officinale
59. Early meadow rue, Thalictrum dioicum
60. Basswood, Tilia americana
61. Nodding trillium, Trillium cernuum
62. American elm, Ulmus americana
63. Stinging nettle, Urtica dioica
64. Yellow bellwort, Uvularia grandiflora
65. Yellow violet, Viola pubescens
66. Grape, Vitis aestivalis
67. Prickly ash, Zanthoxylum americana
68. Blackberry, Rubus species
69. Motherwort, Leonurus
70. Horsetail, Equisetum sp.
71. Figwort, Scrophularia lanceolata

Pastured some 20 years ago. Some trees tapped for maple sap. John logged some maple, oak, and basswood for house construction.

Are these in your woods?

Acer rubrum--Red maple
Actaea rubra--Red baneberry
Adiantum--Maiden-hair fern
Allium tricocum--Wood onion, wild leek
Anemone quinquefolia--wood anemone
Diervilla--Bush-honeysuckle
Onoclea--Sensitive fern
Oryzopsis spp.--Mt. Rice
Panax--ginseng
Pyrola sp.--shin-leaf
Rhus glabra--smooth sumach

Did not list weeds of the disturbed areas around buildings.

RADICAL IRON
E.

When Mother Rylander's house and cabin sold, the new people did not want the kitchen wood stove. So we hauled it over to Earthward and installed it in Birch House.

It was a product of the St. Paul Stove Company, built, I believe, sometime in the 1920's. It had a firebox, an oven, a water reservoir, and a warming shelf on top. The solid parts were boxy iron; the trim and legs and shelf showed neo-Edwardian curves. The stove was faced in white enamel printed with the brand name SANICO.

I would cook later on wood stoves which had names that were grander (Monarch) and cozier (Home Comfort, Warm Morning) and wood stoves that were more ornate and had more features. But Mother's old stove was the first wood stove on which I ever cooked. On this stove I learned the intricacies of differential stoking for fast heat and steady heat, of shaking down the cinders, of emptying the ash hopper. I had cooked both humbly and grandly on the old Sanico.

Of course Mother had cooked plenty before me. Whenever she came to the cottage on the lake, unless the weather was absolutely stifling, she started a fire in the kitchen woodstove. The big tea kettle would go on over the firebox and the enamel-ware dishpan would go on the part above the oven. She had an electric range in the cabin, but why buy water-heating power from the electric company when you could heat it off your own good stovewood, paying nothing but a little sweat? It was like her practice of saving the water in which garden vegetables were rinsed, along with any good black dirt which had washed off those vegetables, and using it to water the flowerbeds by the kitchen door. Why would a person want to throw away any good thing?

John remembers that wood stove as a regular feature in the cottage kitchen, from the time the cottage was built. I don't know whether Mother bought it second hand, or whether it came out of her parent's house. In any case, I was at least the third woman to shake down the cinders, empty the ash-hopper, lay in the tinder and kindling, start the fire, adjust the draft, stoke as needed.

It came from an era when women were short. Even with a couple of bricks under its feet to give it extra height, I always got a crick in the back, bending over to feed it or cook on it. Come to think of it, Mother Rylander was taller than me. So maybe it was manufactured by people who believed in "the little woman", without checking the actual dimensions of that hypothetical user.

It was the stove I came back to, when I left behind the Aztec Bronze gas kitchen range with all modern conveniences circa 1964.

When we built the kitchen in the big house, it included space for a kitchen wood stove, which I used regularly all winter. But there was really not enough space for a wood kitchen range in Earthward, and the house was so snugly built that a cooking fire would have roasted us out of the place.

Everybody in the family, not just us, had a deep sentimental attachment to Mother's old cottage stove, even the sisters-in-law and nieces who had not the slightest interest in ever cooking on it. One of the nephews kept saying, "Hold it for me, I'll pick it up," but he didn't, and apparently, attached as he was to the old piece of iron, he had no real place for it in his current home either.

Cast-iron stoves deteriorate over time, especially when they sit over winter in unheated buildings. The freezing and thawing loosens their joints. Condensation settles on their surfaces, turns to rust, and gradually corrodes them. Truth to tell, the old Sanico had always been a little rattly around the edges and leaked a little smoke.

We needed a stove in Birch House which would hold heat for more than the hour or two of the small firebox in Mother's old stove. So, sentiment aside, we needed to move that stove out. We could stick it up in the sap shack or the tractor shed, to rust away on the vague hope that some member of the family would want it someday, or we could sell it.

So we put our "for sale" ad in the local shopper, the Dairyland Peach, and now a potential buyer was driving his pickup down next to Birch House, where he could load the stove.

The pickup, a full-sized old rustbucket well-patched with Bondo, drove by Earthward. I noticed our customer's bumper stickers, BO GRITZ FOR PRESIDENT and something about the Federal Reserve.

He was probably around forty, a sturdy, bearded, short-haired man accompanied by his teen-aged son. He carried a big-handled knife at his belt. A good sharp knife is always handy in the country, but I have found that a pock-etknife does just fine. He and the boy, who also had a knife at his belt, were dressed in camouflage gear, as if at any minute they might need to fade into the woods around Birch House.

He inspected the stove. I opened and closed doors for him and began explaining how to shake down the cinders, how to empty the ash hopper, but he was looking past me toward John and talking, not so much about the stove as about the importance, indeed the essentialness, of leading an independent life. "Just got the boy away from his Mom," he said, jerking his head toward the son, who had a raw-looking Marine-style haircut and a look of profound self-con-sciousness. "From California." He said the state name as if it dripped slime. "Gonna home-school him, teach him to take care of himself—"

I shut up. I was the one who had done most of the cooking on this stove and knew its peculiarities, but if Camo-man couldn't take advice from a woman, let him figure out the drafts by himself. Let him fill the room with piss-elm smoke, as we had done once, and learn from his mistakes.

He was looking with a kind of hunger, at the compact room, at the garden outside the window, at the end berm of Earthward. "You folks did this all by yourselves? Build all this? You off the grid?"

I actually got the approving corner of an eye, as if I was maybe some small part of "You folks".

"We did most of the building," John said shortly; then (never miss a teachable moment in making the world a greener place), "We've got a composting toilet on the porch you came in."

"One of them Swedish jobs?"

210

"No, I designed it and we built it. It's very low tech, anybody can build one—"

A brief tour of the composter. Then bills changed hands.

Wood kitchen ranges of the Sanico vintage have lots of detachable parts. Off came the warming shelf, out came the lids and tools, which went into a box. (I put aside the handsomest of the old lid-lifters. Mother's sad iron, which used to sit on this stove, was already next door.)

Listen, I kept wanting to say, as the various parts of my first wood cook-stove were muscled up over the bumper stickers, into the rusty pickup bed. Listen, this is not just any old piece of iron.

This is the stove that taught me, through the dumb intransigence of inert objects, that transferring energy from sun to tree to fire to coffeepot and skillet is not an easy and automatic process. This is the stove I came back to, when I wanted to learn how to be more than the little woman and the smart shopper.

Yes, it is true, we came to a wood-stove centered life in flight from a superficial, commercialized community, but we were aiming ourselves toward a different kind of community, an older and deeper and more comprehensive one. This stove made the skillet sizzle as we talked about a more accepting, more diverse America, about what traditions were honorable and worthy of retention. This stove heated the water we dipped out for our children's baths, with hope for a peaceful world in every wipe of the washcloth. The soft conversation of its firebox soothed us when we came back to the cabin in our griefs, after the head-bashings and assassinations of the sixties and early seventies. With its smells of good oak and hot iron in our nostrils, we decided that it was not really a fascist country, not yet, nor would be if we had anything to say about it. That it was still our country. That if we were not part of the solution, we were part of the problem.

Listen, dude, I want to say, this is not a know-nothing stove, a leave-me-be stove, a paranoid stove. Wherever you're going in your self-chosen combat gear, remember this is radical iron in the back of your truck.

Technologies have no politics. The same flint blade could slaughter dinner or brother. The Wright Brothers' marvelous machines and their spacefaring offspring could reveal the world as a single sphere, washed by the same seas, wrapped by the same air, its borders invisible. Or they could find the target and drop the payload anywhere, regardless of camouflage.

Everything was loaded and tied down. John slammed the tailgate. He had been talking about maintenance. "Take good care of her," he said.

The truck lumbered up the hill, leaving ruts in the soft turf. Father and son rattled off down the county road in the company of my first wood stove. Camouflaged, armed, getting ready to take care of themselves.

A FEW WORDS ABOUT AUGUST
J.

August, one of my old friends from Grey Eagle, died on the fourth of July in his ninety-ninth year. He was a few months short of his hundredth birthday. Until just days before his death he kept busy with his yard, his woodwork, and caring for his wife, herself well into her nineties and suffering from Alzheimer's Disease.

For many of his working years, August was a telegrapher for railroads. Later he became a jeweler, doing watch repair and building timepieces. Then he expanded his lifelong interest in hunting (he quit deer hunting at ninety-four, when he bagged his one hundredth deer) by learning gunsmithing.

Finally, in his eighties, he turned to woodworking because, as he said, "My eyes aren't good enough for watch repair and gunsmith work anymore." But his eyes were still good enough to do intricate wood inlays on small jewelry boxes he designed and built.

When we built Earthward August heard about the project and got curious. He asked me to show him my new "earth house", as a lot of local people called it, the year after it was done. I brought August out for his inspection somewhat apprehensively. August was a man with a critical eye, used to working well with small detail at fine tolerances. My own habits and aesthetics in domestic carpentry are best summed up by something I heard from a carpenter friend, when we were trying to fit paneling into a new bathroom in an old and very unsquare house. After several cut-and-try efforts, Ralph said, "Goddamnit, John, nail her down. We ain't buildin' no piano."

Some of the things August made were delicate and elegant enough to meet piano-building specifications.

My trepidation was unwarranted. August obviously admired the unusual design of Earthward and our prolific use of native lumber. But what really excited him was the ironwood (Eastern Hophornbeam) support post which stands in the middle of the living room. The post is about a foot in diameter and nearly eight feet tall. The bark has been peeled from the original tree and the post is varnished, but otherwise it stands just as nature created it, with its frost cracks and protuberances, a unique sculptural form which is also a structural member. We call it the Mother Post.

August liked it. He spent twenty minutes viewing the Mother Post from different angles, running his hands over it, trying to imagine what someone with a need and an eye for natural beauty might be willing to pay for it. He declared he'd never seen such an interesting, appealing tree trunk in his long life.

Of course we were pleased. August was a man who knew wood.

About a month later I saw August in town. He said he had something to show me in his house. In his living room was a new, striking floor lamp. The base was a black ash burl, the grain of the wood twisted and curling; the shaft was a highly figured piece of diamond willow. And the shade was amazing. It was rounded, basketlike, twenty inches in diameter curving in to a six inch top opening. Caning strips were interwoven with basswood withes at two inch inter-

213

vals, which connect top and bottom of the shade. It was clearly meant as a complement to the Mother Post. It would have been a gorgeous lamp in any case, but knowing August was ninety-seven when his accurate, untiring fingers peeled that bark and wove those splints and withes gives it an extra dimension in our minds.

I think of August a lot. He lived all his life in small immigrant towns which were just past the frontier stage of building. His world gave him no esthetic justification, beyond the economic one, for the woodwork to which he turned his eye and hand.

It is easy to sentimentalize the past. His time certainly encouraged thrift and hard work. It also, very often, encouraged a hard, limited, exploitative utilitarianism. It was not comfortable with concepts like beauty, let alone art.

August is gone, but his spirit and message live in the beautiful things he made and in many of us who remember him. The life-course of this small town artisan reminds us that taste and artistry are not the special preserve of the highly educated, that life is full of possibilities, and that boredom is self-inflicted.

Long live August!

ACERTILIA, NEW FOUND LAND
E., J.

This narrative began with two youngish people loading up their children and household goods and lighting out for the territory. It ends with two oldish people in a self-built house, surrounded by books and manuscripts, beautiful wood and interesting stones and kids' pictures, dug into a hillside for the duration.

From one point of view, we have simply done with our lives what most people who wind up happy in old age do. We have looked for work we enjoyed, without too much concern for what it would pay, or, indeed, if it would pay anything. Finding it, we have done it with all our might. We have sustained each other in the enthusiasms of youth and the intensities of parenthood, and now begin to support each other in the infirmities of age. We have, on the basis of our own moral standards, tried to live as good citizens of our place and time. We have tried to teach our children well, and they have responded with love, if not always with total understanding, and have made good lives of their own.

What could be more ordinary, less worthy of anyone's attention?

Yet it is also true that we have lived out a thirty-eight year experiment. We have turned our backs on much that our fellow citizens, at the end of the twentieth century and the second millennium, regard as essential.

This particular experiment began with lists—Thoreau's lists of expenses at Walden Pond, Edie's mother's grocery lists on the Big Chief tablets, those endless lists we both have made over the years. Without lists any complex life would fall into confusion. Our lists have had items as diverse as "worm puppies", "kids to dr.", "build sap shack", "choose poems for Loft reading" and "finish Earthward book".

If the unexamined life is not worth living, perhaps it is time we examined ours, putting the positives and negatives of this thirty-eight year experiment into appropriate columns of debit and credit.

Some parts of it have been clear successes. Our crops have mostly grown, our animals mostly been healthy. The buildings we built have not fallen down. Our composters turn out excellent, odorless, pathogen-free fertilizers. We have, over the long haul and by and large, had a good time. We look back over what we have done with satisfaction.

On the other hand, we have not lived at "good" addresses. We have not sent our children to well-known schools, though two of them, on their own, gained doctoral degrees from excellent universities, and the third, again on his own, has become a topflight marine diesel mechanic. We have not worn fashionable clothing, changed our home decor often, or driven high performance cars. We have lived by an axiom Dan brought home from kindergarten: "Use it up, wear it out, make it do, or do without." We have shamelessly shopped in thrift stores.

We have, more often than not, voted for losers—that is to say, for people who did not triumph in the political arena. We have seen our country flirt briefly with conservation. Americans in general seemed, for an eyeblink of public attention, to have looked at those pictures from space and understood their inescapable message, that we live in a closed and limited world. Then all of a sudden the cars and houses got bigger, the servings in restaurants got enormous, greed got good, and the prime duties of the citizen became consumption and investment. Instead of "In Wildness is the preservation of the world", or "Power to the people", we are being told incessantly, "Let the market sort it out."

As a result, most people in this country eat too much food sold at too cheap a price, have many more items of apparel than they can properly hang and shelve, live in more space than they need filled with more household goods than they use or can keep track of, and busy themselves with travel and electronic diversions, to numb their awareness of what they are doing to the world. Far from making them feel free and powerful, as advertising promises, all this too-much makes the average consumer feel oppressed and exhausted.

In the late fifties and early sixties, social planners used to worry about what would happen, when productivity increases allowed the average worker so much leisure time he wouldn't know what to do with it. In an economy without job security, where, for many workers, the forty hour week is a nostalgic fiction, I wonder how many people waiting out stoplights in endless commutes worry about what they'll do with their leisure time.

Most of our time has been our own, but then the two of us are not and never have been cutting edge. In the national dialogue, people like us are drowned out.

When we were both in college, in the 1950s, the word "alienation" was in the air. All truly educated persons were alienated. Alienation was apparently as essential to a literary career as black turtleneck sweaters and tobacco addiction. The alternative to alienation was to be "well-adjusted", like the high school cheerleader who wrote a book report for John on Catcher in the Rye. The trouble with Holden Caulfield, she said, was that he had no school spirit!

If we had been well-adjusted, I suppose we would never have left California. But no truly alienated person would ever find himself in the middle of a swamp, conscious that his feet had grown into the ground.

Several years ago, John taught at an Elderhostel. On a bright June afternoon, Edith found herself standing in front of a huge map, reading poems about lambs and weeds.

The audience was splendid. But the map was better. It was Max Partch's map of Minnesota, and instead of the usual town and county names, it had names of dominant plant communities on it.

Diagonally up the state, terminating a little northwest of where we live, ran an irregular spur of land labeled "Acertilia." It was named for the climax trees in the woods which it had been before it was cut over and cultivated, the woods it attempts again to be, whenever human vigilance falters. "Acer", the maples. "Tilia", the basswoods.

But when the visiting poet saw the name like that, like the name of a state or nation, she thought, "Yes! Acertilia, that's our country! Oh sure, we're Americans, Minnesotans, Todd Countians, Grey Eagle residents, all of that, but first and last and always and most important, we are citizens of Acertilia!"

It is wonderful to have discovered where you belong, where you are at home. And we are at home in the earth.

Not in the world, probably. The world is largely a human construct. Most human beings are not at home in the earth. If they were, they would not find it necessary to continuously change it, to cut it down, mine it up, to make its deserts bloom and its cities bleed, to fill its air with noise and its skies with waste, to continuously label it and then to kill each other in massive quantities fighting over the labels.

One of the delights of being an Acertilian is that you have no history, or at least none in the ordinary human sense. Acertilia was here before there were people with maps. There is no Acertilian flag. There is no Acertilian national anthem. There never has been a Committee on Un-Acertilian Activities. There never has been an Acertilian war. Indeed, there never could be an Acertilian war. Humans at peace are tremendously destructive to biotic communities. Only humans at war are worse. You cannot defend a place you love by blowing it up.

Acertilianism has nothing to do with nationalism. The nationalist is in love with the idea of the nation, the flag, the anthem, the lines on the map—often so much in love with the idea of the nation that true nationalists are willing not only to die for their countries, but to offer their cities for bombing, their farm-lands for poisoning, and their fellow citizens as cannon fodder. Nationalists are willing to destroy and ruin their actual nations, in the name of imagined future grandeur for those nations.

Acertilians don't care about lines on maps. They love the physical place, the leaves in the wind, the tree shapes and land forms, the actual dumb dirt. They are not just tree-huggers, but earth huggers.

There are disadvantages to being an Acertilian. Nationalistic patriots may dream of indefinite futures, thousand year Reichs, for the political/geo-graphical entities they claim to love, but any good Acertilian knows that biomes change. Just as the lakes and hills of Acertilia are the results of the last glacier, which the next glacier will no doubt change, so her plant/animal communities are the result of climate changes in the seventeenth century. Global warming is changing Acertilia even as I write, and may yet eliminate it entirely.

If this were a natural change, it would be a slow pendulum swing, maple-basswood forests becoming again oak savanna. But human-induced change does not wait for nature to evolve, for successor biomes to move in. Humans take what they want, then say, "Oh, Jeez, I didn't know that was going to happen." At least, that is what most of them have done, so far.

The natural world moves at its own pace. We humans, for reasons of commerce and comfort and also no doubt because we can, want to speed up that pace with genetic engineering. We do this without a clue as to what this tam-pering will do to life systems refined over eons.

You might assume that "Operation Budworm" and similar debacles would have taught us to move slowly and with extreme caution, when we inter-fere with the processes of life. Unfortunately there is no profit and not much glory in what physicians call, "Watchful waiting." And the long human practice of leaving our messes for posterity to clean up is hard to outgrow.

As we worked our way through this book, we have been reminded forcibly, again and again, of the moment when our European ancestors found themselves in a new continent. The shock of that time when suddenly the world opened up permeated every aspect of western culture. It registered in the writings of men who would never set foot on the new world, giving us Shakespeare's magical "vexed Bermoothes", giving us John Donne in bed with his mistress, crying out, "Oh my America, my new found land!"

All of a sudden there were all those wonders and mysteries. Here and there someone of a curious or reverential turn of mind tried to chronicle them, even spoke for preserving them. But mostly there was all that new good Stuff out there, furs, gold, land which no Lord controlled, land free for the breaking, if you did not mind having to kill off a few indigenes first.

The Old World raced into the new like a flock of hungry slum kids charging into a palace which was also a church, a museum, and a living community. Of course they saw themselves as bearers of the True Faith and high culture. They did not stop to read the legends on the cases, which were in a language strange to them. They smashed and grabbed, they fought each other, they dropped and trampled underfoot.

In addition to all that actual wealth, they brought back the idea of the frontier, the wild lands, the territory a man could light out for, the map blank for writing on. The impact of these ideas, breaking into a closed society, is still powerful, and there are parts of the world where the idea of the open society is still radical and dangerous.

Equally powerful is the idea of the discovered fortune, the wealth for which you do not have to labor, the virgin forest for the cutting, the bonanza farm, the gold strike, the Lost Dutchman's mine, the hot insider stock tip waiting out there, somewhere.

The wild, of course, is also the waste, the place you can throw things. Every farm used to have its trash-heap, usually in a gully, as every town had its dump, often in a swamp. Where do you throw things? Away.

But on a globe which is known to be a closed system, where is away? There is none. We now know (or would know, if we paid any attention to such things) that we will live with our own waste of all sorts forever. If we bury waste which will be dangerously radioactive for ten thousand years, in what language should we print the warning signs? This is not a hypothetical question, but one which government agencies have seriously discussed.

The era of New Found Lands is finished. We have what we have.

John's mother used to drive into church in Little Falls from her home at Big Swan Lake, deliberately taking a back-road route through woods. She particularly loved the spring flowers and the colors of the leaves in fall.

Then several homes were built along that road. And, as she said, "I don't drive that way anymore. They've improved it, and it's all ruined."

We can "develop", of course, and we are hell-bent on doing just that. (The market requires it. The market will set every backwoodsman, every subsistence farmer and surviving hunter-gatherer free, whether those persons desire that sort of freedom or not. It will destroy a great many endangered species in their native regions. But it will put the surviving specimens in zoos.)

We will be left with Noah's ark and no Ararat. We can develop, all right. It remains to be seen whether we can improve.

Human "improvements" take place against a backdrop of national and international terrorism and warfare, fueled by centuries of mistrust and hatred. They take place in a world where half or more of a population of six billion and growing is poorly fed, clothed, and housed, has nothing to lose, and has no effective representation at the decision-making levels where grand "improvements" are planned.

We live in a place where the process of discovery and exploitation is still close to us in time. The pelts, the pinery, the five-foot diameter oaks incinerated to clear the land, the topsoil built up over ages which was eroded away within a few years, all these things have happened within a blazingly brief time, here in Acertilia, by Wabizi Sagaiigun. It is impossible to read those accounts of the market hunters and lumbermen without thinking of what has been lost.

The process continues today, without the glamour of the past, without the voyageur's canoe, the scream of the Red River cart, Paul Bunyan plying his trade. In our thirty-six years of residence in Grey Eagle, we have lived through wave after wave of farm sales and foreclosures which occasionally reached a pitch that attracted national interest. But over and around and in between these periods of national concern, the land was being depopulated, the acreage was being concentrated into a few hands, and the production of food was becoming more and more centralized, less and less related to local communities, either human communities or biotic communities.

When we moved here in 1964, Grey Eagle was a functioning market town. It had four groceries and a butcher shop on Main Street, along with a car agency, a bank, a lumber yard, a farm implement dealer, two garages (not filling stations, garages), a cafe, a bar, a dry goods and clothing store, two hardware stores, August's watch repair and gunsmith shop, Tony's salvage emporium, and a pharmacy, with soda fountain. A feed mill and grain elevator, a creamery, and a facility where cucumbers were collected for shipment to a pickle packer served local farmers. Freight and some passenger service was provided by the Burlington Northern Railway. The community supported three churches, a public school with grades from kindergarten through twelve, a mortuary, and a local weekly newspaper.

It now has one grocery, one bar, one hardware store, a lumberyard, a beauty salon, an automotive repair shop, a bank, a credit union, a gift shop, a mortuary, and two filling stations which are also convenience stores. The feedmill still functions as a retail outlet, but it no longer grinds and mixes feed or serves as a shipping point for local grain. The railroad line is gone.

Grey Eagle does not have the depressed, deserted-looking main street of many small towns, because many of the older buildings have been torn down or renovated. The local school has managed to stay open, serving grades K-Six, by pairing with Long Prairie, fourteen miles away. The churches share clergy with other towns, instead of having resident pastors.

There are also public institutions that didn't exist in 1964, like the senior citizen's center, the public library, three children's day care centers, and a medical clinic. A clothing manufacturer on the edge of town employs about a hundred local women. This factory still carries the name of its Minnesota founding company, but now belongs to a multi-national corporation.

The population numbers are about the same, though the general population is older.

From a certain point of view, this hollowing-out of small towns (and large cities, as far as that goes) is a necessary part of the market in operation. People have simply gone to other places for their goods and services. Nothing to worry about there.

That the process is wasteful both ecologically and humanly, and excruciating for the people who have to go through it, appears to be something which the market finds irrelevant.

It is certainly true that you can now buy good wine in central Minnesota, and restaurant cuisine is much more varied than it was in 1964. You can buy kiwi fruit and fresh deli, but not on a hometown main street that has mostly vanished. There are more books and now videos available, but fewer people have their own gardens. Cappuccino is everywhere, but it's harder to find homegrown tomatoes and farm-fresh eggs. More local people get more education; fewer local people make a living by cultivating their own land. It is very much easier to get to almost any place in the world you want to go, but when you get there, it is often remarkably like the place you left behind.

There are also much better environmental protection laws, better (though not nearly good enough) environmental education. The wolves are coming back. Reliable reports not far from us suggest that we may yet see a black bear, on the land where Orley Huffman surprised one in his spring house.

Songbirds are in decline. Seventy per cent of all eastern bird species have seen population declines since the 1960s. Amphibians are in precipitous and scary decline. The small dabbling ducks, like teal and scaup, do not seem likely ever again to descend in their chattering joyous hordes, as they did on Big Swan Lake in the spring of 1965. But the deer herd is large and healthy, Canada geese (which we saw rarely and distantly in the sixties) are abundant local residents. Last spring, a young male wild turkey wakened us at several daybreaks, gobbling in our front yard.

And for the last six or seven years, bald eagles have nested in southern Todd County. Banning DDT brought them back.

Our woods are in the best shape they have been, probably, since they regrew after the lumbermen cleared them. But partly that is because they are our woods.

So; here we are, hunkered down in Earthward, sending out our communiqués from Acertilia to the fatlands of the well-adjusted and the flying battalions of the alienated. To paraphrase a Frost poem, we are, about most things, "Only more sure of all we thought we knew." Here we are, here we stay.

We know that in the geologic long run, all of humankind are privileged to be part of the life system here on this small planet. We are at the mercy of long range cosmic forces over which we will never have any control.

Let us help make this good life last while we can.

The reader must judge the success of our experiment. We have enjoyed
it.

MESSAGE ENCLOSED IN A WALL
IN A HOUSE CALLED "EARTHWARD"
E.

Whoever you are,
Archaeologist or wrecker,
Here are some words from 1988,
Written on the fifth of February
With the thermometer well below zero,
And the sun bright on drifted snow
In the woods around this house
Which we named for our compulsions
And a poem by Robert Frost.
(American poet, 1874-1963).

This house buried in earth,
With its exposed beams, south-facing windows,
And walls of cordwood masonry,
Was not typical of its time and region,
Nor can the builders who lived in it
Be taken as a baseline norm.
We were teacher and poet;
We had raised three children before we built this place.
We built as much as we could
With our own hands.

We cut the trees for this house,
We gathered its stones
From the worked-over country
Of a place called Minnesota.
Half-expecting the nuclear death of everything
At the hands of our own species,
We built as we could.

(As I write this, my husband is waiting
With the finishing trowel in his hand.)

Listen. As you take the old paper
Out of the old bottle, out of this wall
We dreamed and sweated,
Our message is, we were homo sapiens.
We loved each other thirty years.
When we made something, we cleaned up after ourselves.